THE GLOBALISATION OF POVERTY

THE GLOBALISATION OF POVERTY

Impacts of IMF and World Bank Reforms

Michel Chossudovsky

Pluto Press
Australia

IPSR Books
Cape Town

Fernwood Publishing
Halifax, Nova Scotia

Zed Books Ltd
London and New Jersey

The Globalisation of Poverty: Impacts of IMF and World Bank Reforms is published by Zed Books Ltd, 7 Cynthia Street, London N1 9JF, UK and Room 400, 175 Fifth Avenue, New York, NY10010, USA in 1998.

Published in Canada by Fernwood Publishing Ltd, PO Box 9409, Station A, Halifax, Nova Scotia, Canada, B3K 5S3.

Published in South Africa by the Institute for Policy and Social Research (IPSR), 41 Salt River Road, Salt River 7925, Cape Town.

Published in Australia by Pluto Press, 6a Nelson Street, Annandale, NSW 2038, Sydney, Australia

Second impression, 1998

Cover design by Chin Mun Woh
Printed by Biddles Ltd, Guildford and Kings Lynn

A catalogue record for this book is available from the British Library.

Library of Congress Cataloging-in-Publication Data

Chossudovsky, Michel.
The Globalisation of Poverty: Impacts of IMF and World Bank Reforms/Michel Chossudovsky.
p. cm.
Includes bibliographical references and index.
ISBN 1-85649-401-2 (hardbound). -ISBN 1-85649-402-0 (paperback)
1. International Monetary Fund—Developing countries.2.International Monetary Fund—Europe, Eastern.3. World Bank—Developing Countries. 4.World Bank—Europe, Eastern.5.Poverty-—Developing countries. 6 Poverty—Europe, Eastern.
I. International Monetary Fund. II. World Bank. III. Title.
HG3881.5.I58C47 1996
339.4'6—dc20 96-22287
CIP

Canadian Cataloging in Publication Data

Chossudovsky, Michel.
The Globalisation of Poverty
Includes bibliographical references and index.
ISBN 1-55266-004-4
1. Poverty — Developing countries. 2. Poverty — Europe, Eastern. 3. International Monetary Fund. 4. International Bank for Reconstruction and Development. 5. Macro-economics. I. Title.
HG3881.5.I58C47 1998 339.4'6 C98-950148-5

Canadian ISBN 1 55266 004 4 (Pb)
South African ISBN 0 9584224 6 X (Hb)
ISBN 0 9584224 5 1 (Pb)
Australian ISBN 1 86403 057 7 (Pb)

ISBN 1 85649 401 2 (Hb)
ISBN 1 85649 402 0 (Pb)

Acknowledgement

I AM indebted to many people in many countries who provided me with insights on the economic reforms and assisted me in carrying out the country-level research. In the course of my field work initiated in 1988, I came in contact with members of peasant communities and workers' organisations, teachers, health workers, civil servants, members of research institutes, university professors, members of non-governmental organisations, with whom I developed ties of friendship and solidarity. This book is dedicated to their struggle.

The support of the Social Sciences and Humanities' Research Council of Canada (SSHRC) and the University of Ottawa, Faculty of Social Sciences' Research Committee is gratefully acknowledged. The views expressed in this book are those of the author.

To my parents

CONTENTS

PART III: SOUTH AND SOUTH-EAST ASIA

PART IV: LATIN AMERICA

Introduction

THE global crisis is not centred on any single region of the world. National economies are interlocked, commercial banking and business ownership (controlled by some 750 global corporations) transcend economic borders, international trade is integrated and financial markets around the world are connected through instant computer link-up. The present crisis is far more complex than that of the interwar period, its social consequences and geo-political implications, far-reaching, particularly in the uncertain aftermath of the Cold War.

The movement of the global economy is "regulated" by "a worldwide process of debt collection" which constricts the institutions of the national state and contributes to destroying employment and economic activity. *In the developing world, the burden of the external debt has reached two trillion dollars:*[1] *entire countries have been destabilised as a consequence of the collapse of national currencies, often resulting in the outbreak of social strife, ethnic conflicts and civil war.* This book highlights the process of economic restructuring imposed by international creditors on developing countries since the beginning of the 1980s.

The macro-economic reforms are a concrete reflection of the post-war capitalist system and of its destructive evolution. Macro-economic management adopted at the national and international levels plays a central role in the emergence of a new global economic order: the reforms "regulate" the process of capitalist accumulation at a world level. This is not, however, a "free" market system: while supported by neoliberal discourse, the so-called "structural adjustment programme" sponsored by the Bretton Woods institutions constitutes a new interventionist framework.

Since the debt crisis of the early 1980s, the search for maximum profit has been engineered by macro-economic policy, leading to the dismantling of state institutions, the tearing down of economic borders and the impoverishment of millions of people.

The Internationalisation of Macro-economic Reform

The Bretton Woods institutions have played a key role in this process of economic restructuring. While the International Monetary Fund (IMF) and the World Bank constitute a powerful international bureaucracy (formally under an inter-governmental umbrella), the seat of political power does not rest with the international financial institutions and their major share-holders (i.e. the governments of the rich countries). The IMF, the World Bank and the World Trade Organisation (WTO) are administrative structures, they are *regulatory bodies* operating within a capitalist system and responding to dominant economic and financial interests. What is at stake is the ability of this international bureaucracy to supervise national economies through the deliberate manipulation of market forces.

The first part of this book addresses the nature of this global economic system and examines the actual instruments of policy intervention. Focusing on major regions of the developing world, the book proceeds to examine the revamping of national economies including the destruction of entire countries (e.g. Somalia, Rwanda and Yugoslavia), under the impetus of the IMF/World Bank-sponsored reforms.

The Cheap-Labour Economy

Our analysis of the global economic system centres on the role of world unemployment. In this context, the IMF-sponsored reforms have played a decisive role in "regulating labour costs" in a large number of individual countries. Yet this "minimisation of labour costs" undermines the expansion of consumer markets, – i.e. the impoverishment of large sectors of the world population under the brunt of macro-economic reform has been conducive to a dramatic contraction of purchasing power.

In turn, in both developing and developed countries, the low levels of earnings backlash on production contributing to a further string of plant closures and bankruptcies. At each phase of this crisis, the movement is towards global overproduction and decline of consumer demand. By reducing society's capacity to consume, the macro-economic reforms applied worldwide ultimately obstruct the expansion of capital.

Under a system which generates overproduction, international corporations and trading companies can only "expand" their markets by concurrently undermining or destroying the domestic productive base of developing countries, – i.e. through the disengagement of domestic production geared towards the internal market. In this system, the expansion of exports in developing countries is predicated on the contraction of internal purchasing power. Poverty is an input on the supply side. The "emerging markets" are opened up through the concurrent displacement of a pre-existing productive system, small and medium-sized enterprises are pushed into bankruptcy or obliged to produce for a global distributor, state enterprises are privatised or closed down, independent agricultural producers are impoverished.

The global economic system is thus characterised by two contradictory forces: *the consolidation of a global cheap-labour economy* on the one hand and *the search for new consumer markets* on the other. The former undermines the latter. The extension of markets for the global corporation requires the fragmentation and destruction of the domestic economy. Barriers to the movement of money and goods are removed, credit is deregulated, land and state property are taken over by international capital...

Debt and Macro-economic Reform in the Developed Countries

Our investigation in this book has focused largely on the experiences of developing countries. Yet since the collapse of the Berlin Wall in 1989 and the demise of the Soviet Union, the process of restructuring of the world economy has taken on a different face. A "political consensus" on macro-economic policy has developed, governments throughout the world have unequivocally embraced the neoliberal policy agenda. Since the early 1990s, the macro-economic reforms adopted in the OECD countries have contained many of the essential ingredients of the "structural adjustment programmes" applied in the Third World and Eastern Europe.

The institutional mechanics, however, are different to those described in this book, – i.e. in the developed countries, the Bretton Woods institutions have not played a significant role in "policy surveillance". Creditors in the West tend to exert their pressures on national governments without the intermediation of the Washington-based bureaucracy. The debts of parastatal enterprises, public utilities, state, provincial and municipal governments are carefully categorised and "rated" by financial markets (e.g. Moody's and Standard and Poor ratings). Moreover, ministers of finance are increasingly expected to report to the large investment houses and commercial banks. Moody's downgrading of Sweden's sovereign debt rating in 1995 was instrumental in the decision of the minority Social Democratic government to curtail core welfare programmes, including child allowances and unemployment insurance benefits.[2] Similarly, Moody's credit rating of Canada's public debt was a major factor in the adoption of Canada's 1995-1996 structural adjustment programme involving massive cuts in social programmes and lay-offs of civil servants. In the US, the controversial "balanced budget amendment" demanded by Wall Street (which was narrowly defeated in the Senate) in 1995 would have entrenched the rights of the state's creditors in the US Constitution.

In the group of OECD countries, public debts increased beyond bounds throughout the 1980s (in excess of US$13 trillion in 1995).[3] Ironically, the very process of "reimbursing this global debt" has been conducive to its enlargement through the systematic creation of new debts. In the US – which is by far the largest debtor nation – the public debt increased fivefold during the Reagan-Bush era (US$5 trillion in 1996).[4] In turn, the accumulation of large public debts in Western countries has provided financial and banking interests with "political leverage" as well as the power to dictate government economic and social policy.

Global Monopolies

As the recession deepens, the world economy is overshadowed by a handful of international banks and global monopolies. These powerful industrial and financial interests are increasingly in conflict with those of civil society. While the spirit of Anglo-Saxon liberalism is committed to "fostering competition", G-7 macro-economic policy (through tight fiscal and monetary controls) has in practice supported a wave of corporate mergers and acquisitions as well as the planned bankruptcy of small and medium-sized enterprises.

In turn, large multinational companies (particularly in the US and Canada) have taken control of local-level markets (especially in the service economy) through the system of corporate franchising.[5] Small enterprises are either eradicated or impounded as so-called "*franchisees*" into the net of a global distributor. This process enables large corporate capital ("the franchiser") to gain control over human capital and entrepreneurship. A large share of the earnings of small firms and/or retailers is thereby appropriated while the bulk of investment outlays is assumed by the independent producer.

A parallel process can be observed in Western Europe. With the Maastricht Treaty, the process of political restructuring in the European Union increasingly heeds dominant financial interests at the expense of the unity of European societies. In this system, state power has deliberately sanctioned the progress of private monopolies: large capital destroys small capital in all its forms. With the drive towards the formation of economic blocs both in Europe and North America, the regional and local-level entrepreneur is uprooted, city life is transformed and individual small-scale ownership is wiped out. "Free trade" and economic integration provide greater mobility to the global enterprise while at the same time suppressing (through non-tariff and institutional barriers) the movement of small local-level capital.[6] "Economic integration" (under the dominion of the global enterprise), while displaying a semblance of political unity, often promotes factionalism and social strife between and within national societies.

Financial Instability

The disintegration of "the real economy" under the brunt of macro-economic reform is matched by a highly unstable global financial system. Since Black Monday, 19 October 1987, considered by analysts to be very close to a total meltdown of the New York stock exchange, a highly volatile pattern has unfolded marked by frequent and increasingly serious convulsions on major bourses, the ruin of national currencies in Eastern Europe and Latin America, not to mention the plunge of the new "peripheral financial markets" (e.g. Mexico, Bangkok, Cairo, Bombay) precipitated by "profit taking" and the sudden retreat of the large institutional investors. The peripheral stock markets have thereby become a new means of extracting surplus from developing countries.

A new global financial environment has also unfolded: the wave of corporate mergers in the late 1980s paved the way for the consolidation of a new generation of financiers clustered around the merchant banks, the institutional investors, the stock brokerage firms, the large insurance companies, etc. In this process, commercial banking functions have coalesced with those of the investment banks and stock brokers.[7]

While these "money managers" play a powerful role in financial markets, they are, however, increasingly removed from entrepreneurial functions in the real economy. Their activities (which escape state regulation) include speculative transactions in commodity futures and derivatives and the manipulation of currency markets. Major financial actors are routinely involved in "hot money deposits" in "the emerging markets" of Latin America and South-East Asia, not to mention money laundering and the development of (specialised) "private banks" ("which advise wealthy clients") in the many offshore banking havens. The daily turnover of foreign exchange transactions is of the order of $1 trillion a day of which only 15 per cent corresponds to actual commodity trade and capital flows.[8] Within this global financial web, money transits at high speed from one banking haven to the next, in the intangible form of electronic transfers. "Legal" and "illegal" business activities have become increasingly intertwined and vast amounts of unreported private wealth have been accumulated. Favoured by the structural adjustment programme and the concurrent deregulation of the financial system, the criminal mafias have expanded their role in the spheres of international banking.[9] In several developing countries, national governments are under the trusteeship of such criminal factions. The latter have also acquired large amounts of state property under the World Bank-sponsored privatisation programmes. Our analysis of Peru, Bolivia and the former Soviet Union (Chapters 10,11,12) identifies the relationship between macro-economic policy and the laundering of dirty money by the criminal mafias.

Collecting Debt at a World Level

The global financial system has reached a dangerous cross-roads: at the very heart of the economic crisis are the markets for public debt where hundreds of billions of dollars of government bonds and treasury bills are transacted on a daily basis. In turn, the plight of the bond market and the massive trade in US-dollar denominated debts are accompanied (in an almost symbiotic relationship) by intense rivalries between America, Europe and Japan on the world's currency markets. The plunge of the US dollar is also a consequence of the large share of the US public debt held by German and Japanese financial institutions, not to mention the huge amounts of US dollar banknotes in circulation in the Third World and Eastern Europe. The depreciation of the American dollar while not formally acknowledged as "default on sovereign debt", nonetheless denotes a de facto contraction in the real value of US public debt transacted on international capital markets.[10]

Moreover, in the uncertain aftermath of the Mexican financial crisis of 1995 nothing has been resolved: the "rescue package" supported by the US Treasury, the IMF and the Bank for International Settlements was largely intended to allow Mexico to meet its debt servicing obligations (in short-term dollar-denominated *tesobonos*) with international creditor banks and financial institutions. Private debts were conveniently recycled and transformed into public debts. The Mexican economy will be crippled for years to come, leading to a far deeper political and social fracturing: under the deal, Mexican banks will be thrown open to foreign ownership and the country's entire oil export earnings will be deposited into a bank account in New York managed by its international creditors.

The Mexican crisis, however, is but one fragment of a complex financial jigsaw: the *same* mechanism of debt collection has been replicated alongside the adoption of IMF-style market reforms in all major regions of the developing world. The IMF intimated in this regard that other indebted countries could meet the same fate as Mexico: "we will therefore introduce still stronger surveillance to be sure that the convalescence goes well...".[11]

The Conversion of Private Debts

Since the early 1980s, large amounts of the debt of large corporations and commercial banks in the developed countries were erased and transformed into public debt. Similarly, multilateral and bilateral loans to developing countries were granted to enable countries to reimburse the commercial banks, – i.e. commercial debt was conveniently transformed into official debt (bilateral and multilateral) thereby reducing the "exposure" of the commercial banks.

This process of "debt conversion" is a central feature of the crisis: business and bank losses including non-performing loans have been systematically transferred to the state. The Mexican "bail-out" is but one example of this process.

Similarly, in the US during the merger boom of the late 1980s, the burden of corporate losses was shifted to the state through the acquisition of bankrupt enterprises. The latter could then be closed down and written off as tax losses. In turn, the "non-performing loans" of the large commercial banks were routinely transformed into pre-tax losses. The "rescue packages" for troubled corporations and commercial banks are largely based on the same principle of shifting the burden of corporate debts on to the state treasury.

In turn, the many state subsidies in the OECD countries, rather than stimulating job creation, were routinely used by large corporations to finance their mergers, introduce labour-saving technology and relocate production to cheap labour havens in the Third World and Eastern Europe. Not only were the costs associated with corporate restructuring borne by the state, public spending contributed directly to increased concentration of ownership and a significant contraction of the industrial workforce. In turn, the string of bankruptcies of small and medium-sized enterprises and the lay-off of workers (who are also tax payers) were also conducive to a significant contraction in tax revenues.

Fiscal Crisis of the State

The debt crisis in the West had also triggered the development of a highly regressive tax system, which has also contributed to the enlargement of the public debt. While corporate taxes were curtailed, the new tax revenues appropriated from the (lower- and middle-) salaried population (including the value-added taxes) were recycled towards the servicing of the public debt.[12] While the state was collecting taxes from its citizens, "a tribute" was being paid by the state (in the form of hand-outs and subsidies) to big business.

In turn, spurred by the new banking technologies, the flight of corporate profits to offshore banking havens in the Bahamas, Switzerland, the Channel Islands, Luxembourg, etc. contributed to exacerbating the fiscal crisis further. The Cayman Islands, a British Crown colony in the Caribbean, for instance, is the fifth largest banking centre in the world (i.e. in terms of the size of its deposits, most of which are by Shell corporations).[13] The enlargement of the budget deficit in the US bears a direct relationship to massive tax evasion and the flight of unreported corporate profits. In turn, large amounts of money deposited in the Cayman Islands and the Bahamas (part of which is controlled by criminal organisations) are used to fund business investments in the US.

Under the Political Trusteeship of Finance Capital

In the developed countries, a vicious circle had been set in motion. The recipients of government "hand-outs" had become the state's creditors. Public debt issued by the Treasury to fund big business had been acquired by banks and financial institutions, which were simultaneously the recipients of state subsidies. An absurd situation: the state was "financing its own indebtedness", government "hand-outs" were being recycled towards the purchase of bonds and treasury bills. The government was being squeezed between business groups lobbying for subsidies on the one hand and its financial creditors on the other hand. And because a large portion of the public debt was held by private banking and financial institutions, the latter were also able to pressure governments for an increased command over public resources.

The Illusory "Independence" of the Central Bank

The statutes of central banks in both developing and developed countries had been modified to meet the demands of financial markets. Central banks are increasingly under the trusteeship of the state's creditors. In the Third World and Eastern Europe, central banks are largely regulated by the IMF on behalf of the Paris and London Clubs.

In the West, central banks are to become "independent" and "shielded from political influence".[14] What this means in practice is that the national Treasury is increasingly at the mercy of private commercial creditors. The Central Bank cannot under its new statutes be used to provide credit to the state. Under article 104 of the Maastricht Treaty, for instance,"[c]entral bank credit to the government is entirely discretionary, the central bank cannot be forced to provide such credit".[15] These statutes are therefore directly conducive to the enlargement of the public debt held by private financial and banking institutions.

In practice, the Central Bank (which is neither accountable to the government nor to the legislature), operates as an autonomous bureaucracy under the trusteeship of private financial and banking interests. The latter (rather than the government) dictate the direction of monetary policy.

In both developing and developed countries, monetary policy no longer exists as a means of state intervention: it belongs largely to the realm of private banking. In contrast to the marked scarcity of state funds, "the creation of money" (implying a command over real resources) occurs within the inner web of the international banking system with the sole pursuit of private wealth. Powerful financial actors have the ability not only of creating and moving money without impediment, but also of manipulating interests rates and precipitating the decline of major currencies, as occurred with the spectacular tumble of the pound sterling in September 1992. What this signifies, in practice, is that central banks are no longer able to regulate the creation of money in the broad interests of society (e.g. mobilising production or generating employment).

The supply of money is a fundamental instrument which regulates the mobilisation of human and material resources. This instrument is in the hands of private creditors. In both the Third World and Eastern Europe, the IMF-imposed "freeze on money creation" (i.e. used to finance government expenditure) constitutes a powerful instrument capable of paralysing entire economies. In the Russian Federation, for instance, the IMF-sponsored credit restrictions by the Central Bank to state enterprises have been conducive since 1992 to the disintegration of entire sectors of the Russian economy (see Chapter 12).

Crisis of the State

In the West, the democratic system has been steered into a quandary: those elected to high office act increasingly as bureaucrats. The state's creditors have become the depositaries of real political power operating discretely in the background. In turn, a uniform political ideology has unfolded. A "consensus" on macro-economic reform extends across the political spectrum. In the United States, Democrats and Republicans have joined hands; in the European Union, socialist governments have become the protagonists of "strong economic medicine". The fate of public policy is transacted on the US and Eurobond markets, policy options are presented mechanically through the same stylised economic slogans: "we must reduce the deficit, we must combat inflation"; "the economy is overheating: put on the brakes!".

The interests of the financial establishment (particularly in the United States) have also permeated the top echelons of the Treasury and the multilateral banks: the US Treasury Secretary, Mr Robert Rubin under the Clinton Administration, was a senior banking executive at Goldman Sachs, former president of the World Bank, Mr Lewis Preston, was chief executive at J. P. Morgan, and so on. While financiers are involved in politics, politicians have increasingly acquired a financial stake in the business community. Marred by conflicts of interest, the state system in the West is in crisis as a result of its ambivalent relationship to private economic and financial concerns. Under these conditions, the practice of democracy in the developed countries has also become a ritual. No policy alternative is offered to the electorate. As in a one-party state, the results of the ballot have virtually no impact on the actual conduct of state economic and social policy. In turn, the state under the neoliberal policy agenda has become increasingly repressive in curbing the democratic rights of its citizens.

The Global Economic Crisis

The depression of the 1930s – centred largely in the advanced capitalist countries – witnessed (despite the collapse of commodity prices) an easing of colonial dependency thereby providing many developing countries with a temporary "breathing space". During the 1930s, significant economic growth was recorded in countries which were partially "delinked" (e.g. Latin America) from the world market or (politically) isolated (e.g. the Soviet Union under the first five-year plans). In sharp contrast, the present economic crisis has tightened the clutch of the rich countries over their former colonies while bringing the former "socialist" countries within the orbit of world market. With some exceptions, the global market system marks the demise of the "national economy" (i.e. national industry geared towards the domestic market). In the Third World and the former Communist bloc, regional trading structures have been abolished and a large part of the industrial base (which previously supplied the internal market) has been dismantled.

In both the South and the East, the compression of living standards since the early 1980s (not to mention the breakdown of institutions) has been considerably greater than that experienced by the rich countries during the 1930s. The globalisation of poverty in the late 20th century is unprecedented in world history. This poverty is not, however, the consequence of a "scarcity" of human and material resources. Rather it is the result of a system of global oversupply predicated on unemployment and the worldwide minimisation of labour costs.

There are no straightforward and easy "solutions" to a global financial crisis which looms dangerously in the years ahead. The mere indictment of national governments and of the Washington-based bureaucracy cannot constitute the basis of social action. Financial actors, including banks and transnational corporations, must be pinpointed. Social movements and people's organisations, acting in solidarity at national and international levels, must target the various financial interests which feed upon this destructive economic model.

Concrete financial mechanisms which secure the cancellation of the external debt of developing countries and the write-down of the public debts of the developed are required alongside regulatory policies, which carefully monitor the activities of the Bretton Woods institutions and "democratise" the structures of central banks.[16] Yet these measures in themselves are not enough, they do not question the role and legitimacy of the creditors, they do not modify the workings of global capitalism. The accumulation of large public debts (and the pressures exercised by creditors on the national state throughout the world) is at the heart of this crisis, requiring effective "social regulation" and intervention in financial markets, namely a form of "financial disarmament" adopted forcefully by society and in opposition to those financial interests.[17]

The world community should recognise the failure of the dominant neoliberal system. As the economic crisis deepens, there are increasingly fewer policy-avenues available. Yet in the absence of fundamental economic and social reforms, a worldwide financial meltdown cannot be ruled out. Of crucial importance is the articulation of new rules governing world trade as well as the development of an expansionary ("demand side") macro-economic policy-agenda geared towards the alleviation of poverty and the worldwide creation of employment and purchasing power.[18]

The question remains whether this global economic system based on the relentless accumulation of private wealth can be subjected to a process of meaningful reform, namely whether alterations in the rules of world trade and finance (implying a revamping of the WTO and the Bretton Woods institutions) are at all feasible under the existing political and social set-up.

There are no "technical solutions" to this crisis. Meaningful reforms are not likely to be implemented without an enduring social struggle. What is at stake is the massive concentration of financial wealth and the command over real resources by a social minority. The latter also controls the "creation of money" within the international banking system.

The "reappropriation of monetary policy" by society removing the Central Bank from the grip of private creditors is an integral part of this struggle. The latter must be broad-based and democratic, encompassing all sectors of society at all levels, in all countries, uniting in a major thrust workers, farmers, independent producers, professionals, artists, civil servants, members of the clergy, students and intellectuals. The "globalisation" of this struggle is fundamental, requiring a degree of solidarity and internationalism unprecedented in world history. The global economic system feeds on social divisiveness between and within countries. Unity of purpose and worldwide coordination among diverse groups and social movements is crucial. A major thrust is required which brings together social movements in all major regions of the world in a common pursuit and commitment to the elimination of poverty and a lasting world peace.

Endnotes

1. The total debt stock of all developing countries is of the order of US$1.9 billion (1994). See World Bank, *World Debt Tables, 1994-95*, Washington, 1994.
2. See Hugh Carnegy, "Moody's Deals Rating Blow to Sweden", *Financial Times*, London, 6 January 1995, p. 16. see also Hugh Carnegy, "Swedish Cuts Fail to Convince Markets", *Financial Times*, London, 12 January 1995, p. 2.
3. General government gross liabilities for all OECD countries combined was of the order of 72.9 per cent of Gross Domestic Product. See OCDE, *Perspectives de l'OCDE*, Number 56, December 1994, Annex: Table 33.
4. Projection of the US public debt corresponding to July-September 1995. See "The Debt's the Limit", *Investor's Business Daily*, 13 April 1995, p. B1.
5. See *Franchise Directory Handbook*, Fall 1992.
6. For instance, while the large multinational enterprises move freely within the North-American free trade area, non-tariff restrictions prevent small-scale local capital in one Canadian province extending its activities to another Canadian province.
7. In the US, the division between commercial and investment banking is regulated by the Glass Steagall Act enacted in 1933 during the Great Depression to ensure the separation of securities underwriting from lending, to avoid conflicts of interest and to prevent the collapse of commercial banks. The Banking Association has recently pointed to the importance of amending the Glass Steagall Act to allow for the full integration of commercial and investment banking. See American Banking Association President's Position, "New Ball Game in Washington", *ABA Banking Journal*, January 1995, p. 17.
8. The daily turn-over of foreign exchange transactions (including derivative trade in futures, options and swaps) is of the order of US$900 billion (1992 estimate). Of this amount, less than five per cent relates to commodity trade and 10 per cent pertains to capital flows. See *Economist*, 15 August 1992, p. 61.
9. For detailed analysis on the role of criminal organisations in banking and finance, see Alain Labrousse and Alain Wallon (editors), *La planète des drogues*, Editions du Seuil, Paris, 1993 and Observatoire géopolitique des drogues, *La drogue, nouveau désordre mondial*, Hachette, coll. pluriel-Intervention, Paris, 1993.
10. For further details see D. H. Gowland, *International Bond Markets*, Routledge, New York, 1991. See also Hayes Hubbard, *Investment Banking*, Harvard Business School Press, Boston, 1990.

11. See David Duchan and Peter Norman, "IMF Urges Close Watch on Weaker Economies", *Financial Times*, London, 8 February 1995, p.1.
12. In the US, the contribution of corporations to federal revenues declined from 13.8 per cent in 1980 (including the taxation of windfall profits) to 8.3 per cent in 1992. See *US Statistical Abstract*, 1992.
13. Estimate of Jack A. Blum presented at Jornadas: *Drogas, desarrollo y estado de derecho*, Bilbao, October 1994. See also Jack Blum and Alan Bloch, "Le blanchiment de l'argent dans les Antilles" in Alain Labrousse and Alain Wallon (editors), *La planète des drogues*, Editions du Seuil, Paris, 1993.
14. See Carlo Cottarelli, *Limiting Central Bank Credit to the Government*, International Monetary Fund, Washington, 1993, p. 5.
15. Ibid. p. 5.
16. See the proposal contained in *The Copenhagen Alternative Declaration* adopted by some 620 non-governmental organisations and networks at the World Summit for Social Development, March 1995.
17. The term "financial disarmament" was coined by the Ecumenical Coalition for Social Justice, "The Power of Global Finance", *Third World Resurgence*, No. 56, March 1995, p. 21.
18. This requires substantive modifications of the rules of international trade as defined in the Final Act of the Uruguay Round and the articles of agreement of the World Trade Organisation.

PART I

Global Poverty and Macro-economic Reform

Chapter 1

The Globalisation of Poverty

SINCE the early 1980s, the "macro-economic stabilisation" and "structural adjustment" programmes imposed by the IMF and the World Bank on developing countries (as a condition for the renegotiation of their external debt) have led to the impoverishment of hundreds of millions of people. Contrary to the spirit of the Bretton Woods agreement which was predicated on "economic reconstruction" and the stability of major exchange rates, the structural adjustment programme has contributed largely to destabilising national currencies and ruining the economies of developing countries.

Internal purchasing power has collapsed, famines have erupted, health clinics and schools have been closed down, hundreds of millions of children have been denied the right to primary education. In several regions of the developing world, the reforms have been conducive to a resurgence of infectious diseases including tuberculosis, malaria and cholera. While the World Bank's mandate consists of "combating poverty" and protecting the environment, its support for large-scale hydroelectric and agro-industrial projects has also speeded up the process of deforestation and the destruction of the natural environment, leading to the forced displacement and eviction of several million people.

Global Geopolitics

In the aftermath of the Cold War, macro-economic restructuring also supports global geopolitical interests. Structural adjustment is used to undermine the economy of the former Soviet bloc and dismantle its system of state enterprises. Since the late 1980s, the IMF-World Bank "economic medicine" has been imposed on Eastern Europe, Yugoslavia and the former Soviet Union with devastating economic and social consequences.

While the mechanism of enforcement is distinct, the structural adjustment programme has since the 1990s been applied also in the developed countries. Whereas the macro-economic therapies (under the jurisdiction of national governments) tend to be less brutal than those imposed on the South and the East, the theoretical and ideological underpinnings are broadly similar. The same global financial interests are served. Monetarism is applied on a world scale and the process of global economic restructuring strikes also at the very heart of the rich countries. The consequences are unemployment, low wages and the marginalisation of large sectors of the population. Social expenditures are curtailed and many of the achievements of the welfare state are repealed. State policies have encouraged the destruction of small and medium-sized enterprises. Low levels of food consumption and malnutrition are also hitting the urban poor in the rich countries. According to a recent study, 30 million people in the United States are classified as "hungry".[1]

Since the mid-1980s, the impact of structural adjustment, including the derogation of the social rights of women and the detrimental environmental consequences of economic reform, have been amply documented. While the Bretton Woods institutions have acknowledged "the social impact of adjustment", no shift in policy direction is in sight. In fact since the late 1980s, coinciding with the collapse of the Eastern block, the IMF-World Bank policy prescriptions (now imposed in the name of "poverty alleviation") have become increasingly harsh and unyielding.

Social Polarisation and the Concentration of Wealth

In the South, the East and the North, a privileged social minority has accumulated vast amounts of wealth at the expense of the large majority of the population. This new international financial order feeds on human poverty and the destruction of the natural environment. It generates social apartheid, encourages racism and ethnic strife, undermines the rights of women and often precipitates countries into destructive confrontations between nationalities. Moreover, these reforms – when applied simultaneously in more than 100 countries – are conducive to a "globalisation of poverty", a process which undermines human livelihood and destroys civil society in the South, the East and the North.

The Role of Global Institutions

Global institutions play an important role in the process of restructuring national economies. The ratification of the GATT agreement and the formation of the World Trade Organisation (WTO) in 1995 marks a landmark in the development of the global economic system. The WTO's mandate consists of regulating world trade to the benefit of the international banks and transnational corporations as well as "supervising" the enforcement of national trade policies. The GATT agreement violates fundamental peoples' rights, particularly in the areas of foreign investment, bio-diversity and intellectual property rights.

In other words, a new "triangular division of authority" has unfolded based on the close collaboration of the IMF, the World Bank and the WTO in the "surveillance" of developing countries' economic policies. Under the new trade order (which emerged from the completion of the Uruguay Round at Marrakesh and the establishment of the WTO in 1995), the relationship of the Washington-based institutions to national governments has been redefined. Enforcement of IMF-World Bank policy prescriptions no longer hinges solely upon ad hoc country-level loan agreements (which are not "legally binding" documents). Many of the clauses of the structural adjustment programme (e.g. trade liberalisation and the foreign investment regime) have become permanently entrenched in the articles of agreement of the WTO. These articles have laid the foundations for "policing" countries (and enforcing "conditionalities") according to international law.

The IMF Menu

The same "menu" of budgetary austerity, devaluation, trade liberalisation and privatisation is applied simultaneously in more than 100 indebted countries. Debtor nations forego economic sovereignty and control over fiscal and monetary policy, the Central Bank and the Ministry of Finance are reorganised (often with the complicity of the local bureaucracies), state institutions are undone and an "economic tutelage" is installed. A "parallel government" which bypasses civil society is established by the international financial institutions (IFIs). Countries which do not conform to the IMF's "performance targets" are blacklisted.

While adopted in the name of "democracy" and so-called "good governance", the structural adjustment programme requires the strengthening of the internal security apparatus: political repression – with the collusion of the Third World élites – supports a parallel process of "economic repression".

"Good governance" and the holding of multi-party elections are added conditions imposed by the donors and creditors, yet the very nature of the economic reforms precludes a genuine democratisation, – i.e. their implementation invariably requires (contrary to the "spirit of Anglo-Saxon liberalism") the backing of the military and of the authoritarian state. Structural adjustment promotes bogus institutions and a fake parliamentary democracy which in turn supports the process of economic restructuring.

Throughout the Third World, the situation is one of social desperation and the hopelessness of a population impoverished by the interplay of market forces. Anti-SAP riots and popular uprisings are brutally repressed: Caracas, 1989. President Carlos Andres Perez after having rhetorically denounced the IMF of practising"an economic totalitarianism which kills not with bullets but with famine", declares a state of emergency and sends regular units of the infantry and the marines into the slum areas (*barrios de ranchos*) on the hills overlooking the capital. The Caracas anti-IMF riots had been sparked off as a result of a 200 per cent increase in the price of bread. Men, women and children were fired upon indiscriminately: "The Caracas morgue was reported to have up to 200 bodies of people killed in the first three days ... and warned that it was running out of coffins". Unofficially more than a thousand people were killed. Tunis, January 1984: the bread riots instigated largely by unemployed youth protesting the rise of food prices; Nigeria, 1989: the anti-SAP student riots leading to the closing of six of the country's universities by the Armed Forces Ruling Council; Morocco, 1990: a general strike and a popular uprising against the government's IMF-sponsored reforms; Mexico, 1993: the insurrection of the Zapatista Liberation Army in the Chiapas region of southern Mexico; protest movements in the Russian Federation and the storming of the Russian parliament in 1993, and so on. The list is long.

Economic Genocide

Structural adjustment is conducive to a form of "economic genocide" which is carried out through the conscious and deliberate manipulation of market forces. When compared to genocide at various periods of colonial history (e.g. forced labour and slavery), its social impact is devastating. Structural adjustment programmes affect directly the livelihood of more than four billion people. The application of the structural adjustment programme in a large number of individual debtor countries favours the "internationalisation" of macro-economic policy under the direct control of the IMF and the World Bank acting on behalf of powerful financial and political interests (e.g. the Paris and London Clubs, the G7). This new form of economic and political domination – a form of "market colonialism" – subordinates people and governments through the seemingly "neutral" interplay of market forces. The Washington-based international bureaucracy has been entrusted by international creditors and multinational corporations with the execution of a global economic design which affects the livelihood of more than 80 per cent of the world's population. At no time in history has the "free" market – operating in the world through the instruments of macro-economics – played such an important role in shaping the destiny of "sovereign" nations.

Destroying the National Economy

The restructuring of the world economy under the guidance of the Washington-based financial institutions increasingly denies individual developing countries the possibility of building a national economy: the internationalisation of macro-economic policy transforms countries into open economic territories and national economies into "reserves" of cheap labour and natural resources. The application of the IMF's "economic medicine" tends to further depress world commodity prices because it forces individual countries to simultaneously gear their national economies towards a shrinking world market.

At the heart of the global economic system, lies an unequal structure of trade, production and credit which defines the role and position of developing countries in the global economy. What is the nature of this unfolding world economic system, on what structure of global poverty and income inequality is it based? By the turn of the century, the world population will be over six billion of which five billion will be living in poor countries. While the rich countries with some 15 per cent of the world population control close to 80 per cent of total world income, some 56 per cent of the world population representing the group of "low-income countries" (including India and China), with a population of over three billion people, received in 1993 approximately 5 per cent of total world income, less than the GDP of France and its overseas territories. With a population of more than 600 million people, the gross product of the entire sub-Saharan African region is approximately half that of the state of Texas. Together, the lower and middle-income countries (including the former "socialist" countries and the former Soviet Union) representing some 85 per cent of world population receive approximately 20 per cent of total world income (see Table 1.1).

In many indebted Third World countries, real salaried earnings in the modern sector have declined by more than 60 per cent since the beginning of the 1980s. The situation of the informal sector and the unemployed is even more critical. In Nigeria under the military government of General Ibrahim Babangida, for instance, the minimum wage declined by 85 per cent in the course of the 1980s. Wages in Vietnam were below US$10 a month while the domestic price of rice had risen to the world level as a result of the IMF programme carried out by the Hanoi government: a Hanoi secondary school teacher, for instance, with a university degree, received in 1991 a monthly salary of less than US$15[2] (see Chapter 12). In Peru, in the aftermath of the IMF-World Bank sponsored *Fujishock* implemented by President Alberto Fujimori in August 1990, fuel prices increased 31 times overnight whereas the price of bread increased 12 times. The real minimum wage had declined by more than 90 per cent (in relation to its level in the mid-1970s) (see Chapter 10).

The Dollarisation of Prices

While there are sizeable variations in the cost of living between developing and developed countries, devaluation combined with trade liberalisation and the deregulation of domestic commodity markets (under the structural adjustment programme) is conducive to the

Table 1.1: The Distribution of World Income (1993)

	Population (Millions) Mid-1993	Share of World Population	Per Capita Income (in US$)	Total Income Billion dollars	Share of World Income
Low-Income Third World	3,077.8	56.0	379	1,166.5	4.9
Sub-Saharan Africa	599.0	10.9	520	311.5	1.3
South Asia	1,194.4	21.7	310	370.3	1.5
China	1,178.4	21.4	490	577.4	2.4
Middle-Income Third World	1,218.9	22.2	2,397	2,921.7	12.2
Total Third World	4,296.7	78.1	951	4,088.6	17.1
Eastern Europe and Ex-USSR	392.3	7.1	2,665	1,045.5	4.4
Total Poor Countries*	4,689.0	85.2	1,095	5,133.7	21.5
OECD Countries**	812.2	14.7	22,924	18,618.9	77.9
Total Rich Countries	812.4	14.8	23,090	18,758.3	78.5
World Total	5,501.5	100.0	4,343.0	23,892.0	100.0

Source: Estimated from World Bank data in *World Development Report*, 1995, Washington DC, 1995, pp. 162-163

* Excludes low income countries of the Ex-USSR

• Total poor countries is the sum of total Third World and Eastern Europe and Ex-USSR.

** Excluding Iceland, Mexico and Turkey.

Note: The categories and weights differ from those of the World Bank; Tajikistan, Georgia and Armenia are included in Eastern Europe and Ex-USSR.

Figure 1.1: Shares of World Population and Income (1993)

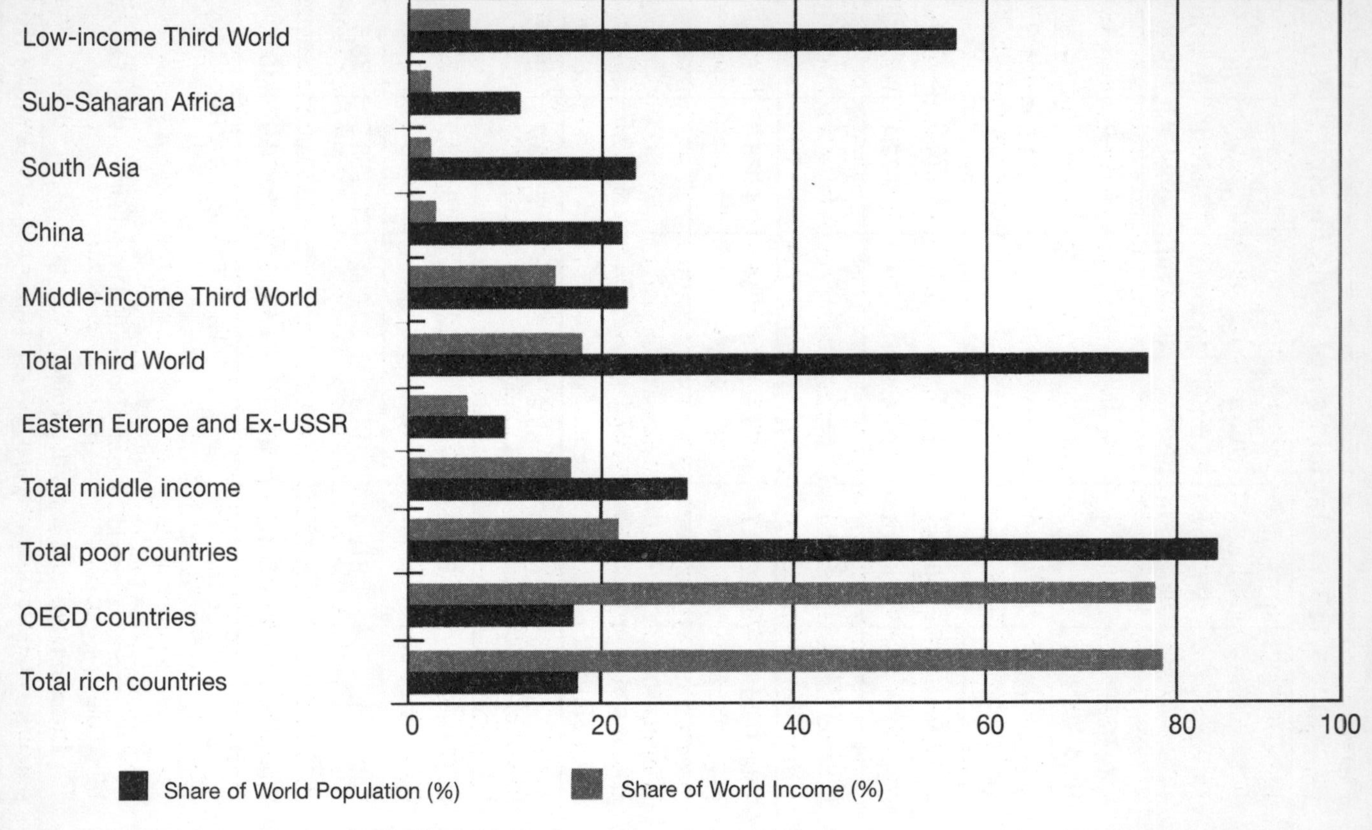

Source: World Bank, *World Development Report, 1995*

"dollarisation" of domestic prices. Increasingly, the domestic prices of basic food staples are brought up to their world market levels. This new world economic order, while based on the internationalisation of commodity prices and a fully integrated world commodity market, functions increasingly in terms of a watertight separation between two distinct "labour markets". In other words, this global market system is characterised by a duality in the structure of wages and labour costs between rich and poor countries. Whereas prices are unified and brought up to world levels, wages (and labour costs) in the Third World and Eastern Europe are as much as 70 times lower than in the OECD countries.

Income disparities between nations are superimposed on extremely wide income disparities between social-income groups within nations. In many Third World countries, at least 60 per cent of national income is concentrated in the upper 20 per cent of the population. In many low and middle-income developing countries, 70 per cent of rural households have a per capita income which is between 10 and 20 per cent of the national average. These vast disparities in income between and within countries are the consequence of the structure of commodity trade and the unequal international division of labour which imparts to the Third World, and more recently to the countries of the former Soviet bloc, a subordinate status in the global economic system. The disparities have widened in the course of the 1980s and 1990s as a result of the "remoulding" of national economies under the structural adjustment programme.[3]

The "Thirdworldisation" of the Former Eastern Bloc

The end of the Cold War has had a profound impact on the global distribution of income. Until recently, Eastern Europe and the Soviet Union were considered as part of the developed "North", – i.e. with levels of material consumption, education, health, scientific development, etc. broadly comparable to those prevailing in the OECD countries. Whereas average incomes were on the whole lower, Western scholars nonetheless acknowledged the achievements of the Eastern-bloc countries, particularly in the areas of health and education.

Impoverished as a result of the IMF-sponsored reforms, the countries of the former socialist bloc are now categorised by the World

Bank as "developing economies", alongside the "low" and "middle-income countries" of the Third World. The Central Asian republics appear next to Syria, Jordan and Tunisia in the "lower middle-income" category, whereas the Russian Federation is next to Brazil with a per capita income of the order of US$3,000. This shift in categories reflects the outcome of the Cold War and the underlying process of "thirdworldisation" of Eastern Europe and the former Soviet Union.

Economic Ideology Distorts the Causes of Global Poverty

The dominant economic discourse has, since the early 1980s, reinforced its hold in academic and research institutions throughout the world: critical analysis is strongly discouraged, social and economic reality is to be seen through a single set of fictitious economic relations which serve the purpose of concealing the workings of the global economic system. Mainstream economic scholarship produces theory without facts ("pure theory") and facts without theory ("applied economics"). The dominant economic dogma admits neither dissent from nor discussion of its main theoretical paradigm: the universities' main function is to produce a generation of loyal and dependable economists who are incapable of unveiling the social foundations of the global market economy. Similarly, Third World intellectuals are increasingly enlisted in support of the neoliberal paradigm; the internationalisation of economic "science" unreservedly supports the process of global economic restructuring.

This "official" neoliberal dogma also creates its own "counter-paradigm" embodying a highly moral and ethical discourse. The latter focuses on "sustainable development" and "poverty alleviation" while distorting and "stylising" the policy issues pertaining to poverty, the protection of the environment and the social rights of women. This "counter-ideology" rarely challenges neoliberal policy prescriptions. It develops alongside and in harmony rather than in opposition to the official neoliberal dogma.

Within this counter-ideology (which is generously funded by the research establishment) development scholars find a comfortable niche. Their role is to generate (within this counter-discourse) a semblance of critical debate without addressing the social foundations of the global market system. The World Bank plays in this regard a key role by promoting research on poverty and the so-called "social dimensions of adjustment". This ethical focus and the underlying categories (e.g. poverty alleviation, gender issues, equity, etc.) provide a "human face" for the Bretton Woods institutions and a semblance of commitment to social change. However, inasmuch as this analysis is functionally divorced from an understanding of the main macro-economic reforms, it rarely constitutes a threat to the neoliberal economic agenda.

Manipulating the Figures on Global Poverty

Whereas social and income disparities between and within nations have widened, the realities of world poverty are increasingly concealed by the manipulation of income statistics.

The World Bank "estimates" that 18 per cent of the Third World is "extremely poor" and 33 per cent is "poor". In a major World Bank study which has served as a reference on issues of global poverty, the "upper poverty line" is arbitrarily set at a per capita income of US$1 a day corresponding to an annual per capita income of US$370 per annum.[4] Population groups in individual countries with per capita incomes in excess of US$1 a day are arbitrarily identified as "non-poor". In other words, through the manipulation of income statistics, the World Bank figures serve the useful purpose of representing the poor in developing countries as a minority group.

Double standards abound in the "scientific measurement of poverty". The World Bank, for instance, "estimates" that in Latin America and the Caribbean only 19 per cent of the population is "poor": a gross distortion when we know for a fact that in the United States (with an annual per capita income of approximately US$20,000) one American in five is defined (by the Bureau of the Census) to be below the poverty line.[5]

Endnotes

1. According to the Tufts University Centre on Hunger, Poverty and Nutrition Policy.
2. Interviews conducted by author in Hanoi and Ho Chi Minh City in January 1991.
3. It is worth noting in this regard that the share of developing countries in total world income have declined substantially since the onslaught of the debt crisis. Whereas the group of low-income countries increased its share of world population by more than 2 per cent in the three-year period between 1988 and 1991, its share of world income declined from 5.4 to 4.9 per cent. Similarly, sub-Saharan Africa's share of world income declined in the same period from 0.9 to 0.7 per cent. In 1993, the World Bank redefined the basis of measuring and comparing per capita income. The figures contained in Table 1.1 have been corrected for differences in purchasing power parity.
4. See World Bank, *World Development Report 1990*, *Poverty*, Washington DC., 1990.
5. The US Bureau of the Census estimated (based on an achievement of a minimum food bundle) the level of poverty in the US at 18.2 per cent in 1986; see Bruce E. Kaufman, *The Economics of Labor and Labor Markets*, second edition, Orlando, 1989, p. 649. More recent official estimates confirm a level of poverty of the order of 20 per cent.

Chapter 2

Policing Countries Through Loan "Conditionalities"

The Global Debt

HOW were sovereign countries brought under the tutelage of the international financial institutions? Because countries were indebted, the Bretton Woods institutions were able to oblige them through the so-called "conditionalities" attached to the loan agreements to "appropriately" redirect their macro-economic policy in accordance with the interests of the official and commercial creditors.

The debt burden of developing countries has increased steadily since the early 1980s despite the various rescheduling, restructuring and debt-conversion schemes put forward by the creditors. In fact, these procedures when combined with IMF-World Bank policy-based lending (under the structural adjustment programme) were conducive to enlarging the outstanding debt of developing countries while ensuring prompt reimbursement of interest payments.

The total outstanding long-term debt of developing countries (from official and private sources) stood at approximately US$62 billion in 1970. It increased sevenfold in the course of the 1970s to reach $481 billion in 1980. The total debt (including the short-term debt) of developing countries stood at more than $2 trillion (1996) a 32-fold increase in relation to 1970 (see Table 2.1).

A Marshall Plan for the Rich Countries

While commodity prices tumbled leading, since the early 1980s, to a decline in the value of exports, an increasingly larger share of export earnings had been earmarked for debt-servicing (see Figures 2.1 – 2.4).

Table 2.1: Developing Countries' External Debt (in US$ billions)

	Total external debt	Long-term debt	Short-term debt	Use of IMF credit
1980	658	481	164	12
1981	672	498	159	14
1982	745	557	168	20
1983	807	633	140	33
1984	843	675	132	36
1985	990	809	141	40
1986	1218	996	179	43
1987	1369	1128	198	43
1988	1375	1127	213	35
1989	1427	1151	244	32
1990	1539	1226	278	35
1991	1627	1286	303	38
1992	1696	1328	329	38
1993	1812	1424	349	39
1994*	1945	1538	366	41

* Projected.

Technical Note: The pre-1985 data are based on all countries reporting to the World Bank and are not directly comparable to the post-1985 data.

Source: World Bank, *World Debt Tables,* several issues,Washington DC.

Figure 2.1: Developing Countries' External Debt

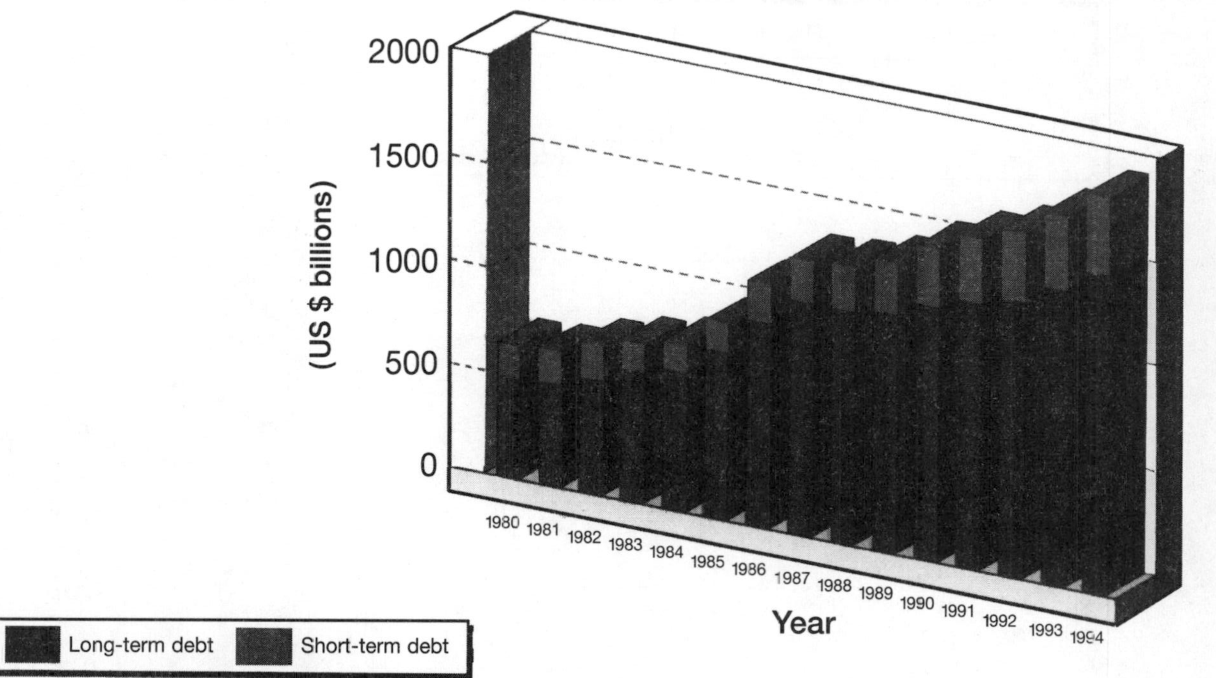

- The pre-1985 data are based on all countries reporting to the World Bank and are not directly comparable to the post-1985 data.

Source: World Bank, *World Debt Tables*

Figure 2.2: The Ratio of Total External Debt to Exports of Goods and Services (in per cent)

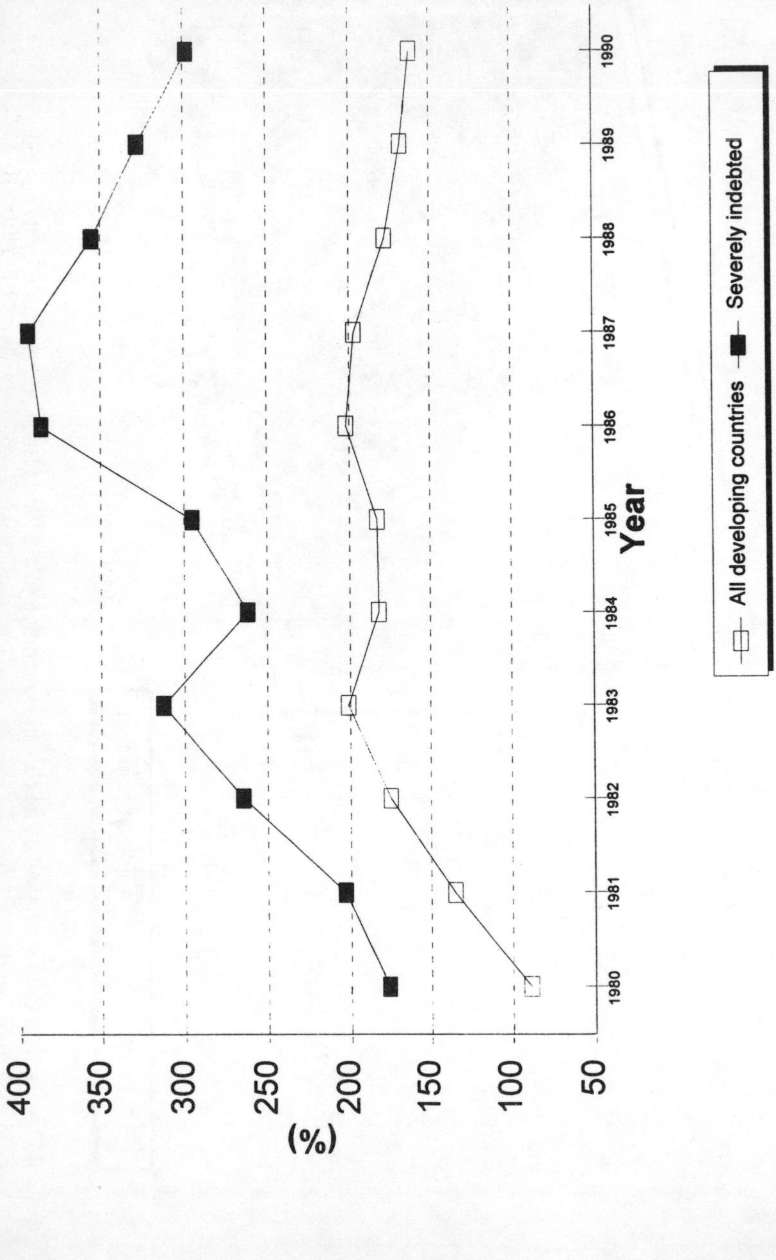

Source: World Bank, *World Debt Tables*

Figure 2.3: Share of Exports Allocated to Debt Servicing (in per cent)

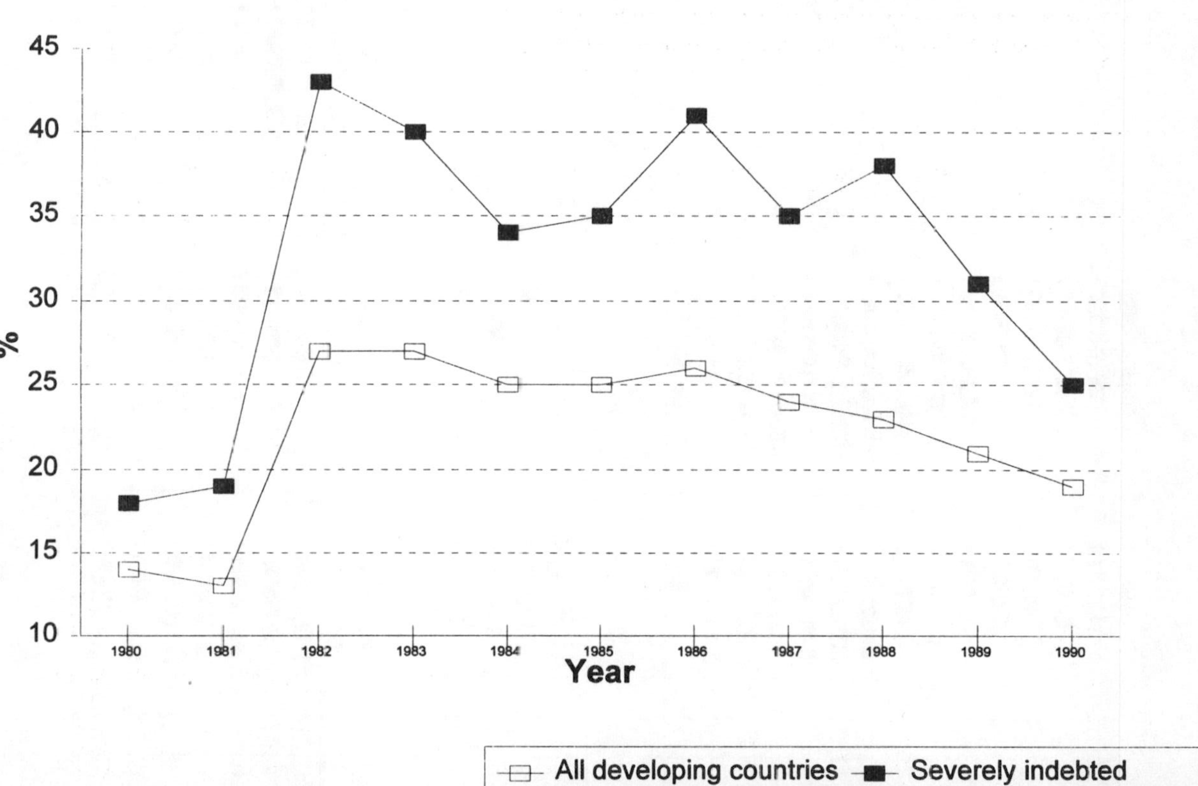

Source: World Bank, *World Debt Tables*

Figure 2.4: Share of Exports Allocated to Debt Servicing by Geographical Region (in per cent)*

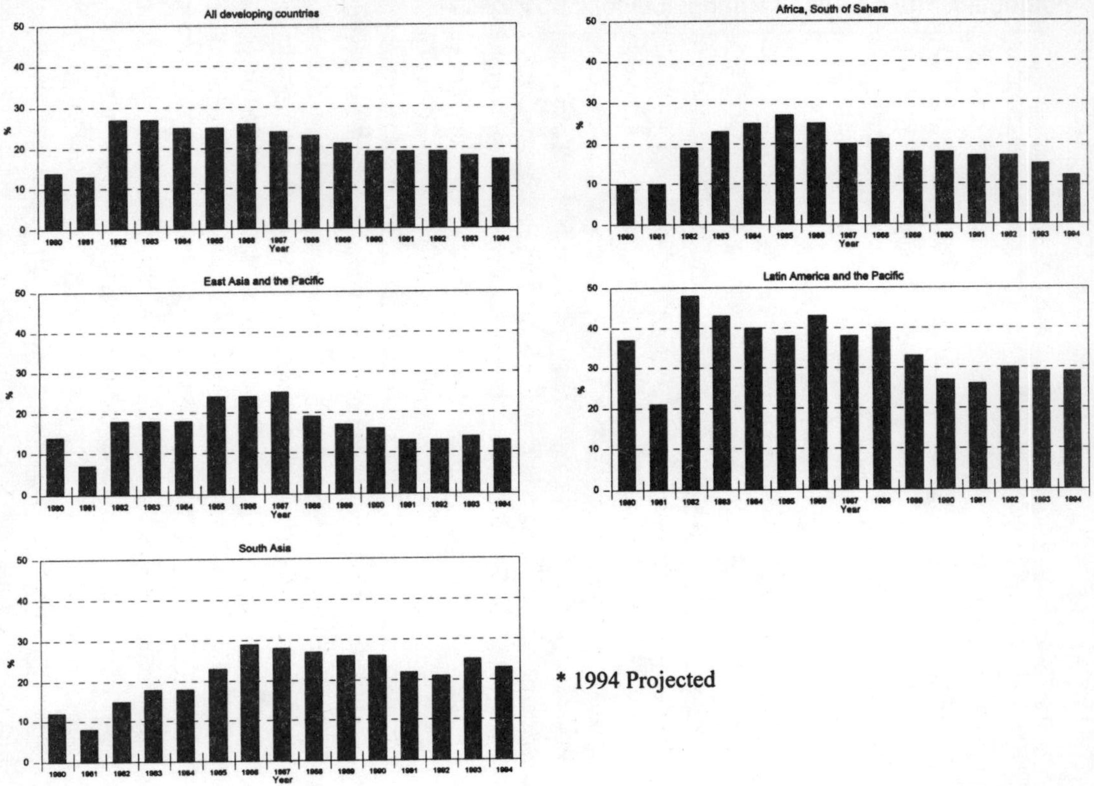

All developing countries

Africa, South of Sahara

East Asia and the Pacific

Latin America and the Pacific

South Asia

% 0 10 20 30 40 50

Year 1980 1981 1982 1983 1984 1985 1986 1987 1988 1989 1990 1991 1992 1993 1994

* 1994 Projected

Source: World Bank, *World Debt Tables*

By the mid-1980s, developing countries had become net exporters of capital in favour of the rich countries. In other words, the flow of actual debt servicing was in excess of the new inflows of capital (in the form of loans, foreign investment and foreign aid).[1] Up until the mid-1980s, the international financial institutions (IFIs) had re-financed debt largely in the name of the commercial bank and official creditors. However, many of the loans granted by the multilateral institutions at the outset of the debt crisis became due and the Washington-based IFIs demanded the reimbursement of these loans. Under the articles of agreement of the Bretton Woods institutions, these loans cannot be rescheduled.

Policy-based Lending

There is a close, almost "symbiotic" relationship between debt-management policy and macro-economic reform. Debt management is confined to ensuring that individual debtor nations continue formally to abide by their financial obligations. Through "financial engineering" and the careful art of debt rescheduling, repayment of the principal is deferred while interest payments are enforced, debt is swapped for equity and "new" money is "lent" to nations on the verge of bankruptcy to enable them to pay off their interest arrears on "old" debts so as to temporarily avert default, and so on. In this process, the formal loyalty of individual debtors is paramount. The creditors accept to reschedule only if debtor nations abide by the "policy conditionalities" attached to the loan agreements.

The objective consists in enforcing the legitimacy of the debt-servicing relationship while maintaining debtor nations in a strait-jacket which prevents them from embarking upon an independent national economic policy. A new generation of "policy-based loans" was devised. Money was provided "to help countries to adjust". These World-Bank loan agreements included tight "conditionalities": the money was granted only if the government complied with the structural adjustment reforms while at the same time respecting very precise deadlines for their implementation.

In turn, the adoption of the IMF's policy prescriptions under the structural adjustment programme was not only conditional for obtaining new loans from multilateral institutions, it also provided "the green light" to the Paris and London Clubs, foreign investors, commercial banking institutions and bilateral donors. Countries which refused to accept the Fund's corrective policy measures faced serious difficulties in rescheduling their debt and/or obtaining new development loans and international assistance. The IMF also had the means of seriously disrupting a national economy by blocking short-term credit in support of commodity trade.

So-called "conditionalities" were attached to "the quick disbursing policy-based loans". In other words, these loans by the IFIs were granted subject to the adoption of a comprehensive programme of macro-economic stabilisation and structural economic reform, – i.e. the loan agreements were not in any way related to an investment programme as in conventional project lending. The loans were intended to support policy changes: the latter were tightly monitored by the Bretton Woods institutions, their evaluation being based on "policy performance". In other words, once the loan agreement had been signed, disbursements could be interrupted if the government did not conform, with the danger that the country would be blacklisted by the so-called "aid coordination group" of bilateral and multilateral donors.[2]

The nature of these loan agreements did not favour the real economy, since none of the money was channelled into investment. Another important objective was served, however: the adjustment loans diverted resources away from the domestic economy and encouraged countries to keep on importing large quantities of consumer goods, including food staples, from the rich countries. In other words, the money granted in support of the "adjustment" of agriculture, for instance, was not meant for investment in agricultural projects. The loans could be spent freely on commodity imports including consumer durables and luxury goods.[3] The result of this process was stagnation of the domestic economy, enlargement of the balance of payments crisis and growth of the debt burden.

Enlarging the Debt

The new "quick disbursing loans" (theoretically earmarked for commodity imports) represented "fictitious money" because the amounts granted to debtor nations were invariably lower than the amounts reimbursed in the form of debt servicing. Envisage, for instance, a developing country which has a total debt stock of US$10 billion and owes $1 billion in (annual) debt-servicing obligations to the Paris and London Clubs. With depressed export earnings, however, the country is unable to meet these obligations. And unless new loans "to pay back old debts" are forthcoming, arrears will accumulate and the country will be placed on an international blacklist.

In our example, a quick disbursing loan of US$500 million is granted in the form of balance of payments support earmarked for the purchase of commodity imports. The loan acts as "*a catalyser*": it allows the country's foreign exchange earnings from exports to be redirected towards interest payments, thereby enabling the government to meet the deadlines of commercial and official creditors. A billion dollars of debt-servicing is collected through a new loan of US$500 million.

The net outflow of resources is US$500 million. The loan is "fictitious" because the money which had been advanced (i.e. by the IMF or the World Bank) is immediately reappropriated by the official and/or commercial creditors. Moreover, this process has resulted in a $500 million increase in the debt stock because the new loan was used to pay back the interest portion of debt servicing and not the principal.

The IMF Shadow Programme

Invariably, substantial reforms will be required prior to the holding of actual loan negotiations. The government has to provide evidence to the IMF that it is "seriously committed to economic reform". This process often takes the form of a so-called "Letter of Intent" submitted to the IMF identifying the government's major orientations in macroeconomic policy and debt management. This process was also carried out in the context of the so-called "IMF Shadow Programme" in which the IMF provided policy guidelines and technical advice to the government without formal loan support. The Shadow Programme applies to countries whose economic reforms are (according to the IMF) "not on track" [e.g. Peru under Alberto Fujimori (1990-91) or Brazil under Fernando Collor de Mello and Itamar Franco (1990-94)]. The Shadow Programme was also implemented in countries of the former Soviet bloc in the form of IMF-World Bank technical assistance prior to their formal membership of the Bretton Woods institutions and/or the signing of loan agreements.

"Satisfactory performance" under the Shadow Programme is a prerequisite (i.e. a prior condition) to formal loan negotiations. Once the loan has been granted, policy performance is tightly monitored on a quarterly basis by the Washington institutions. The disbursements granted in several "tranches" can be interrupted if the reforms are "not on track" in which case the country is back "on the blacklist" with the danger of reprisals in the area of trade and capital flows. The disbursements can also be interrupted if the country falls behind in its current debt-servicing obligations. The country may, nonetheless, continue to receive IMF-World Bank technical assistance, – i.e. a new Shadow Programme (as in the case of Kenya in 1991) is set up leading to a new round of policy negotiations.

The Policy Framework Paper

In many indebted countries, the government is obliged under its agreement with the Washington-based institutions to outline its priorities in a so-called "Policy Framework Paper" (PFP). Although officially a government document determined by the national authorities, the PFP is written under the close supervision of the IMF and the World Bank according to a standard pre-set format. There is, in this context, a clear division of tasks between the two sister organisations. The IMF is involved in key policy negotiations with regard to the exchange rate and the budget deficit whereas the World Bank is far more involved in the actual reform process through its country-level representative office and its numerous technical missions.

The IMF monitors a country's economic performance in the context of "Article IV consultations" (regular review of a member country's economy) on an annual basis. This review provides – in addition to the more stringent quarterly monitoring of performance targets under loan agreements – the basis of so-called "IMF surveillance activities" of members' economic policies.

The World Bank is present in many of the ministries: the reforms in health, education, industry, agriculture, transportation, the environment, etc. are under its jurisdiction. Moreover, since the late 1980s, the World Bank supervises the privatisation of state enterprises, the structure of public investment and the composition of public expenditure through the so-called Public Expenditure Review (PER).

The IFIs' Lending Facilities

Various "lending facilities" were used by the Bretton Woods institutions in support of policy-based loans:

> **International Monetary Fund**
> Stand-by arrangements, the Compensatory and Contingency Financing Facility (CCFF), the Extended Fund Facility (EFF), IMF structural adjustment and enhanced structural adjustment facilities (SAF and ESAF), the Systemic Transformation Facility (STF), Emergency Lending Facility for Post-Conflict countries.
>
> **World Bank**
> Structural adjustment loans (SAL) and sector adjustment loans (SECAL).

The Systemic Transformation Facility (STF) applied in the former Eastern bloc countries operates broadly with the same conditionalities as the structural adjustment loans.

Phase One: "Economic Stabilisation"

Structural adjustment is viewed by the IFIs as consisting of two distinct phases: "Short-term" macro-economic stabilisation (implying devaluation, price liberalisation and budgetary austerity) to be followed by the implementation of a number of more fundamental (and so-called "necessary") structural reforms. More often, however, these "structural" reforms are carried out concurrently with the "economic stabilisation" process. The IMF-World Bank stabilisation exercise addresses both the budget deficit and the balance of payments. According to the World Bank, this requires: "Getting macro-economic policy right... Keeping budget deficits small helps in controlling inflation and avoiding balance of payments problems. Keeping a realistic exchange rate pays off in greater international competitiveness and in supporting convertible currencies".[4]

Destroying A Nation's Currency

The exchange rate is by far the most important instrument of macro-economic reform: currency devaluation (including the unification of the exchange rate and the elimination of exchange controls) affects fundamental supply and demand relations within the national economy. The IMF plays a key political role in decisions to devalue. The rate of exchange regulates the real prices paid to the direct producers as well as the real value of wages.

The IMF invariably argues that the exchange rate is "overvalued". Currency devaluation is often demanded (as a pre-condition) prior to the negotiation of a structural adjustment loan: the destabilisation of the national currency is a key objective of the IMF-World Bank's "hidden agenda". A "maxi-devaluation" – resulting in immediate and abrupt price hikes – is conducive to a dramatic compression of real earnings while at the same time reducing the value of labour costs expressed in hard currency. The devaluation also reduces the dollar value of government expenditure thereby facilitating the release of state revenues towards the servicing of the external debt.

The IMF imposes the unification of the exchange rate in the context of the clauses of Article VIII of the IMF Articles of Agreement. Countries accepting Article VIII are prevented from adopting multiple exchange-rate practices or foreign exchange controls without IMF approval. Eighty-seven member countries of the IMF have accepted the clauses of Article VIII.

The Social Consequences of Devaluation

The social impact of the IMF-sponsored devaluation is brutal and immediate: the domestic prices of food staples, essential drugs, fuel and public services increase overnight. While the devaluation invariably triggers inflation and the "dollarisation" of domestic prices, the IMF obliges the government (as part of the economic package) to adopt a so-called "anti-inflationary programme". The latter has little to do with the real causes of inflation (i.e. the devaluation). It is predicated "on a contraction of demand" requiring the dismissal of public employees, drastic cuts in social-sector programmes and the deindexation of wages. In sub-Saharan Africa, for instance, the devaluation of the Central and West African (CFA) franc imposed by the IMF and the French Treasury in 1994 compressed (with the stroke of a pen) the real value of wages and government expenditure (expressed in hard currency) by 50 per cent while massively redirecting state revenues towards debt-servicing.

In some cases, currency devaluation has provided the basis for a short-term reactivation of commercial agriculture geared towards the export market. More often, however, the underlying benefits accrue to the large commercial plantations and agro-industrial exporters (in the form of lower real wages to agricultural workers). The "short-term gains" from devaluation are invariably wiped out when competing Third World countries are forced to devalue (in similar agreements with the IMF).

The "Dollarisation" of Domestic Prices

The devaluation leads to a "realignment of domestic prices" at the levels prevailing in the world market. This process of "dollarisation" of domestic prices leads to abrupt price hikes in most commodities, including food staples, consumer durables, gasoline, fuel, as well as most inputs and raw materials used in production (e.g. farm inputs, equipment, etc.). In this regard, domestic prices will adjust to their world market levels irrespective of the direction of monetary policy.

The devaluation rather than the supply of money constitutes the main factor which triggers the inflationary spiral. The IMF denies the inflationary impact of currency devaluation: tight restrictions on money supply are imposed in the aftermath of the devaluation once the price hikes have already taken place with a view to "combating inflationary pressures". This freeze on money creation obliges the government to curtail real expenditures, reduce real wages and lay off civil servants.

The Deindexation of Wages

Needless to say, pressures build up within society to increase nominal wages to compensate for the dramatic decline in real earnings, yet the agreement with the IMF formally disallows the indexation of real earnings (and social expenditures). The IMF requires "the liberalisation of the labour market", the elimination of cost of living adjustment clauses in collective agreements and the phasing out of minimum-wage legislation. The argument in favour of deindexation is based on the "inflationary impact of wage demands".

Analysing the Impact of Devaluation

The impact of the devaluation must be analysed in relation to the following variables:

- the level of domestic prices (P),
- nominal wages (W), real wages (W/P),
- nominal government expenditure (G), real government expenditure (G/P),
- the nominal money supply (M), the real money supply (M/P).

The dollarisation of domestic prices leads to a contraction in:

- real wages (W/P) and the real value of government expenditure (G/P).

The nominal supply of money (M) may increase but the real value of the supply of money (M/P) declines dramatically. In other words, the devaluation implies a process of monetary contraction (M/P) and a massive compression of the real value of government expenditure (G/P) and wages (W/P). The real prices paid to direct producers also decline as a result of the devaluation.

Taking Control of the Central Bank

The IMF tightly monitors and provides resources for the restructuring of the Central Bank. The IMF requires so-called "Central Bank independence from political power" "as a remedy against the inflationary bias of governments".[5] In practice this means that the IMF rather than the government controls money creation. In other words, the agreement signed between the government and the IMF prevents the funding of government expenditure and the provision of credit by the Central Bank through money creation, – i.e. the IMF on behalf of the creditors is in a position virtually to paralyse the financing of real economic development. Incapable of using domestic monetary policy to mobilise its internal resources, the country becomes increasingly dependent on international sources of funding which has the added consequence of increasing the level of external indebtedness.

Another important condition put forth by the IMF is that "Central Bank independence holds also with respect to parliament".[6] Namely, once the senior officials of the Central Bank have been appointed, they are neither accountable to the government nor to parliament. Increasingly, their allegiance is to the IFIs. In many developing countries, senior officials of the Central Bank are former staff members of the IFIs and of the regional development banks. Moreover, Central Bank officials often receive "salary supplements" in hard currency financed from multilateral and bilateral sources.

Destabilising a Nation's Public Finances

The dismissal of public employees and drastic cuts in social-sector programmes are imposed by the Bretton Woods institutions. These austerity measures hit all categories of public expenditure. At the outset of the debt crisis, the IFIs would limit their intervention to setting an overall target for the budget deficit in view of releasing state revenues for debt servicing. Since the late 1980s, the World Bank has monitored closely the structure of public expenditure through the so-called Public Expenditure Review (PER). In this context, the composition of expenditure in each of the ministries is under the supervision of the Bretton Woods institutions. The World Bank recommends "a cost effective" transfer from regular expenditure categories to "targeted expenditures". According to the World Bank, the PER is to "promote the reduction of poverty in a cost effective and efficient fashion".

With regard to the social sectors, the IFIs insist on the principle of cost recovery and the gradual withdrawal of the state from basic health and educational services. The concept of targeting in the social sectors pertains to the identification of so-called "vulnerable groups". The austerity measures in the social sectors – requiring a shift from regular to targeted programmes – has largely been responsible for the collapse of schools, health clinics and hospitals, while providing a semblance of legitimacy to the Washington-based institutions.

The Budget Deficit: A Moving Target

Initial targets are set in the loan agreements for the budget deficit. However, since the early 1990s, the IMF has applied the concept of a "moving target" for the budget deficit: a target of 5 per cent of GDP is first set, the government meets the IMF target; in subsequent loan negotiations or within the same loan agreement, the IMF lowers the target to 3.5 per cent on the grounds that government expenditure patterns are "inflationary"; once the 3.5 per cent target has been met, the IMF will insist on reducing the budget deficit to 1.5 per cent of GDP, and so on. This exercise ultimately exacerbates the fiscal crisis of the state leading to the collapse of state programmes while releasing state revenue (in the short-run) for the payment of interest on the external debt.

Engineering the Collapse of State Investment

The budget targets imposed by the Bretton Woods institutions combined with the effects of the devaluation trigger the collapse of public investment. New rules pertaining to both recurrent and development expenditures are established: precise "ceilings" are placed on all categories of expenditure, the state is no longer permitted to mobilise its own resources for the building of public infrastructure, roads or hospitals, etc. – i.e. the creditors not only become the "brokers" of all major public investment projects, they also decide in the context of the "Public Investment Programme" (PIP) (established under the technical auspices of the World Bank) on what type of public infrastructure should or should not be funded by the "donor community". The concept of targeted investment is put forth and capital formation in necessary economic and social infrastructure is dramatically curtailed.

Under the PIP, all project loans require a system of procurement and international tender ("competitive bidding") which allocates the entire execution of public works projects to international construction and engineering firms. The latter in turn skim off large amounts of money into a variety of consulting and management fees. Local construction companies (whether public or private) tend to be excluded from the tendering process although much of the actual construction work will be undertaken by local companies (using local labour at very low wages) in separate sub-contracting deals reached with the transnationals. In other words, loan money earmarked for infrastructural projects is largely "recycled" in favour of multinational contractors.

While project financing is granted in the form of "soft loans" at concessional interest rates with extended repayment periods, the actual costs (and the imputed interest rate which underly these costs) to the country are exceedingly high. In other words, the PIP under the supervision of the World Bank is predicated on enlarging the external debt while contributing to the demobilisation of domestic resources.

Price Liberalisation

The IMF-World Bank claims that it is necessary to eliminate so-called price distortions. "Getting Prices Right" consists in the elimination of all subsidies and price controls. The impact on levels of real earnings (in both the formal and informal sectors) is immediate.

The deregulation of domestic grain prices as well as the liberalisation of staple food imports are an essential feature of this programme. The liberalisation programme also pertains to the prices of inputs and raw materials. Combined with the devaluation, the underlying measures lead to substantial hikes in the domestic prices of fertiliser, farm inputs, equipment, etc. which have an immediate impact on the cost structure in most areas of economic activity.

The Pricing of Petroleum Products and Public Utilities

The price of petroleum products is regulated by the state under the supervision of the World Bank. The price hikes both in fuel and public utilities (often of several hundred per cent) invariably contribute to destabilising domestic production, – i.e. the high domestic price of gasoline (substantially above world market levels) backlashes on the cost structure of domestic industry and agriculture. The production costs are often artificially pushed up above the domestic sale price of the commodity thereby precipitating a large number of small and medium-sized producers into bankruptcy.

Moreover, the periodic price hikes of petroleum products imposed by the World Bank (adopted concurrently with the liberalisation of commodity imports) operates as an "internal transit duty" which serves the purpose of cutting domestic producers off from their own market. The high price of gasoline contributes to the disruption of internal freight. Exceedingly high petrol and diesel prices (i.e. in relation to very low wages) combined with the numerous user fees and tolls for bridges, roads, inland waterways, etc. affect the entire cost structure of domestically produced goods largely to the advantage of imported commodities. In sub-Saharan Africa, the high cost of transportation imposed by the IFIs is one of the key factors which prevent farmers from selling their produce in the urban market in direct competition with heavily subsidised agricultural commodities imported from Europe and North America.

Although the modalities differ, the tariff on fuel and public utilities has similar consequences to the internal transit duty imposed in India by the British East India Company in the late 18th century.

Phase Two: "Structural Reform"

The application of macro-economic "stabilisation" (which is a condition for the granting of bridge financing by the IMF and the rescheduling of the external debt with the Paris and London Clubs) is followed by the implementation of so-called "necessary" structural reforms. There is a division of tasks between the IMF and the World Bank. These "necessary" economic reforms are "supported" by World Bank SALs and sectoral adjustment loans (SECALs). The package of structural reforms discussed below consists of measures pertaining to trade liberalisation, the deregulation of the banking sector, the privatisation of state enterprises, tax reform, the privatisation of agricultural land, "poverty alleviation" and "good governance".

Trade Liberalisation

The Bretton Woods institutions argue that the tariff structure constitutes a so-called "anti-export bias" which discourages the development of the export economy, – i.e. it favours the development of the domestic market at the expense of the export sector leading to a misallocation of resources. There is little evidence to suggest, however, that the elimination of tariffs has facilitated "the switch of resources" in favour of exports.

The trade liberalisation programme invariably consists of the elimination of import quotas and the reduction and unification of tariffs. The consequent decline in customs' revenues also has a significant impact on the state's public finances. Not only do these measures backfire on the budget deficit, thus exacerbating fiscal imbalances; they also prevent the authorities from selectively "rationing" (through tariffs and quotas) the use of scarce foreign exchange.

While the elimination of quotas and the reduction of protective tariff barriers are intended "to make domestic industry more competitive", the liberalisation of trade invariably leads to the collapse of domestic manufacturing (geared towards the internal market). The measures also fuel the influx of luxury goods; while the tax burden of the upper income groups is reduced as a result of the lowering of import tariffs on automobiles and consumer durables. Imported consumer goods not only replace domestic production. This consumer frenzy sustained on borrowed money (through the various quick disbursing loans) ultimately contributes to swelling the external debt....

Divestiture and Privatisation of State Enterprises

Structural adjustment constitutes a means for taking over the real assets of indebted countries through the privatisation programme as well as collecting debt servicing obligations. The privatisation of state enterprises is invariably tied to the renegotiation of the country's external debt. The most profitable parastatals are taken over by foreign capital or joint ventures often in exchange for debt. The proceeds of these sales deposited in the Treasury are channelled towards the London and Paris Clubs. International capital gains control and/or ownership over the most profitable state enterprises at a very low cost. Moreover, with a large number of indebted countries selling (or trading) their public enterprises at the same time, the price of state assets tumbles.

In some countries, state ownership over "strategic sectors" (e.g. oil, gas, telecommunications) and public utilities is entrenched in the constitution. Privatisation of these sectors may require, as in the case of Brazil, the prior amendment of the constitution (see Chapter 9).

Tax Reform

Under the guidance of the World Bank, a number of fundamental changes are implemented in the fiscal structure. These changes tend to undermine domestic production both on the demand and supply sides. The introduction of a value-added or sales tax and changes in the structure of direct taxation invariably imply a greater tax burden for the lower- and middle-income groups. Included in the World Bank framework is the registration for tax purposes of small agricultural producers and units of the informal urban sector. While domestic producers are subjected to government taxes, joint ventures and foreign capital invariably enjoy generous tax holidays as a means of "attracting foreign investment".

Land Tenure and the Privatisation of Agricultural Land

The reforms are conducted in the context of the World Bank's sectoral adjustment loans. The relevant legislation on the ownership of land is often developed with technical support provided by the World Bank's Legal Department. The reforms consist in issuing land titles to farmers while at the same time encouraging the concentration of farm-land in fewer hands. Customary land rights are also affected. The tendency is towards the forfeiture and/or mortgaging of land by small farmers, the growth of the agro-business sector, and the formation of a class of landless seasonal agricultural workers.

Moreover, the measures often contribute – under the disguise of modernity – to the restoration of the rights of the "old-time" landlord class. Ironically, the latter is often the champion of economic "liberalisation".

The privatisation of land also serves the objective of debt servicing since the proceeds of public land sales under advice from the World Bank are used to generate state revenues which are channelled by the national Treasury to the international creditors.

Deregulation of the Banking System

The Central Bank loses control over monetary policy: interest rates are determined in the "free market" by the commercial banks. Concessional credit to agriculture and industry is phased out. The underlying measures are usually conducive to significant hikes in both real and nominal interest rates. The movement of interest rates interacts with that of domestic prices. Nominal interest rates are pushed up to abnormally high levels as a result of periodic devaluations and the resulting "dollarisation" of domestic prices. The deregulation of the banking system also leads to the influx of "hot money" attracted by artificially high interest rates. The commercial banks are no longer in a position to provide credit to the real economy at reasonable rates.

This policy – combined with the phasing out of the state development banks – leads to the collapse of credit to both agriculture and domestic industry. Whereas short-term credit to merchants involved in the export trade is maintained, the domestic banking sector is no longer geared towards providing credit to local producers.

The international financial institutions will also require the privatisation of state development banks and the deregulation of the commercial banking system. It is worth noting that under the Uruguay Round agreement conducted under the umbrella of the GATT and signed in 1994, foreign commercial banks are allowed free entry into the domestic banking sector.

The movement is towards the divestiture of state banking institutions (under the privatisation programme) as well as the displacement of private domestic banks. The restructuring of the banking sector is implemented in the context of a Financial Sector Adjustment programme (FSAP). The latter includes the divestiture and sale of all state banks under the supervision of the IFIs with key state banking institutions taken over by foreign financial interests.

The process of divestiture is related directly to the collection of debt servicing obligations. The restructuring of the commercial debt under the Brady Plan, for instance, was often conditional upon the prior privatisation of state banking institutions under the clauses of the FSAP, with the proceeds of these sales channelled into the servicing of the commercial debt.

Liberalising Capital Movements

The IMF insists on the "transparency" and "free movement" of foreign exchange in and out of the country (through electronic transfers). This process enables foreign companies freely to repatriate their profits in foreign exchange.

Recycling Dirty Money Towards Debt Servicing

Another important objective, however, is served: the liberalisation of capital movements encourages the "repatriation of capital flight", namely the return of "black" and "dirty money" which had been deposited by the Third World élites since the 1960s in offshore bank accounts. "Dirty money" constitutes the proceeds of illegal trade and/or criminal activity whereas "black money" is money which has escaped taxation.

The crisis of the legal economy under the brunt of the macro-economic reforms is related directly to the rapid growth of illicit trade. Moreover, the convenience and speed at which dirty money transactions can be undertaken (through electronic transfers) tend to facilitate the development of illicit trade at the expense of the legal economy.

The liberalisation of capital movements serves the interests of the creditors. It constitutes a means for channelling "dirty" and "black money" deposited offshore towards the servicing of the external debt while providing the privileged social classes with a convenient mechanism for laundering large amounts of money which were obtained illegally.

This process works as follows: hard currency is transferred from an offshore bank account into the interbank market of a developing country ("no questions asked"). The foreign exchange is then converted into local currency and used to purchase state assets and/or public land put on the auction block by the government in the context of the World Bank-sponsored privatisation programme. In turn, the foreign exchange proceeds of these sales are channelled towards the national Treasury where they are earmarked for debt-servicing.

"Poverty Alleviation" and the "Social Safety Net"

Since the late 1980s, "poverty alleviation" has become a "conditionality" of World Bank loan agreements. "Poverty alleviation" supports the objective of debt-servicing: "sustainable poverty reduction" under the dominion of the Bretton Woods institutions is predicated on slashing social-sector budgets and redirecting expenditure on a selective and token basis "in favour of the poor". The "Social Emergency Fund" established (on the Bolivia-Ghana model) is intent on providing "a flexible mechanism" for "managing poverty" while at the same time dismantling the state's public finances. The poor are defined in this framework as "target groups".

The Social Emergency Fund (SEF) requires a "social engineering" approach, a policy framework for "managing poverty" and attenuating social unrest at minimal cost to the creditors. So-called "targeted programmes" earmarked "to help the poor" combined with "cost recovery" and the "privatisation" of health and educational services are said to constitute "a more efficient" way of delivering social programmes. The state withdraws and many programmes under the jurisdiction of line ministries will henceforth be managed by the organisations of civil society under the umbrella of the SEF. The latter also finances, under the "social safety net", severance payments and/ or minimum-employment projects earmarked for public-sector workers laid off as a result of the adjustment programme.

The SEF officially sanctions the withdrawal of the state from the social sectors and "the management of poverty" (at the micro-social level) by separate and parallel organisational structures. Various non-governmental organisations (NGOs) funded by international "aid programmes" have gradually taken over many of the functions of local-level governments. Small-scale production and handicraft projects, sub-contracting for export processing firms, community-based training and employment programmes, etc. are set up under the umbrella of the "social safety net". A meagre survival to local-level communities is ensured while at the same time the risk of social upheaval is contained.

"Good Governance": Promoting Bogus Parliamentary Institutions

"Democratisation" has become the motto of the free market. So-called "governance" and the holding of multi-party elections are added as conditionalities to the loan agreements. The nature of the economic reforms, however, prevents a genuine democratisation.

The Consequences of Structural Adjustment

The solution to the debt crisis becomes the cause of further indebtedness. The IMF's economic stabilisation package is in theory intended to assist countries in restructuring their economies with a view to generating a surplus on their balance of trade so as to pay back the debt and initiate a process of economic recovery. Exactly the opposite occurs. The very process of "belt-tightening" imposed by the creditors undermines economic recovery and the ability of countries to repay their debt.

In other words, the underlying measures contribute to enlarging the external debt:

1) The new policy-based loans granted to pay back old debt contribute to increasing the debt stock.

2) Trade liberalisation tends to exacerbate the balance of payments crisis. Domestic production is replaced by imports (in a wide range of commodities) and new quick-disbursing loans are granted to enable countries to continue importing goods from the world market.

3) With the completion of the Uruguay Round and the formation of the World Trade Organisation, a much larger share of the import bill is made up of "services", including the payment of intellectual property rights. In other words, the import bill will increase without a corresponding influx of ("produced") commodities.

4) The structural adjustment programme has implied a significant shift out of project lending and a consequent freeze on capital formation in all areas which do not directly serve the interests of the export economy.

The economic stabilisation package destroys the possibility of an "endogenous national economic development process" controlled by national policy-makers. The IMF-World Bank reforms brutally dismantle the social sectors of developing countries, undoing the efforts and struggles of the post-colonial period and reversing "with the stroke of the pen" the fulfilment of past progress. Throughout the developing world, there is a consistent and coherent pattern: the IMF-World Bank reform package constitutes a coherent programme of economic and social collapse. The austerity measures lead to the disintegration of the state, the national economy is remoulded, production for the domestic market is destroyed through the compression of real earnings and domestic production is redirected towards the world market. These measures go far beyond the phasing out of import-substituting industries. They destroy the entire fabric of the domestic economy.

The IMF Tacitly Acknowledges Policy Failure

Ironically, policy failure is tacitly acknowledged by the IMF and the World Bank:

> Although there have been a number of studies on the subject over the past decade, one cannot say with certainty whether programs have "worked" or not.... On the basis of existing studies, one certainly cannot say whether the adoption of programs supported by the Fund led to an improvement in inflation and growth performance. In fact it is often found that programs are associated with a rise in inflation and a fall in the growth rate.[7]

While calling for the development of "improved methods of evaluation" of fund-supported programmes, the empirical tests proposed by the IMF Research Department are not able to refute the evidence.

The Counterfactual Argument

The measures are justified by the Bretton Woods institutions on the grounds of micro-economic efficiency. According to the IFIs, the "social costs" must be balanced against the "economic benefits" of macro-economic stabilisation. The IMF-World Bank motto is "short-term pain for long-term gain".

While recognising the "social dimensions of adjustment", the Bretton Woods institutions have also underscored the so-called "counterfactual argument": "the situation is bad, but it would have been far worse had the structural adjustment measures not been adopted". According to a recent World Bank report:

> Africa's disappointing economic performance in the aggregate represents a failure to adjust [rather than] a failure of adjustment...: More Adjustment – Not Less – Would Help the Poor and the Environment... Adjustment is the necessary first step on the road to sustainable poverty reduction....[8]

Whereas the economic policy package is in principle intended to promote efficiency and a more rational allocation of productive resources based on the market mechanism, this objective is brought about through a massive disengagement of human and material resources. The counterpart of "micro-economic efficiency" is programmed austerity at the macro-economic level. It is consequently difficult to justify these measures on the grounds of efficiency and resource allocation.

The Social Impact of Macro-economic Reform

The social implications of these reforms (including their impact on health, education, the social rights of women and the environment) have been amply documented.[9] Educational establishments are closed down and teachers are laid off due to lack of funds; in the health sector, there is a general breakdown in curative and preventive care as a result of the lack of medical equipment and supplies, poor working conditions and the low pay of medical personnel. The lack of operating funds is in part "compensated" by the exaction of registration and user fees – e.g. the "drug cost recovery scheme" under the Bamako Proposal and the Parent Teachers Associations' (PTA) levies exacted by local communities to cover expenses previously incurred by the Ministry of Education.

This process, however, implies the partial privatisation of essential government social services and the de facto exclusion of large sectors of the population (particularly in rural areas) which are unable to pay the various fees attached to health and educational services.[10]

It should be emphasised that the structural adjustment programme not only results in increased levels of urban and rural poverty. It also implies a reduced capacity of people (including middle-class households) to pay for health and educational services associated with the cost recovery scheme.

Freezing the number of graduates of the teacher training colleges and increasing the number of pupils per teacher are explicit conditions of World Bank social-sector adjustment loans. The educational budget is curtailed, the number of contact-hours spent by children in school is cut down and a "double shift system" is installed: one teacher now does the work of two, the remaining teachers are laid off and the resulting savings to the Treasury are funnelled towards the external creditors.

These "cost effective" initiatives, however, are still considered to be incomplete: in sub-Saharan Africa, the donor community has recently proposed a new imaginative ("cost-effective") formula which consists in eliminating the teachers' meagre salary altogether (in some countries as low as US$15-20 a month) while granting small loans to enable unemployed teachers to set up their own informal "private schools" in rural backyards and urban slums. Under this scheme, the Ministry of Education would nonetheless still be responsible for monitoring "the quality" of teaching.

The Restructuring of the Health Sector

A similar approach prevails in the area of health: state subsidies to health are said to create undesirable "market distortions" which "benefit the rich". Moreover, according to the World Bank, an expenditure of US$8 per person per annum is amply sufficient to meet acceptable standards of clinical services.[11] Moreover, user fees for primary health care to impoverished rural communities should be exacted both on the grounds of "greater equity" and "efficiency". These communities should also participate in the running of the primary health care units by substituting the qualified nurse or medical auxiliary (hitherto paid by the Ministry of Health) by an untrained and semi-illiterate health volunteer.

The results: with the exception of a small number of externally funded "showpieces", health establishments in sub-Saharan Africa have de facto become a source of disease and infection. The shortage of funds allocated to medical supplies, including disposable syringes, as well as the price hikes (recommended by the World Bank) in electricity, water and fuel (e.g. required to sterilise needles) increase the incidence of infection (including HIV transmission). In sub-Saharan Africa, for instance, the inability to pay for prescription drugs tends to reduce the levels of attendance and utilisation in government health centres to the extent that health infrastructure and personnel is no longer utilised in a cost-effective fashion.[12]

While the cost recovery scheme may ensure the limited operational viability of a select number of health centres, the tendency is towards a) increased social polarisation in the health-care delivery system, b) a reduction in health coverage and an increase in the already large percentage of the population which has no access to health. In other words, macro-economic policy is conducive to a major disengagement of human and material resources in the social sectors.

The Resurgence of Communicable Diseases

In sub-Saharan Africa there has been a resurgence of a number of communicable diseases which were believed to be under control. These include cholera, yellow fever and malaria. Similarly, in Latin America the prevalence of malaria and dengue has worsened dramatically since the mid-1980s in terms of parasite incidence. Control and prevention activities (directly associated with the contraction of public expenditure under the structural adjustment programme) have declined dramatically. The outbreak of bubonic and pneumonic plague in India in 1994 has been recognised as "the direct consequence of a worsening urban sanitation and public health infrastructure which accompanied the compression of national and municipal budgets under the 1991 IMF/World Bank-sponsored structural adjustment programme...."[13]

The social consequences of structural adjustment are fully acknowledged by the IFIs. The IMF-World Bank methodology considers, however, the "social sectors" and "the social dimensions of adjustment" as something "separate", – i.e. according to the dominant economic dogma, these "undesired side effects" are not part of the workings of an economic model. They belong to a separate "sector": the social sector.

Endnotes

1. See World Bank, *World Debt Tables*, several issues.
2. The loan disbursements are nomally granted in several tranches. The release of each tranche is conditional upon the implementation of precise economic reforms.
3. These loans constitute so-called "balance of payments aid".
4. World Bank, *Adjustment in Africa*, Oxford University Press, Washington, 1994, p. 9.
5. Carlo Cottarelli, *Limiting Central Bank Credit to the Government*, IMF, Washington DC, 1993, p. 3.
6. Carlo Cotarrelli, *op. cit.*, p. 26.
7. Mohsin Khan, "The Macroeconomic Effects of Fund Supported Adjustment Programs", *IMF Staff Papers*, Vol. 37, No. 2, 1990, p. 196, p. 222.
8. World Bank, *Adjustment in Africa*, Oxford University Press, Washington 1994, p. 17.
9. Various studies including a major study by UNICEF entitled "Structural Adjustment with a Human Face" have examined the impact of macroeconomic policy on a number of social indicators including morbidity and the frequency of infectious diseases, infant mortality, levels of child nutrition, levels of education.
10. It is worth noting that under a scheme of cost recovery proposed by the international financial institutions to indebted countries, the Ministry of Health would reduce its disbursements and transfer the cost of running the health centres to impoverished rural and urban communities. Under the cost-recovery scheme, there would be "decentralisation of decision-making" and "community involvement and control": what this means is that impoverished rural and urban communities – while becoming formally "self-reliant" – would bear the burden of subsidising the Ministry of Health.
11. See World Bank, *World Development Report, 1993: Investing in Health,* Washington DC, 1993, p. 106.
12. On the issue of cost recovery see UNICEF, "Revitalising Primary Health Care/Maternal and Child Health, the Bamako Initiative", report by the Executive Director, February 1989, p. 16.
13. See *Madrid Declaration of Alternative Forum, The Other Voices of the Planet*, Madrid, October 1994.

Chapter 3

The Global Cheap-Labour Economy

Introduction

THE globalisation of poverty is accompanied by the reshaping of national economies of developing countries and the redefinition of their role in the new world economic order. The national level macro-economic reforms (discussed in the previous Chapter) applied simultaneously in a large number of individual countries play a key role in regulating wages and labour costs at a world level. Global poverty is an input on the supply side, the global economic system feeds on cheap labour.

The world economy is marked by the relocation of a substantial share of the industrial base of the advanced countries to cheap-labour locations in developing countries. The development of the cheap-labour export economy was launched in South-East Asia in the 1960s and 1970s largely in "labour-intensive manufacturing". Initially limited to a few export enclaves (e.g. Hong Kong, Singapore, Taiwan and South Korea), the development of offshore cheap-labour production gained impetus in the 1970s and 1980s.

Since the late 1970s, a "new generation" of free trade areas has developed with major growth poles in South-East Asia and the Far East, China, Brazil, Mexico and Eastern Europe. This globalisation of industrial production affects a wide range of manufactured goods. Third World industry encompasses most areas of manufacturing (automobiles, ship-building, aircraft assembly, arms production, etc).[1]

Whereas the Third World continues to play a role as a major primary producer, the contemporary world economy is no longer structured along traditional divisions between "industry" and "primary production" (e.g. the debate on the terms of trade between primary and industrial producers). An increasingly large share of world manufacturing is undertaken in South-East Asia, China, Latin America and Eastern Europe.

This worldwide development of cheap-labour industries (in increasingly sophisticated and heavier areas of manufacturing) is predicated on the compression of internal demand in individual Third World economies and the consolidation of a cheap, stable and disciplined industrial labour force in a "secure" political environment. This process is based on the destruction of national manufacturing for the internal market (i.e. import-substituting industries) in individual Third World countries and the consolidation of a cheap-labour export economy. With the completion of the Uruguay Round at Marrakesh and the establishment of the World Trade Organisation (WTO) in 1995, the frontiers of these cheap labour "free trade zones" have been extended to the entire national territory of developing countries.

Macro-economic Reform Supports the Relocation of Industry

The restructuring of individual national economies under the auspices of the Bretton Woods institutions contributes to the weakening of the state. Industry for the internal market is undermined and national enterprises are pushed into bankruptcy. The compression of internal consumption resulting from the structural adjustment programme (SAP) implies a corresponding reduction in labour costs; therein lies the "hidden agenda" of the SAP: the compression of wages in the Third World and Eastern Europe supports the relocation of economic activity from the rich countries to the poor countries.

The globalisation of poverty endorses the development of a worldwide cheap-labour export economy; the possibilities of production are immense given the mass of cheap impoverished workers throughout the world. In contrast, poor countries do not trade among themselves: poor people do not constitute a market for the goods they produce.

Consumer demand is limited to approximately 15 per cent of the world population, confined largely to the rich OECD countries (see Table 1.1). In this system and contrary to the famous dictum of the French economist Jean Baptiste Say (Say's Law), supply does not create its own demand. On the contrary, poverty means "low costs of production": poverty is "an input" into the cheap-labour economy ("on the supply side").

Industrial Export Promotion

"Die or Export" is the motto, import substitution and production for the internal market are obsolete concepts. "Countries should specialise according to their comparative advantage",which lies in the abundance and low price of their labour; the secret of "economic success" is export promotion. Under the close watch of the World Bank and the IMF, the same "non-traditional" exports are promoted simultaneously in a large number of developing countries. The latter now joined by cheap-labour producers in Eastern Europe are forced into cut-throat competition. Everybody wants to export to the same European and North American markets: oversupply obliges Third World producers to cut their prices; the factory prices of industrial goods tumble on world markets much in the same way as those of primary commodities. Competition between and within developing countries contributes to depressing wages and prices. Export promotion (when applied simultaneously in a large number of individual countries) leads to overproduction and the contraction of export revenues. Ironically, the promotion of exports leads ultimately to lower commodity prices and less export revenue from which to repay the external debt.

Moreover, the economic stabilisation measures imposed on the South and the East backfire on the economies of the rich countries: poverty in the Third World contributes to a global contraction in import demand which in turn affects economic growth and employment in the OECD countries.

Structural adjustment transforms national economies into open economic spaces and countries into territories. The latter are "reserves" of cheap labour and natural resources. But because this process is based on the globalisation of poverty and the worldwide compression of consumer demand, export promotion in the developing countries can succeed only in a limited number of cheap-labour locations. In other words, the simultaneous development of new export activities in a large number of locations is conducive to greater competition between developing countries in both primary production and manufacturing. In as much as world demand is not expanding, the creation of new productive capacity in some countries will be matched by economic decline (and disengagement) in competing Third World locations.

Global Adjustment

What happens when macro-economic reform is applied simultaneously in a large number of countries? In an interdependent world economy, the "summation" of national-level SAPs is conducive to a "global adjustment" in the structures of world trade and economic growth.

The impact of "global adjustment" on the terms of trade is fairly well understood: the simultaneous application of export promotion policies in individual Third World countries is conducive to oversupply in particular commodity markets coupled with further declines in world commodity prices. In many countries subjected to structural adjustment, the volume of exports has gone up substantially, but the value of export revenues has deteriorated. In other words, this "global structural adjustment" (predicated on the internationalisation of macro-economic policy) further depresses commodity prices and promotes a negative transfer of economic resources between debtor and creditor nations.

"Decomposition" of National Economies

SAPs play a key role in the "decomposition" of the national economy of an indebted country and in the "recomposition" of a "new relationship" to the global economy. In other words, the economic reforms imply the "decomposition/recomposition" of the structures of national production and consumption. Compression of real earnings is conducive to a lowering of labour costs and a decline in the levels of necessary mass consumption (basic human needs) by the large majority of the population. On the other hand, the "recomposition" of consumption is characterised by the enlargement of "high-income consumption" through the liberalisation of trade and the dynamic influx of imported consumer durables and luxury goods for a small segment of society. This "decomposition/recomposition" of the national economy and its insertion into the global cheap-labour economy is predicated on the compression of internal demand (and of the levels of social livelihood): poverty, low wages and an abundant supply of cheap labour are "inputs" on the supply side. Poverty and the reduction of production costs constitute the instrumental basis (on the supply side) for reactivating production geared towards the external market.

The simultaneous application of SAPs in debtor countries accelerates the relocation of manufacturing industry to cheap-labour locations in Third World countries and Eastern Europe from existing production sites in the developed countries. Yet the new (export oriented) productive capacity which results is developed against a general background of slow and/or depressed growth of world demand. This positive "engagement" in the creation of new productive capacity (for export) in one or more individual Third World countries is matched by a process of "disengagement of productive resources" and decline elsewhere in the world economic system.

Decomposition does not ensure "successful" recomposition. In other words, the phasing out of domestic industry for the internal market does not ensure the development of a new "viable" and stable relationship to the world market – i.e. the compression of labour costs (in support of supply) does not in itself ensure the growth of the export sector and the insertion of the national Third World economy into the international market (nor does it for that matter ensure the development of industrial exports). Complex economic, geo-political and historical factors will determine the geographical location of these new poles of cheap-labour production geared towards the world market.

"Recomposition" tends to take place in specific functional regions of the global economy. The formation of new dynamic poles of the cheap-labour economy in Mexico, Eastern Europe and South-East Asia is in marked contrast to the situation prevailing in most of sub-Saharan Africa and parts of Latin America and the Middle East.

World Unemployment

Many regions of the world – although not "actively" inserted into the global cheap-labour economy – nonetheless contain important "reserves of cheap labour" which play an important role in regulating the costs of labour at a world level. If labour unrest, including social pressures on wages, occurs in one Third World location, transnational capital can switch its production site or subcontract (through outsourcing) to alternative cheap-labour locations. In other words, the existence of "reserve countries" with abundant supplies of cheap labour tends to dampen the movement of wages and labour costs prevailing in the more active (cheap-labour) export economies (e.g. South East Asia, Mexico, China, Eastern Europc).

In other words, the determination of national wage levels in individual developing countries not only depends on the structure of the national labour market but also on the level of wages prevailing in competing cheap-labour locations. The level of labour costs is therefore conditioned by the existence of a "global reserve pool of cheap labour" made up of the "reserve armies" of labour in different countries. This "world surplus population" conditions the international migration of productive capital in the same branch of industry from one country to another: international capital (the direct or indirect purchaser of labour power) moves from one national labour market to another. From the point of view of capital, the "national reserves of labour" are integrated into a single international reserve pool where workers in different countries are brought into overt competition with one another.

World unemployment becomes "a lever" of global capital accumulation which "regulates" the cost of labour in each of the national economies. Mass poverty regulates the international cost of labour. Wages are also conditioned at the level of each national economy, by the urban-rural relationship. Namely, rural poverty and the existence of a large mass of unemployed and landless farm-workers tends to promote low wages in the urban-manufacturing economy.

Declining Wages

In many cheap-labour exporting economies, the share of wages in GDP declined dramatically in the course of the 1980s. In Latin America, for instance, the adjustment programmes were conducive to a marked contraction of wages both as a share of GDP and as a percentage of value added in manufacturing. While employee earnings in the developed countries constitute approximately 40 per cent of value added in manufacturing, the corresponding percentage in Latin America and South-East Asia is of the order of 15 per cent.

Plant Closures and Industrial Delocation in the Developed Countries

The development of cheap-labour export factories in the Third World is matched by plant closures in the industrial cities of the advanced countries. The earlier wave of plant closures affected largely the (labour-intensive) areas of light manufacturing. Since the 1980s, however, all sectors of the Western economy (and all categories of the labour force) have been affected: corporate restructuring of the aerospace and engineering industries, relocation of automobile production to Eastern Europe and the Third World, closure of the steel industry, etc.

The development of manufacturing in the *maquilas* and export processing zones, located to the immediate south of the Rio Grande on the US-Mexican border, was matched throughout the 1980s by industrial lay-offs and unemployment in industrial centres in the US and Canada. Under the North American Free Trade Area (NAFTA), this process of relocation has been extended to the entire Mexican economy. Similarly, Japanese transnationals are relocating a significant part of their manufacturing industry to production sites in Thailand or the Philippines where industrial workers can be hired for US$3 or $4 a day.[2] German capitalism is expanding beyond the Oder-Neisse back into its pre-war *Lebensraum.* In assembly plants in Poland, Hungary and the Czech and Slovak republics, the cost of labour (of the order of US$120 a month) is substantially lower than in the European Union. In contrast, workers in German automobile plants have wages of the order of US$28 an hour.

In this context, the former "socialist" countries are integrated into the global cheap-labour economy. Despite idle factories and high levels of unemployment in the former German Democratic Republic, it was more profitable for German capitalism to expand its manufacturing base in Eastern Europe.

For every job lost in the developed countries and transferred to the Third World, there is a corresponding decline of consumption in the developed countries. While plant closures and lay-offs are usually presented in the press as isolated and unrelated cases of "corporate restructuring", their combined impact on real earnings and employment is devastating. Consumer markets collapse because a large number of enterprises (in several countries) simultaneously reduce their workforce. In turn, sagging sales backlash on production, contributing to a further string of plant closures and bankruptcies, and so on.

The Worldwide Compression of Consumer Spending

In the North, the compression in levels of spending is further exacerbated by the deregulation of the labour market: deindexation of earnings, part-time employment, early retirement and the imposition of so-called "voluntary" wage cuts. In turn, the practice of attrition (which shifts the social burden of unemployment onto the younger age groups) bars an entire generation from the job-market.

In other words, the process of phasing-out industry in the developed countries contributes to a contraction of market demand, which in turn undermines the efforts of developing countries to sell manufactured goods to a (shrinking) Western market.

It's a vicious circle: the relocation of industry to the South and the East leads to economic dislocation and unemployment in the developed countries which in turn tends to push the world economy into global recession. This system is characterised by an unlimited capacity to produce yet the very act of expanding production – through relocation of material production from the "high wage" to the "low wage" economies – contributes to a contraction of spending (e.g. by those who have been laid off) which leads the world economy ultimately to the path of global stagnation.

Relocation within Trading Blocs

The delocation of economic activity is increasingly taking place within the continental shelf of each trading bloc. Both Western Europe and North America are respectively developing "cheap-labour hinterlands" on their immediate geographic borders. In the European context, the "Oder-Neisse line" is to Poland what the Rio Grande is to Mexico. The former "iron curtain" performs the same role as the Rio Grande. It separates the high-wage economy of Western Europe from the low-wage economy of the former Soviet bloc.

NAFTA, however, is distinct from the Maastricht Treaty which allows for the "free movement" of labour "within" the countries of the

European Union. Within NAFTA, the Rio Grande separates two distinct labour markets: production units are closed down in the US and Canada and moved to Mexico where wages are at least ten times lower. "The immobility of labour", rather than "free trade", and the removal of tariff barriers, is the central feature of NAFTA.

Under NAFTA, American corporations can reduce their labour costs by more than 80 per cent by relocating to or subcontracting in Mexico. This mechanism is not limited to manufacturing or to activities using unqualified labour: nothing prevents the movement of America's high-tech industries to Mexico where engineers and scientists can be hired for a few hundred dollars a month. Delocation potentially affects a large share of the US and Canadian economies, including the services sector.

NAFTA has from the outset been predicated on a contraction of employment and real wages. Industrial relocation to Mexico destroys jobs and depresses real earnings in the US and Canada. NAFTA exacerbates this economic recession: workers laid off in the US and Canada are not redeployed elsewhere in the economy and no new avenues of economic growth are created as a result of the delocation of industry. The contraction of consumer spending which results from the lay-offs and plant closures leads to a general contraction in sales and employment and to further industrial lay-offs.

Moreover, while NAFTA enables American and Canadian corporations to penetrate the Mexican market, this process is undertaken largely by displacing existing Mexican enterprises. The tendency is towards increased industrial concentration, the elimination of small and medium-sized enterprises, as well as the taking over of part of Mexico's service economy through the system of corporate franchising. The US "exports its recession" to Mexico. With the exception of a small market of privileged consumption, poverty and low wages in Mexico do not favour the expansion of consumer demand. In Canada, the free trade agreement signed with the US in 1989 has led to the phasing out of the branch-plant economy. Canadian subsidiaries are closed down and replaced by a regional sales office.

The formation of NAFTA has contributed to exacerbating the economic recession: the tendency is towards the reduction of wages and employment in all three countries. The potential to produce is enhanced, yet the very act of expanding production (through relocation of production from the US and Canada to Mexico) contributes to a contraction of spending.

The Dynamic Development of Luxury Consumption

The increased concentration of income and wealth in the hands of a social minority (in the advanced countries as well as in small pockets of affluence in the Third World and Eastern Europe) has led to the dynamic growth of the luxury-goods economy: travel and leisure, the automobile, the electronics and telecommunications revolution, etc. The "drive-in" and "duty free" cultures built around the axes of the automobile and air transport are the focal points of the modern "high-income" consumption and leisure economy, towards which massive amounts of financial resources are channelled.

Whereas the range of consumer goods available in support of upper-income lifestyles has expanded almost beyond limit, there has been (since the debt crisis of the early 1980s) a corresponding contraction in the levels of consumption of the large majority of the world population. In contrast to the large diversity of goods available to a social minority, basic consumption (for some 85 per cent of the world population) is confined to a small number of food staples and essential commodities.

This dynamic growth of luxury consumption, nonetheless, provides a temporary "breathing space" to a global economy beset by recession.[3] Rapid growth of luxury consumption, however, contrasts increasingly with the stagnation of the sectors producing necessary goods and services. In the Third World and Eastern Europe, stagnation of food production, housing and essential social services contrasts with the development of small pockets of social privilege and luxury consumption. The élites of indebted countries including the former *apparatchiks* and the new business tycoons of Eastern Europe and the former Soviet Union are both the protagonists and beneficiaries of this process. Social and income disparities in Hungary and Poland are now comparable to those prevailing in Latin America. (For instance, a Porsche-Carrera can now be purchased at Porsche-Hungaria in downtown Budapest for the modest sum of 9,720,000 forints, more than an average Hungarian worker earns in a lifetime – i.e. 70 years earnings at the average (annual) industrial wage).[4]

The low wage structure in the Third World coupled with the effects of economic restructuring and recession in the advanced countries does not favour the development of mass consumption and an overall improvement of purchasing power. The global productive system is thus increasingly geared towards supplying limited markets – i.e. upper-income consumer markets in the North plus small pockets of luxury consumption in the South and the East.

In the foregoing context, low wages and low costs of production are conducive to low purchasing power and deficient demand. This contradictory relationship is an essential feature of the global cheap-labour economy: those who produce are not those who consume.

The Rentier Economy

With the phasing out of manufacturing, a "rentier economy" has developed in the rich countries. This rentier economy – centred in the services sector – syphons off the profits of Third World manufacturing. The high-technology economy based on the ownership of industrial know-how, product designs, Research and Development, etc. subordinates the sectors of "material production". "Non-material production" subordinates "material production"; the services sector appropriates the value added of manufacturing. Moreover, in addition to the payment of royalties and licensing fees for the use of Western and Japanese technology, the earnings of Third World producers are invariably appropriated by distributors, wholesalers and retailers in the developed countries. Industrial production remains subordinate to corporate monopoly capital. The development of so-called "industry" in the Third World is the consequence of a process of global restructuring of production. The growth poles in the advanced countries are in the "non-material sectors" (high technology including product design and innovation, services economy, real estate, commercial and financial infrastructure, communications, transportation) rather than in material manufacturing production *per se*.

This apparent "deindustrialisation" of the industrialised countries should be understood: the meaning of the term "industry" has changed profoundly. The high-technology growth poles are experiencing rapid development at the expense of the old traditional industries which developed historically in the advanced countries from the inception of the industrial revolution.

The Globalisation of Manufacturing

We are dealing with a world economy in which a large number of national economies produce manufactured goods for export to the market of the OECD countries. With some important exceptions (e.g. Korea, Brazil, Mexico), these countries, however, cannot be considered as "newly industrialised": the process of "industrialisation" is largely the consequence of the relocation of production to cheap-labour areas in the Third World. It is conditioned by the reshaping of the global economy.

In other words, the decentralisation and relocation of material production to the Third World were motivated largely by the sizeable differentials in wages between rich and poor countries. The latter have become producers of "industrial staples". In this context, overproduction of industrial commodities takes place on a world level, depressing the prices of manufactured goods much in the same way as the process of oversupply which characterises primary-commodity markets. The entry of China into the international division of labour in the late 1970s has in this regard exacerbated the structures of oversupply.

Import-led Growth in the Rich Countries

The rentier economy appropriates the earnings of the direct producers. Material production takes place off-shore in a Third World cheap-labour economy, yet the largest increases in GDP are recorded in the importing country. GDP growth in the rich countries is in this regard "import led": cheap-labour imports (in primary commodities and manufacturing) generate a corresponding increase in income in the services economy of the rich countries.

The application of the IMF-sponsored SAP in a large number of individual countries also contributes to the consolidatation of this rentier-type economy: each country is obliged to produce (in competition with other developing countries) the same range of staple primary and industrial commodities for the world market. While competition characterises material commodity production in the developing countries, the channels of international trade as well as the wholesale and retail trade markets in the advanced countries are controlled by corporate monopolies. This duality between competition and monopoly is a fundamental feature of the system of global exchange. Cut-throat competition between the "direct producers" often located in different countries under a structure of global oversupply is in contrast to a structure of monopoly control over international trade, industrial patents, wholesale and retail trade, etc. by a small number of global corporations.

The Appropriation of Surplus by non-Producers

Because goods produced in developing countries are imported at very low international (fob) prices, the recorded "value" of OECD imports from developing countries is relatively small (i.e. in comparison to total trade as well as in relation to the value of domestic production). Yet as soon as these commodities enter into the wholesale and retail channels of the rich countries, their prices are multiplied several-fold. The retail price of goods produced in the Third World is often up to 10 times higher than the price at which the commodity was imported. A corresponding "value added" is thus artificially created within the services economy of the rich countries without any material production taking place. This "value" is added to the Gross Domestic Product of the rich country. For instance, the retail price of coffee is seven to 10 times higher than the fob price and approximately 20 times the price paid to the farmer in the Third World (see Table 3.1).

In other words, the bulk of the earnings of primary producers is appropriated by merchants, intermediaries, wholesalers and retailers. A similar process of appropriation exists with regard to most industrial commodities produced in offshore cheap-labour locations.

An Example: the Garment Industry

In the international garment trade, for instance, an international fashion designer will purchase a Paris-designed shirt for US$3 to $4 in Bangladesh, Vietnam or Thailand.[5] The product will then be resold in the European market at five to 10 times its price: the GDP of the importing Western country increases without any material production taking place.

Table 3.1: Coffee – Hierarchy of Prices
(US dollars)

	Price	Cumulative Share of Value Added (%)
Farmgate	0.25-0.50	4.00
International FOB	1.00	10.00
Final Retail	10.00	100.00

Source: Illustration based on approximate fob prices (early 1990s) and retail prices in the North American market (early 1990s). Farmgate prices vary considerably from one country to another.

Data collected at the factory level in Bangladesh enable us roughly to identify the structure of costs and the distribution of earnings in the garment export industry: the factory price of one dozen shirts is US$36 to $40 (fob).[6] All the equipment and raw materials are imported. The shirts are retailed at approximately US$22 a piece or US$266 a dozen in the United States (see Table 3.2). Female and child labour in Bangladeshi garment factories is paid approximately US$20 a month, at least 50 times less than the wages paid to garment workers in North America. Less than two per cent of the total value of the commodity accrues to the direct producers (the garment workers) in the form of wages. Another one per cent accrues as industrial profit to the "competitive" independent Third World producer.

The gross mark-up between the factory price and the retail price (US$266 – $38 = $228) is essentially divided into three components:

1) merchant profit to international distributors, wholesalers and retailers including the owners of shopping centres, etc. (i.e. the largest share of the gross mark-up),
2) the real costs of circulation (transport, storage, etc.).
3) customs duties exacted on the commodity upon entry into the developed countries' markets and indirect (value-added) taxes exacted at the point of retail sale of the commodity.

While the retail price is seven times the factory price, profit does not necessarily accrue to small retailers in the developed countries. A large share of the surplus generated at the levels of wholesale and retail trade is appropriated in the form of rent and interest payments by powerful commercial, real estate and banking interests.

It is worth noting that the flow of imports from the Third World also constitutes a means of generating fiscal revenues for the state in the rich countries in the form of sales and/or value-added taxes. In Western Europe, the VAT is well in excess of 10 per cent of the retail price. The process of tax collection is therefore dependent on the structure of unequal commodity exchange: in the case of the garment trade example, the Treasury of the rich countries appropriates almost as much as the producing country and approximately four times the amount accruing to garment workers in the producing country (see Table 3.3).

Wages and Labour Costs in the Developed Countries

In the global economy, the services of labour are purchased by capital in several separate and distinct national labour markets, – i.e. a part of the labour costs associated with transport, storage, wholesale and retail trade are incurred in the "high-wage" labour market of the rich countries. For instance, retail salesmen in the developed countries receive a daily wage which is at least 40 times higher than that of the Bangladeshi factory worker. A comparatively much larger share of the total (dollar) labour costs of producing and distributing the commodity will accrue, therefore, to service-sector workers in the high-wage countries.

There is, however, no relationship of "unequal exchange" between factory workers in Bangladesh and retail personnel in the US: the available evidence confirms that service workers in the rich countries are heavily underpaid. Moreover, their wages (which constitute a bona fide value-added – i.e. a "real cost") constitute a relatively small percentage of total sales.

In our example, the labour costs associated with the production of one dozen shirts in Bangladesh is US$5 which corresponds to 25 to 30 hours of labour (at 15-20 cents an hour). Assuming a retail worker in

Table 3.2: Cost Structure Third World Garment Exporter (US dollars)

Materials and accessories (imported)	$ 27
Depreciation on equipment	$ 3
Wages	$ 5
Net industrial profit	$ 3
Factory price (one dozen shirts)	$ 38
Gross mark-up	$228
Retail price (per dozen) in the advanced countries	$266
Retail price including sales tax (10 per cent)	$292.60

Source: Based on cost structure and sale prices of Bangladesh garment factory, 1992.

the US is paid US$5 an hour and sells half a dozen shirts per hour, the labour costs of producing a dozen shirts (US$5) is half the cost of retailing (US$10). The latter, however, still represents a relatively small percentage of the total price (US$292.60 including sales tax); i.e. the bulk of the surplus is appropriated in the form of merchant profit and rent by non-producers in the rich countries (see Table 3.2).

Whereas Third World enterprises operate under conditions which approximate "perfect competition", the buyers of their products are trading companies and multinational firms. The net industrial profit accruing to the "competitive" Third World entrepreneur (US$3) is of the order of one per cent of the total value of the commodity. Because Third World factories operate in a global economy marked by over-supply, the factory price tends to decline, pushing industrial profit margins to a bare minimum. This process facilitates the collection and appropriation of surplus by powerful international traders and distributors.

Table 3.3: Third World Manufacturing, the Distribution of Earnings

The distribution of earnings: one dozen shirts produced in a Third World cheap-labour factory	Amount in US dollars	Percentage of sale price
1. Earnings accruing to Third World country	8.00	2.7
1.1 Wages	5.00	1.7
1.2 Net industrial Profit	3.00	1.0
2. Earnings accruing to developed country	284.60	97.3
2.1 Materials, accessories and equipment imported from the rich countries	30.00	10.2
2.2 Freight and commissions	4.00	1.4
2.3 Customs duty on FOB price	4.00	1.4
2.4 Wages to wholesale and retail personnel	10.00	3.4
2.5 Gross commercial profit, rent and other income of distributors	210.00	71.8
2.6. Sales taxes (10% of retail price), accruing to developed-country state Treasury	26.60	9.1
3. Total retail price (including sales taxes)	292.60	100.0

Note: For the purposes of this illustration, the margins for freight and commissions, customs duty and sales taxes have been set at realistic levels (in accordance with available information). No information, however, is available on the wholesale and retail labour costs. In this illustration, the costs of retailing one dozen shirts have been assumed at approximately 25 per cent of the fob price (US$10).

Graph 3.1: The Comparative Cost of Labour in Manufacturing
(nominal wage in US dollars)

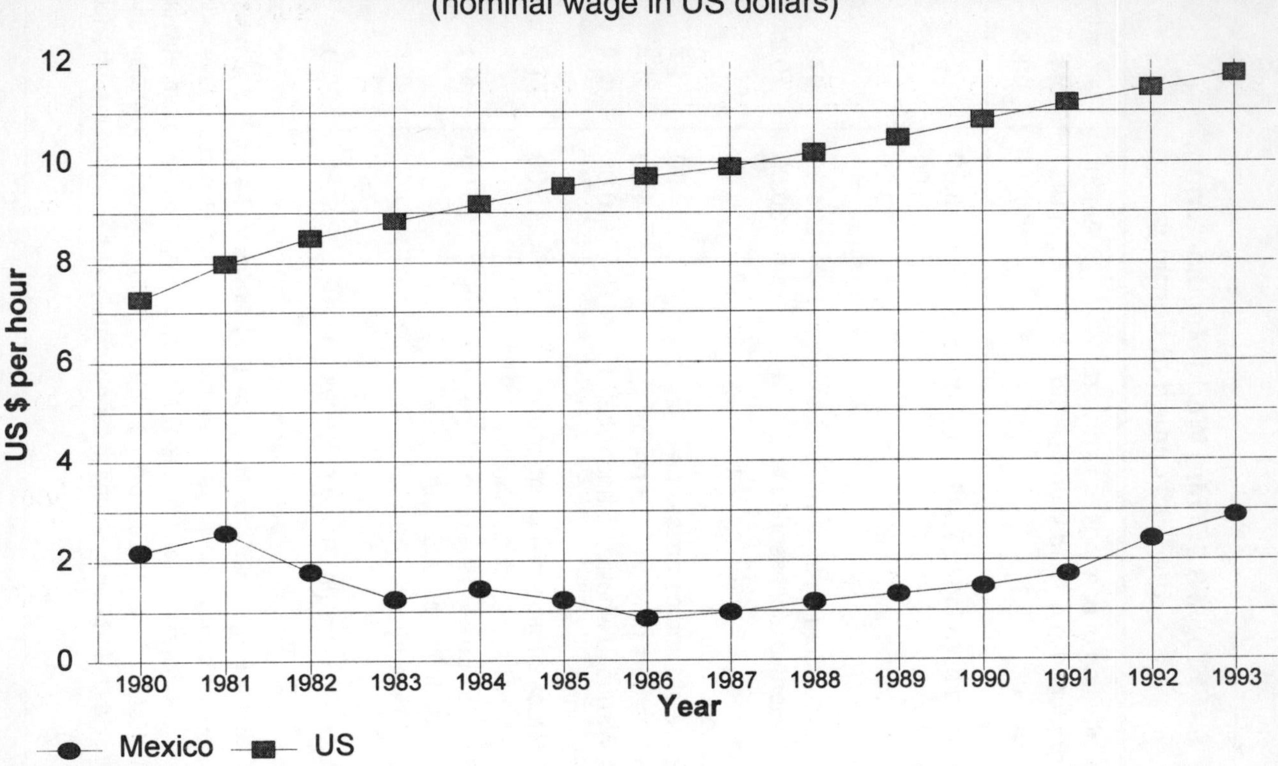

Sources: International Labour Office, Yearbook of Labour Statistics, Geneva, 1980-1994.
International Monetary Fund, International Financial Statistics, Washington, DC, 1995.

Graph 3.2: The Comparative Cost of Labour in Manufacturing
(nominal wage in US dollars)

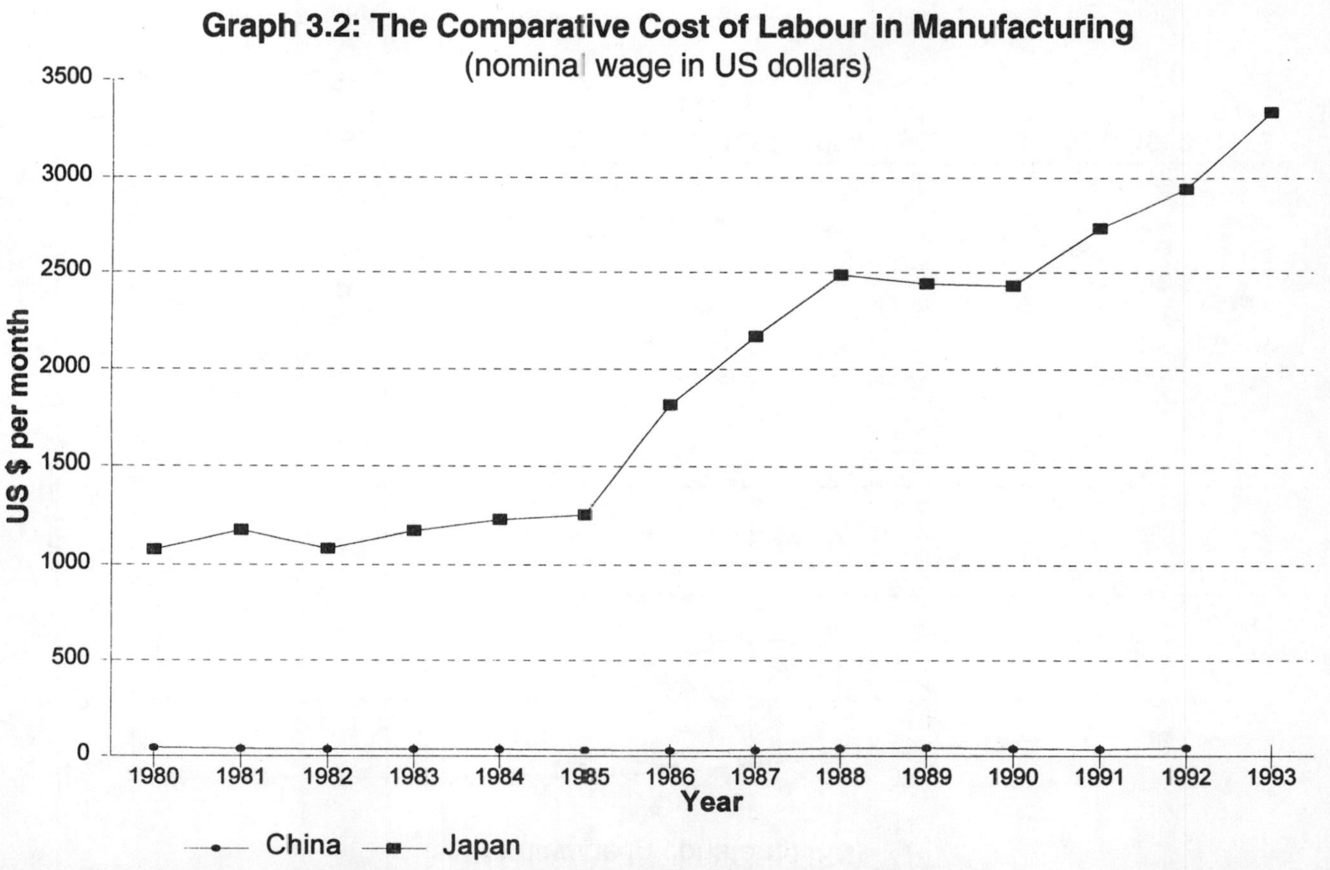

Sources: International Labour Office, Yearbook of Labour Statistics, Geneva, 1980-1994.
International Monetary Fund, International Financial Statistics, Washington, DC, 1995.

Graph 3.3: The Comparative Cost of Labour in Manufacturing

(real wage in constant US$)

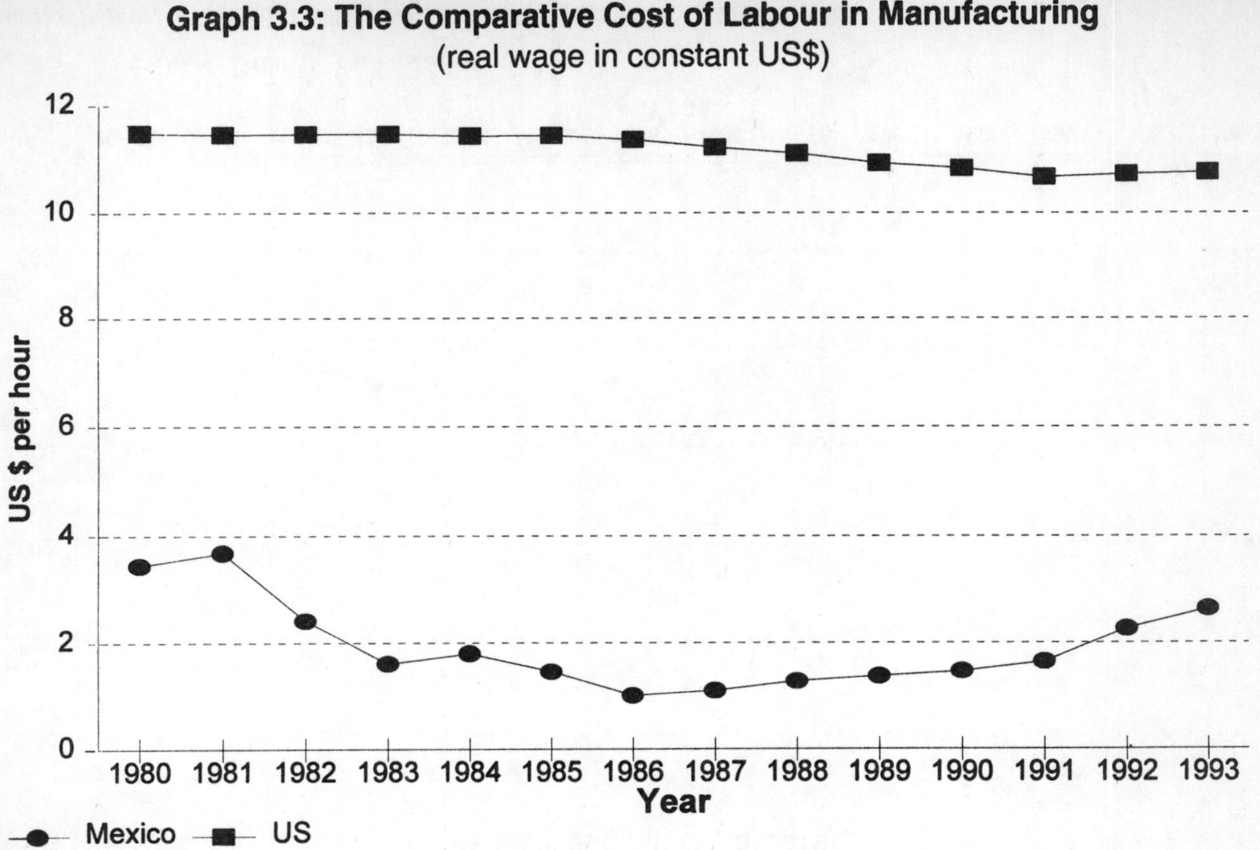

Sources: International Labour Office, Yearbook of Labour Statistics, Geneva, 1980-1994. International Monetary Fund, International Financial Statistics, Washington, DC, 1995.

Graph 3.4: The Comparative Cost of Labour in Manufacturing
(real wage in constant US$)

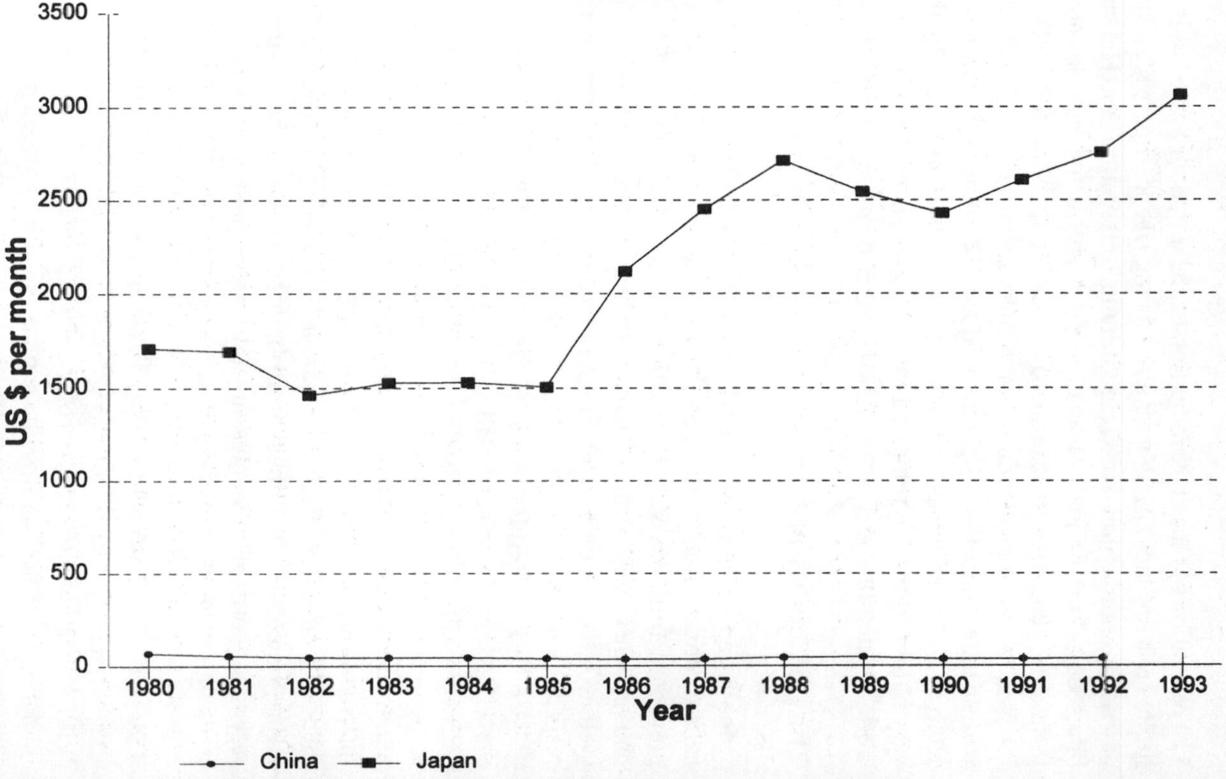

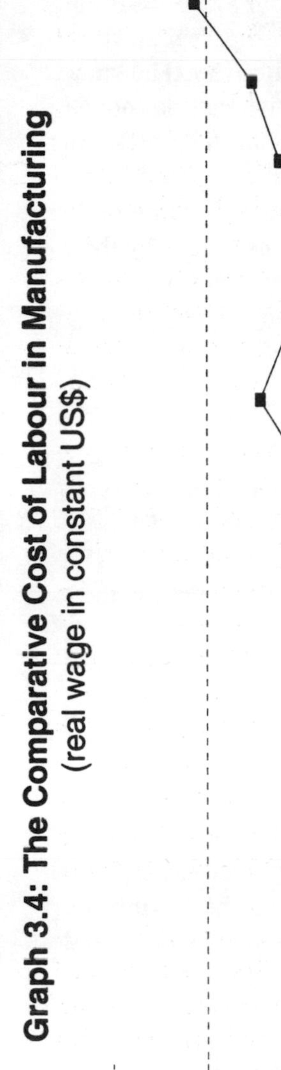

Sources: International Labour Office, Yearbook of Labour Statistics, Geneva, 1980-1994. International Monetary Fund, International Financial Statistics, Washington, DC, 1995.

Mobile and Immobile Sectors

The relocation of material production to cheap-labour locations is not limited to a few areas of light manufacturing. It encompasses all areas of material production which are "mobile" internationally. The "mobile sectors" are defined as sectors of activity which can be moved from one geographic location to another either through offshore investment in a cheap-labour country or by subcontracting production with an independent Third World producer. In contrast, the "immobile sectors" of the advanced countries include activities which by their very nature cannot be relocated internationally: construction, public works, agriculture and most of the services economy.

The Immobility of Labour

"Mobile capital" moves towards "immobile labour reserves". Whereas capital moves "freely" from one labour market to another, labour is prevented from crossing international boundaries. National labour markets are closed compartments with heavily guarded borders. The system is based on keeping national labour reserves within their respective borders.

Under NAFTA, for instance, the movement of Mexicans across the US-Mexican frontier will be tightly restricted so as to retain Mexico's labour force "within the boundaries of the cheap-labour economy". However, in economic activities such as construction, public works and agriculture, which by their very nature are not internationally "mobile", the agreement allows for the selective movement of a contractual seasonal labour force. Manpower exports, (to these "immobile" activities) from both Mexico and the Caribbean, serve the purpose of depressing the wages paid to American and Canadian workers as well as undermining the role of trade unions.

The Sectors of non-Material Production

With delocation, the structure of industry in the advanced countries is fundamentally modified. With the phasing out of material production, the new industries in information systems, telecommunications, etc. become the new growth poles. The old red-brick industrial centres are phased out: the "factory system" is closed down. Material production in manufacturing (which constitutes a "mobile" sector) is relocated to the low-wage economies. A sizeable sector of the labour force in the developed countries is now associated with the services economy and "the non-material sectors" of economic activity. In contrast, the percentage of the labour force in the production of material commodities has declined dramatically.

The duality respectively between "material" and "non-material production" and between "mobile" and "immobile" sectors is central to an understanding of the changing structure of the global economy. Global recession is not incompatible with the dynamic growth of the new high-technology sectors. The designs, technology and know-how are owned and controlled by international corporate capital."Non-material production" and the control over intellectual property rights subordinate "material production". The surplus from material industrial production is appropriated by the non-material sectors.

The Impact of the Scientific Revolution

The late 20th century has witnessed far-reaching progress in telecommunications, computer technology and production engineering. The latter constitute a vital lever in the process of industrial relocation: the centres of corporate decision-making are in instant contact with manufacturing sites and assembly plants around the world. The high-tech innovations of the 1980s and 1990s represent, under global capitalism, a powerful instrument of worldwide corporate control and supervision. The global enterprise minimises labour costs at a world level through its ability to link-up (or subcontract) with cheap-labour production sites around the world: workers are laid off in one (high-wage) country, production is transferred to another (low-wage) country, a smaller number of workers toil for longer hours and receive substantially lower wages.

Moreover, the technological revolution, while opening up new areas of professional work in the advanced countries, significantly reduces the overall labour requirements of industry. New robotised assembly lines are opened while workers in existing production facilities are fired. Technological change combined with delocation and enterprise restructuring tends, thereby, to favour a new wave of mergers and corporate acquisitions in key industries.

The Delocation of the Services Economy

With the revolution in global telecommunications and information technology certain service activities of the advanced capitalist countries are being transferred to cheap-labour locations in the Third World and Eastern Europe. In other words, part of the services economy is no longer an "immobile activity". Commercial and financial establishments can reduce their personnel in a variety of office activities: the accounting systems of large firms, for instance, can now be delocated and managed at considerable savings by computer link-up and electronic mail in developing countries, where qualified accountants and computer specialists can be hired for less than US$100 a month. Similarly, data and word processing can be rapidly subcontracted (e.g. by electronic mail) to office personnel for US$2 or $3 a day in the Philippines, and so on. With more than 70 per cent of the labour force of the advanced capitalist countries in the services sector, the potential impact of delocation on wages and employment (not to mention the social repercussions) is far-reaching.

Endnotes

1. The international relocation of manufacturing was initiated in the 1960s with the four Asian dragons: Hong Kong, Taiwan, Singapore and South Korea. At the outset, it was confined to the "softer" areas of export processing and assembly (such as the garment industry and electronics assembly).
2. The minimum industrial wage in Bangkok of US$4 a day (1991) is not enforced in modern factories.
3. In the face of low civilian spending, military expenditure also plays an important role in reactivating demand.
4. "In zwei Jahren über den Berg", *Der Spiegel*, No. 19, 1991, p. 194.
5. The export-processing fee in Ho Chi Minh City is US80cents per shirt (January 1991).
6. Interviews by author conducted in the Bangladesh garment industry, 1992.

PART II

Sub-Saharan Africa

Chapter 4

Somalia: the Real Causes of Famine

WHAT were the underlying causes? The global TV image spotlights the victims of civil war, drought and flood. Famine in Somalia was ascribed mechanically to "external" political and climatic factors: "the absence of rain-carrying clouds and air pressure anomalies"... History is distorted, only the surface and colour of world events are disclosed. Somalia was self-sufficient in food until the 1970s; what precipitated the collapse of civil society? Why were food agriculture and nomadic pastoralism destroyed? Drought, desertification and civil war were the "official" causes of the Somalian famine. "Operation Restore Hope" and the US military intervention in 1993 were the "solution". What are the origins of the Somalian crisis?

The IMF Intervention in the Early 1980s

Somalia was a pastoral economy based on "exchange" between nomadic herdsmen and small agriculturalists.[1] Nomadic pastoralists accounted for 50 per cent of the population. In the 1970s, resettlement programmes led to the development of a sizeable sector of commercial pastoralism. Livestock contributed to 80 per cent of export earnings until 1983.[2] Despite recurrent droughts, Somalia remained virtually self-sufficient in food until the 1970s.[3]

The IMF-World Bank intervention in the early 1980s contributed to exacerbating the crisis of Somali agriculture. The economic reforms undermined the fragile exchange relationship between the "nomadic economy" and the "sedentary economy", – i.e. between pastoralists and small farmers characterised by money transactions as well as traditional barter. A very tight austerity programme was imposed on the government largely to release the funds required to service Somalia's debt with the Paris Club. In fact, a large share of the external debt was held by the Washington-based financial institutions.[4] According to an ILO mission report:

> ...the Fund alone among Somalia's major recipients of debt service payments, refuses to reschedule... De facto it is helping to finance an adjustment programme, one of whose major goals is to repay the IMF itself....[5]

Towards the Destruction of Food Agriculture

The structural adjustment programme reinforced Somalia's dependency on imported grain. From the mid-1970s to the mid-1980s, food aid increased fifteen-fold, at the rate of 31 per cent per annum.[6] Combined with increased commercial imports, this influx of cheap surplus wheat and rice sold in the domestic market led to the displacement of local producers, as well as to a major shift in food consumption patterns to the detriment of traditional crops (maize and sorghum). The devaluation of the Somali shilling, imposed by the IMF in June 1981, was followed by periodic devaluations, leading to hikes in the prices of fuel, fertiliser and farm inputs. The impact on agriculturalists was immediate particularly in rain-fed agriculture but also in the areas of irrigated farming. Urban purchasing power declined dramatically, government extension programmes were curtailed, infrastructure collapsed, the deregulation of the grain market and the influx of "food aid" led to the impoverishment of farming communities.[7]

Also, during this period, much of the best agricultural land was appropriated by bureaucrats, army officers and merchants with connections to the government.[8] Rather than promoting food production for the domestic market, the donors were encouraging the development of so-called "high value-added" fruits, vegetables, oilseeds and cotton for export, on the best irrigated farmland.

Collapse of the Livestock Economy

As of the early 1980s, prices for imported livestock drugs increased as a result of the depreciation of the currency. The World Bank encouraged the exaction of user fees for veterinarian services to the nomadic herdsmen, including the vaccination of animals. A private market for veterinary drugs was promoted. The functions performed by the Ministry of Livestock were phased out, with the Veterinary Laboratory Services of the ministry to be fully financed on a cost-recovery basis. According to the World Bank:

> ...veterinarian services are essential for livestock development in all areas, and they can be provided mainly by the private sector (...) Since few private veterinarians will choose to practise in the remote pastoral areas, improved livestock care will also depend on "para vets" paid from drug sales.[9]

The privatisation of animal health was combined with the absence of emergency animal feed during periods of drought, the commercialisation of water and the neglect of water and rangeland conservation. The results were predictable: the herds were decimated and so were the pastoralists, who represent 50 per cent of the country's population. The "hidden objective" of this programme was to eliminate the nomadic herdsmen involved in the traditional exchange economy. According to the World Bank, "adjustments" in the size of the herds are in any event beneficial because nomadic pastoralists in sub-Saharan Africa are narrowly viewed as a cause of environmental degradation.[10]

The collapse in veterinarian services also served indirectly the interests of the rich countries: in 1984, Somalian cattle exports to Saudi Arabia and the Gulf countries plummeted as Saudi beef imports were redirected to suppliers from Australia and the European Community. The ban on Somali livestock imposed by Saudi Arabia was not, however, removed once the rinderpest disease epidemic had been eliminated.

Destroying the State

The restructuring of government expenditure under the supervision of the Bretton Woods institutions also played a crucial role in destroying food agriculture. Agricultural infrastructure collapsed and recurrent expenditure in agriculture declined by about 85 per cent in relation to the mid-1970s.[11] The Somali government was prevented by the IMF from mobilising domestic resources. Tight targets for the budget deficit were set. Moreover, the donors increasingly provided "aid" not in the form of imports of capital and equipment but in the form of "food aid". The latter would in turn be sold by the government on the local market and the proceeds of these sales (i.e. the so-called "counterpart funds") would be used to cover the domestic costs of development projects. As of the early 1980s, "the sale of food aid" became the principal source of revenue for the state thereby enabling donors to take control of the entire budgetary process.[12]

The economic reforms were marked by the disintegration of health and educational programmes.[13] By 1989, expenditure on health had declined by 78 per cent in relation to its 1975 level. According to World Bank figures, the level of recurrent expenditure on education in 1989 was about US$4 per annum per primary school student down from about $82 in 1982. From 1981 to 1989, school enrolment declined by 41 per cent (despite a sizeable increase in the population of school age), textbooks and school materials disappeared from the class-rooms, school buildings deteriorated and nearly a quarter of the primary schools closed down. Teachers' salaries declined to abysmally low levels.

The IMF-World Bank programme has led the Somali economy into a vicious circle: the decimation of the herds pushed the nomadic pastoralists into starvation which in turn backlashed on grain producers who sold or bartered their grain for cattle. The entire social fabric of the pastoralist economy was undone. The collapse in foreign exchange earnings from declining cattle exports and remittances (from Somali workers in the Gulf countries) backlashed on the balance of payments and the state's public finances leading to the breakdown of the government's economic and social programmes.

Small farmers were displaced as a result of the dumping of subsidised US grain on the domestic market combined with the hike in the price of farm inputs. The impoverishment of the urban population also led to a contraction of food consumption. In turn, state support in the irrigated areas was frozen and production in the state farms declined. The latter were to be closed down or privatised under World Bank supervision.

According to World Bank estimates, real public-sector wages in 1989 had declined by 90 per cent in relation to the mid-1970s. Average wages in the public sector had fallen to US$3 a month, leading to the inevitable disintegration of the civil administration.[14] A programme to rehabilitate civil service wages was proposed by the World Bank (in the context of a reform of the civil service), but this objective was to be achieved within the same budgetary envelope by dismissing some 40 per cent of public-sector employees and eliminating salary supplements.[15] Under this plan, the civil service would have been reduced to a mere 25,000 employees by 1995 (in a country of six million people). Several donors indicated keen interest in funding the cost associated with the retrenchment of civil servants.[16]

In the face of impending disaster, no attempt was made by the international donor community to rehabilitate the country's economic and social infrastructure, to restore levels of purchasing power and to rebuild the civil service: the macro-economic adjustment measures proposed by the creditors in the year prior to the collapse of the government of General Siyad Barre in January 1991 (at the height of the civil war) called for a further tightening over public spending, the restructuring of the Central Bank, the liberalisation of credit (which virtually thwarted the private sector) and the liquidation and divestiture of most of the state enterprises.

In 1989, debt-servicing obligations represented 194.6 per cent of export earnings. The IMF's loan was cancelled because of Somalia's outstanding arrears. The World Bank had approved a structural adjustment loan for US$70 million in June 1989 which was frozen a few months later due to Somalia's poor macro-economic performance.[17] Arrears with creditors had to be settled before the granting of new loans and the negotiation of debt rescheduling. Somalia was tangled in the straightjacket of debt servicing and structural adjustment.

Famine Formation in Sub-Saharan Africa: The Lessons of Somalia

Somalia's experience shows how a country can be devastated by the simultaneous application of food "aid" and macro-economic policy. There are many Somalias in the developing world and the economic reform package implemented in Somalia is similar to that applied in more than 100 developing countries. But there is another significant dimension: Somalia is a pastoralist economy, and throughout Africa nomadic and commercial livestock are being destroyed by the IMF-World Bank programme in much the same way as in Somalia. In this context, subsidised beef and dairy products imported (duty free) from the European Union have led to the demise of Africa's pastoral economy. European beef imports to West Africa increased seven-fold since 1984: "the low quality EC beef sells at half the price of locally produced meat. Sahelian farmers are finding that no-one is prepared to buy their herds".[18]

The experience of Somalia shows that famine in the late 20th century is not a consequence of "a shortage of food". On the contrary, famines are spurred on as a result of a global oversupply of grain staples. Since the early 1980s, grain markets have been deregulated under the supervision of the World Bank and US grain surpluses are used systematically (as in the case of Somalia) to destroy the peasantry and destabilise national food agriculture. The latter becomes, under these circumstances, far more vulnerable to the vagaries of drought and environmental degradation.

Throughout the continent, the pattern of "sectoral adjustment" in agriculture under the custody of the Bretton Woods institutions has been unequivocally towards the destruction of food security. Dependency *vis-à-vis* the world market has been reinforced,"food aid" to sub-Saharan Africa increased by more than seven times since 1974 and commercial grain imports more than doubled. Grain imports for sub-Saharan Africa expanded from 3.72 million tons in 1974 to 8.47 million tons in 1993. Food aid increased from 910,000 tons in 1974 to 6.64 million tons in 1993.[19]

"Food aid", however, was no longer earmarked for the drought-stricken countries of the Sahelian belt; it was also channelled into countries which were until recently more or less self-sufficient in food. Zimbabwe (once considered the "bread basket" of Southern Africa) was severely affected by the famine and drought which swept Southern Africa in 1992. The country experienced a drop of 90 per cent in its maize crop, located largely in less productive lands.[20] Yet ironically at the height of the drought, tobacco for export (supported by modern irrigation, credit, research, etc.) registered a bumper harvest.[21] While "the famine forces the population to eat termites", much of the export earnings from Zimbabwe's tobacco harvest were used to service the external debt.

Under the structural adjustment programme, farmers have increasingly abandoned traditional food crops; in Malawi, which was once a net food exporter, maize production declined by 40 per cent in 1992 while tobacco output doubled between 1986 and 1993. One hundred and fifty thousand hectares of the best land was allocated to tobacco.[22] Throughout the 1980s, severe austerity measures were imposed on African governments and expenditures on rural development drastically curtailed, leading to the collapse of agricultural infrastructure. Under the World Bank programme, water was to become a commodity to be sold on a cost-recovery basis to impoverished farmers. Due to lack of funds, the state was obliged to withdraw from the management and conservation of water resources. Water points and boreholes dried up due to lack of maintenance, or were "privatised" by local merchants and rich farmers. In the semi-arid regions, this "commercialisation of water" and irrigation leads to the collapse of food security and famine.[23]

Concluding Remarks

While "external" climatic variables play a role in triggering off a famine and heightening the social impact of drought, famines in the age of globalisation are man-made. They are not the consequence of "a scarcity of food" but of a structure of global oversupply which undermines food security and destroys national food agriculture. Tightly regulated and controlled by international agro-business, this oversupply is ultimately conducive to the stagnation of both production and consumption of essential food staples and the impoverishment of farmers throughout the world. Moreover, in the era of globalisation, the IMF-World Bank structural adjustment programme bears a direct relationship to the process of famine formation because it systematically undermines all categories of economic activity, whether urban or rural, which do not directly serve the interests of the global market system.

Endnotes

1. The 1970s witnessed the impoverishment of the nomadic pastoralists, while the privatisation of boreholes and rangelands supported the enrichment of commercial livestock interests. As in other developing countries,

cash crops for export occupied the best land thereby weakening food agriculture and the small peasantry.

2. From the mid-1970s, there was also a surge of cash remittances from Somali workers in the Gulf states bolstered by the oil boom.
3. There was almost no food aid in the early 1970s.
4. The World Bank and the IMF held 20 per cent of the Somali debt during the 1983-85 period. See International Labour Organisation,*Generating Employment and Incomes in Somalia*, Jobs and Skills Programme for Africa, Addis Ababa, 1989, p.5.
5. International Labour Organisation, *op. cit.*, p. 16.
6. By the mid-1980s it was in excess of 35 per cent of food consumption. See Hossein Farzin, "Food Aid: Positive and Negative Effects in Somalia?", *The Journal of Developing Areas*, January 1991, p. 265.
7. According to the ILO, the State Agricultural Development Corporation (ADC) had historically played an important role in supporting high farmgate prices for agriculturalists: "the ADC was encouraging too much production of maize and sorghum, not too little". International Labour Organisation, *op. cit.*, p. 9. World Bank data, on the other hand, suggests an increase in maize and sorghum production after the deregulation of the grain prices in 1983.
8. See African Rights, *Somalia, Operation Restore Hope: A Preliminary Assessment*, London, May 1993, p. 18.
9. World Bank, *Sub-Saharan Africa, From Crisis to Sustainable Growth*, Washington DC, 1989, p. 98.
10. Ibid., p. 98-101. Overgrazing is detrimental to the environment but the problem cannot be solved by curtailing the livelihood of the pastoralists.
11. From 1975 to 1989.
12. Counterpart funds from the various commodity assistance programmes were the sole source of funding of development projects. Most recurrent expenditures were also dependent on the donors.
13. The allocation to defence spending remained high in percentage terms but declined in real terms.
14. Public-sector wages constituted a mere 0.5 per cent of GNP in 1989.
15. Retrenchment of civil servants over a period of five-years (1991-95).
16. A 40 per cent decrease in public-sector employment over a five-year period (1991-95).
17. The first tranche of this IDA credit (ASAP II) was disbursed, the second tranche was frozen in 1990. The credit was cancelled in January 1991 after the collapse of the Syiad Barre government.
18. Leslie Crawford, "West Africans Hurt by EC Beef Policy", *Financial Times*, 21 May 1993.

19. The figures for 1970 are from World Bank, *World Development Report, 1992*. The 1993 figures are from Food and Agricultural Organisation, *Food Supply Situation and Crop Prospects in Sub-Saharan Africa*, Special Report, No. 1, Rome, April 1993, p. 10.
20. See Haut Commissariat des Nations Unies pour les refugiés, "*Afrique australe, la sécheresse du siècle*," Geneva, July 1992.
21. Ibid., p. 5.
22. See "Tobacco, the Golden Leaf ", *Southern African Economist*, May 1993, p. 49-51.
23. See World Bank, *World Development Report, 1992*, ch. 5.

Chapter 5

Economic Genocide in Rwanda

THE Rwandan crisis which led up to the 1994 ethnic massacres has been presented by the Western media as a profuse narrative of human suffering, while the underlying social and economic causes have been carefully ignored by reporters. As in other "countries in transition", ethnic strife and the outbreak of civil war are increasingly depicted as something which is almost "inevitable" and "innate to these societies", constituting "a painful stage in their evolution from a one-party state towards democracy and the free market." The brutality of the massacres shocked the world community, but what the international media failed to mention was that the civil war was preceded by the flare-up of a deep-seated economic crisis. It was the restructuring of the agricultural system which precipitated the population into abject poverty and destitution.

This deterioration of the economic environment which immediately followed the collapse of the international coffee market and the imposition of sweeping macro-economic reforms by the Bretton Woods institutions exacerbated simmering ethnic tensions and accelerated the process of political collapse. In 1987, the system of quotas established under the International Coffee Agreement (ICA) started to fall apart, world prices plummeted and the *Fonds d'égalisation* (the state coffee-stabilisation fund) which purchased coffee from Rwandan farmers at a fixed price started to accumulate a sizeable debt. A lethal blow to Rwanda's economy came in June 1989 when the ICA reached a deadlock as a result of political pressures from Washington on behalf of the large US coffee traders. At the conclusion of a historic meeting of producers held in Florida, coffee prices plunged in a matter of months by more than 50 per cent.[1] For Rwanda and several other African countries, the drop in prices wreaked havoc. With retail prices more than 20 times that paid to the African farmer, a tremendous amount of wealth was being appropriated in the rich countries.

The Legacy of Colonialism

What is the responsibility of the West in this tragedy? First it is important to stress that the conflict between the Hutu and Tutsi was largely the product of the colonial system, many features of which still prevail today. From the late 19th century, the early German colonial occupation had used the *mwami* (King) of the *nyiginya* (monarchy) installed at Nyanza as a means of establishing its military posts. However, it was largely the administrative reforms initiated in 1926 by the Belgians which were decisive in shaping socio-ethnic relations. The Belgians used dynastic conflicts explicitly to reinforce their territorial control. The traditional chiefs in each hill (*colline*) were used by the colonial administration to requisition forced labour. Routine beatings and corporal punishment were administered on behalf of the colonial masters by the traditional chiefs. The latter were under the direct supervision of a Belgian colonial administrator responsible for a particular portion of territory. A climate of fear and distrust was installed, communal solidarity broke down and traditional client relations were transformed to serve the interests of the coloniser. The objective was to fuel inter-ethnic rivalries as a means of achieving political control as well as preventing the development of solidarity between the two ethnic groups which would inevitably have been directed against the colonial regime. The Tutsi dynastic aristocracy was also made responsible for the collection of taxes and the adminstration of justice. The communal economy was undermined and the peasantry forced to shift out of food agriculture into cash crops for export. Communal lands were transformed into individual plots geared solely towards cash-crop cultivation (the so-called *cultures obligatoires*).[2]

Colonial historiographers were entrusted with the task of "transcribing" as well as distorting Rwanda-Urundi's oral history. The historical record was falsified: the *mwami* monarchy was identified exclusively with the Tutsi aristocratic dynasty. The Hutus were represented as a dominated caste.[3]

The Belgian colonialists developed a new social class, the so-called "*nègres évolués*" recruited from among the Tutsi aristocracy, and the school system was put in place to educate the sons of the chiefs and to provide the African personnel required by the Belgians. In turn, the various apostolic missions and vicariats received under Belgian colonial rule an almost political mandate. The clergy, for example, was often used to oblige the peasants to integrate the cash crop economy. These socio-ethnic divisions – which have unfolded since the 1920s – have left a profound mark on contemporary Rwandan society.

Since independence in 1962, relations with the former colonial powers and donors became exceedingly more complex. Inherited from the Belgian colonial period, however, the same objective of pushing one ethnic group against the other ("divide and rule") largely prevailed in the various "military", "human rights" and "macro-economic" interventions undertaken from the outset of the civil war in 1990. The Rwandan crisis became encapsulated in a continuous agenda of donor roundtables (held in Paris), cease-fire agreements and peace talks. These various initiatives were closely monitored and coordinated by the donor community in a tangled circuit of "conditionalities" (and cross-conditionalities). The release of multilateral and bilateral loans since the outbreak of the civil war was made conditional upon implementing a process of so-called "democratisation" under the tight surveillance of the donor community. In turn, Western aid in support of multiparty democracy was made conditional (in an almost "symbiotic" relationship) upon the government reaching an agreement with the IMF, and so on. These attempts were all the more illusive because since the collapse of the coffee market in 1989, actual political power in Rwanda rested largely, in any event, in the hands of the donors. A communiqué of the US State Department issued in early 1993 illustrates this situation vividly: the continuation of US bilateral aid was made conditional on good behaviour in policy reform as well as progress in the pursuit of democracy.

"Democratisation" based on an abstract model of inter-ethnic solidarity envisaged by the Arusha peace agreement signed in August 1993 was an impossibility from the outset and the donors knew it. The brutal impoverishment of the population which resulted both from the war and the IMF reforms precluded a genuine process of democratisation. The objective was to meet the conditions of "good governance" (a new term in the donors' glossary) and oversee the installation of a bogus multiparty coalition government under the trusteeship of Rwanda's external creditors. In fact multipartyism as narrowly conceived by the donors contributed to fuelling the various political factions of the regime. Not surprisingly, as soon as the peace negotiations entered a stalemate, the World Bank announced that it was interrupting the disbursements under its loan agreement.[4]

The Economy since Independence

The evolution of the post-colonial economic system played a decisive role in the development of the Rwandan crisis. While progress since independence in diversifying the national economy was indeed recorded, the colonial-style export economy based on coffee (*les cultures obligatoires*) established under the Belgian administration was largely maintained, providing Rwanda with more than 80 per cent of its foreign exchange earnings. A rentier class with interests in coffee trade and with close ties to the seat of political power had developed. Levels of poverty remained high, yet during the 1970s and the first part of the 1980s, economic and social progress was nonetheless realised: real GDP growth was of the order of 4.9 per cent per annum (1965-89), school enrolment increased markedly and recorded inflation was among the lowest in sub-Saharan Africa, less than 4 per cent per annum.[5]

While the Rwandan rural economy remained fragile, marked by acute demographic pressures (3.2 per cent per annum population growth), land fragmentation and soil erosion, local-level food self-sufficiency had, to some extent, been achieved alongside the development of the export economy. Coffee was cultivated by approximately 70 per cent of rural households, yet it constituted only a fraction of total monetary income. A variety of other commercial activities had been developed including the sale of traditional food staples and banana beer in regional and urban markets.[6] Until the late 1980s, imports of cereals including food aid were minimal compared to the patterns observed in other countries of the region. The food situation started to deteriorate in the early 1980s with a marked decline in the per capita availability of food. In overt contradiction to the usual trade reforms adopted under the auspices of the World Bank, protection to local producers had been provided up to that time through restrictions on the import of food commodities.[7] These were lifted with the adoption of the 1990 structural adjustment programme.

The Fragility of the State

The economic foundations of the post-independence Rwandan state remained extremely fragile. A large share of government revenues depended on coffee, with the risk that a collapse in commodity prices would precipitate a crisis in the state's public finances. The rural economy was the main source of funding for the state. As the debt crisis unfolded, a larger share of coffee and tea earnings had been earmarked for debt servicing, putting further pressure on small-scale farmers.

Export earnings declined by 50 per cent between 1987 and 1991. The demise of state institutions unfolded thereafter. When coffee prices plummeted, famines erupted throughout the Rwandan countryside. According to World Bank data, the growth of GDP per capita declined from 0.4 per cent in 1981-86 to -5.5 per cent in the period immediately following the slump of the coffee market (1987-91).

The IMF-World Bank Intervention

A World Bank mission travelled to Rwanda in November 1988 to review Rwanda's public expenditure programme. A series of recommendations had been established with a view to putting Rwanda back on the track of sustained economic growth. The World Bank mission presented the country's policy options to the government, as consisting of two "scenarios". Scenario I entitled "No Strategy Change" contemplated the option of remaining with the "old" system of state planning, whereas Scenario II labelled "With Strategy Change" was that of macro-economic reform and "transition to the free market". After careful economic "simulations" of likely policy outcomes, the World Bank concluded with some grain of optimism that if Rwanda adopted Scenario II, levels of consumption would increase markedly over 1989-93 alongside a recovery of investment and an improved balance of trade. The "simulations" also pointed to added export performance and substantially lower levels of external indebtedness.[8] These outcomes depended on the speedy implementation of the usual recipe of trade liberalisation and currency devaluation, alongside the lifting of all subsidies to agriculture, the phasing out of the *Fonds d' égalisation*, the privatisation of state enterprises and the dismissal of civil servants.

The "With Strategy Change" (Scenario II) was adopted. The government had no choice.[9] A 50 per cent devaluation of the Rwandan franc was carried out in November 1990 barely six weeks after the incursion from Uganda of the rebel army of the Rwandan Patriotic Front.

The devaluation was intended to boost coffee exports. It was presented to public opinion as a means of rehabilitating a war-ravaged economy. Not surprisingly, exactly the opposite results were achieved, exacerbating the plight of the civil war. From a situation of relative price stability, the plunge of the Rwandan franc contributed to triggering inflation and the collapse of real earnings. A few days after the devaluation, sizeable increases in the prices of fuel and consumer essentials were announced. The consumer price index increased from 1.0 per cent in 1989 to 19.2 per cent in 1991. The balance of payments situation deteriorated dramatically and the outstanding external debt, which had already doubled since 1985, increased by 34 per cent between 1989 and 1992. The state administrative apparatus was in disarray, state enterprises were pushed into bankruptcy and public services collapsed.[10] Health and education disintegrated under the brunt of the IMF-imposed austerity measures: despite the establishment of "a social safety net" (earmarked by the donors for programmes in the social sectors), the incidence of severe child malnutrition increased dramatically; the number of recorded cases of malaria increased by 21 per cent in the year following the adoption of the IMF programme largely as a result of the absence of anti-malarial drugs in the public health centres; and the imposition of school fees at the primary-school level led to a massive decline in school enrolment.[11]

The economic crisis reached its climax in 1992 when Rwandan farmers in desperation uprooted some 300,000 coffee trees.[12] Despite soaring domestic prices, the government had frozen the farmgate price of coffee at its 1989 level (RwF 125/kg), under the terms of its agreement with the Bretton Woods institutions. The government was not allowed (under the World Bank loan) to transfer state resources to the *Fonds d'égalisation*. It should also be mentioned that a significant profit was appropriated by local coffee traders and intermediaries serving to put further pressure on the peasantry.

In June 1992, a second devaluation was ordered by the IMF,

leading – at the height of the civil war – to a further escalation of the prices of fuel and consumer essentials. Coffee production tumbled by another 25 per cent in a single year.[13] Because of over-cropping of coffee trees, there was increasingly less land available to produce food, but the peasantry was not able easily to switch back into food crops. The meagre cash income derived from coffee had been erased yet there was nothing to fall back on. Not only were cash revenues from coffee insufficient to buy food, the prices of farm inputs had soared and money earnings from coffee were grossly insufficient. The crisis of the coffee economy backlashed on the production of traditional food staples leading to a substantial drop in the production of cassava, beans and sorghum. The system of savings and loan cooperatives which provided credit to small farmers had also disintegrated. Moreover, with the liberalisation of trade and the deregulation of grain markets as recommended by the Bretton Woods institutions, (heavily-subsidised) cheap food imports and food aid from the rich countries were entering Rwanda with the effect of destabilising local markets.

Under "the free market" system imposed on Rwanda, neither cash crops nor food crops were economically viable. The entire agricultural system was pushed into crisis. The state administrative apparatus was in disarray due not only to the civil war but also as a result of the austerity measures and sinking civil service salaries, a situation which contributed inevitably to exacerbating the climate of generalised insecurity which had unfolded in 1992.

The seriousness of the agricultural situation had been amply documented by the FAO which had warned of the existence of widespread famine in the southern provinces.[14] A report released in early 1994 also pointed to the total collapse of coffee production as a result of both the war and the failure of the state marketing system which was being phased out with the support of the World Bank. Rwandex, the mixed enterprise responsible for the processing and export of coffee, had become largely inoperative.

The decision to devalue (and "the IMF stamp of approval") had already been reached on 17 September 1990, prior to the outbreak of hostilities, in high-level meetings held in Washington between the IMF and a mission headed by Rwandan Minister of Finance Mr Ntigurirwa. The "green light" had been granted: as of early October, at the very moment when the fighting started, millions of dollars of so-called "balance of payments aid" (from multilateral and bilateral sources) came pouring into the coffers of the Central Bank. These funds administered by the Central Bank had been earmarked (by the donors) for commodity imports, yet it appears likely that a sizeable portion of these "quick disbursing loans" had been diverted by the regime (and its various political factions) towards the acquisition of military hardware (from South Africa, Egypt and Eastern Europe).[15] The purchases of Kalaṣhnikov guns, heavy artillery and mortar were undertaken in addition to the bilateral military aid package provided by France which included, *inter alia,* Milan and Apila missiles (not to mention a Mystère Falcon jet for President Habyarimana's personal use).[16] Moreover, since October 1990, the armed forces had expanded virtually overnight from 5,000 to 40,000 men requiring inevitably (under conditions of budgetary austerity) a sizeable influx of outside money. The new recruits were largely enlisted from the ranks of the urban unemployed of which the numbers had dramatically swelled since the collapse of the coffee market in 1989. Thousands of delinquent and idle youths from a drifting population were also drafted into the civilian militia responsible for the massacres. And part of the arms' purchases enabled the armed forces to organise and equip the militiamen.

In all, from the outset of the hostilities (which coincided chronologically with the devaluation and the initial "gush of fresh money" in October 1990), a total envelope of some US$260 million had been approved for disbursal (with sizeable bilateral contributions from France, Germany, Belgium, the European Community and the US). While the new loans contributed to releasing money for the payment of debt servicing as well as equipping the armed forces, the evidence would suggest that a large part of this donor assistance was neither used productively nor was it channelled into providing relief in areas affected by famine.

It is also worth noting that the World Bank (through its soft-lending affiliate, the International Development Association (IDA)) had ordered in 1992 the privatisation of Rwanda's state enterprise Electrogaz. The proceeds of the privatisation were to be channelled towards debt servicing. In a loan agreement co-financed with the European Investment Bank (EIB) and the Caisse française de développement (CFD), the Rwandan authorities were to receive in return (after meeting the "conditionalities") the modest sum of US$39 million which could be spent freely on commodity imports.[17] The privatisation carried out at the height of the civil war also included dismissals of personnel and an immediate hike in the price of electricity which further contributed to paralysing urban public services. A similar privatisation of Rwandatel, the state telecommunications company under the Ministry of Transport and Communications was implemented in September 1993.[18]

The World Bank had carefully reviewed Rwanda's public investment programme. The *fiches de projet* having been examined, the World Bank recommended scrapping more than half the country's public investment projects. In agriculture, the World Bank had also demanded a significant down-sizing of state investment including the abandonment of the inland swamp reclamation programme which had been initiated by the government in response to the severe shortages of arable land (and which the World Bank considered "unprofitable"). In the social sectors, the World Bank proposed a so-called "priority programme" (under "the social safety net") predicated on maximising efficiency and "reducing the financial burden of the government" through the exaction of user fees, lay-offs of teachers and health workers and the partial privatisation of health and education.

The World Bank would no doubt contend that things would have been much worse had Scenario II not been adopted. This is the so-called "counterfactual argument". Such a reasoning, however, sounds absurd particularly in the case of Rwanda. No sensitivity or concern was expressed as to the likely political and social repercussions of economic shock therapy applied to a country on the brink of civil war. The World Bank team consciously excluded the "non-economic variables" from their "simulations".

While the international donor community cannot be held directly responsible for the ethnic massacres and tragic outcome of the Rwandan civil war, the austerity measures combined with the impact of the IMF-sponsored devaluations contributed to impoverishing the Rwandan people at a time of acute political and social crisis. The deliberate manipulation of market forces destroyed economic activity and people's livelihood, fuelled unemployment and created a situation of generalised famine and social despair.

Economic Genocide

To lay the blame solely on deep-seated tribal hatred not only exonerates G-7 governments and the donors, it also distorts an exceedingly complex process of economic, social and political disintegration affecting an entire nation of more than seven million people. Rwanda, however, is but one among many countries in sub-Saharan Africa (in, for example, Burundi famine and ethnic massacres are rampant) which are facing a similar predicament. And in many respects the Rwandan 1990 devaluation appeared almost as a "laboratory test case" as well as a threatening "danger signal" for the devaluation of the Central and West African (CFA) franc implemented on the instructions of the IMF and the French Treasury in January 1994 by the same amount, 50 per cent.

In Somalia in the aftermath of "Operation Restore Hope", the absence of a genuine economic recovery programme by the USAID mission in Mogadishu – outside the provision of short-term emergency relief and food aid – was the main obstacle to resolving the civil war and rebuilding the country (see Chapter 4). In Somalia, because of the surplus of relief aid which competed with local production, farmers remained in the relief camps instead of returning to their home villages. What are the lessons for Rwanda? As humanitarian organisations prepared for the return of the refugees, the prospects for rebuilding the Rwandan economy outside the framework determined by the IMF and Rwanda's international creditors were extremely bleak. Even in the event that a national unity government is installed and the personal security of the refugees can be ensured, the two million Rwandans cramped in camps in Zaire and Tanzania have nothing to return to, nothing to look forward to: agricultural markets have been destroyed, local-level food production and the coffee economy have been shattered, urban employment and social programmes have been erased. The reconstruction of Rwanda will require "an alternative economic programme" implemented by a genuinely democratic government (based on inter-ethnic solidarity and free from donor interference). Such a programme presupposes erasing the external debt, together with an unconditional infusion of international aid. It also requires lifting the straitjacket of budgetary austerity imposed by the IMF, mobilising domestic resources, and providing for a secure and stable productive base for the rural people.

Endnotes

1. The system of export quotas of the International Coffee Organisation (ICO) was lifted in the aftermath of the Florida meetings in July 1989. The fob price in Mombasa declined from US$1.31 a pound in May 1989 to $0.60 in December, *Marchés tropicaux*, 18 May 1990, p. 1369; 29 June 1990, p. 1860.
2. See Jean Rumiya, *Le Rwanda sous le régime du mandat belge (1916-1931)*, L'Harmattan, Paris, 1992, pp. 220-26; Andre Guichaoua, *Destins paysans et politiques agraires en Afrique centrale,* L'Harmattan, Paris, 1989.
3. See Ferdinand Nahimana, *Le Rwanda, Emergence d'un Etat*, L'Harmattan, Paris, 1993.
4. *New African*, June 1994, p. 16.
5. See United Nations Conference on the Least Developed Countries, *Country Presentation by the Government of Rwanda*, Geneva, 1990, p. 5. See also République Rwandaise, Ministère des Finances et de l'Economie, *L'Economie rwandaise, 25 ans d'efforts* (1962-87), Kigali, 1987.
6. See the study of A. Guichaoua, *Les paysans et l'investissement-travail au Burundi et au Rwanda*, Bureau international du Travail, Geneva, 1987.
7. United Nations Conference on the Least Developed Countries, *op. cit.*, p. 2.
8. A 5 per cent growth in exports was to take place under Scenario II as opposed to 2.5 per cent under Scenario I.
9. Debt forgiveness amounting to US$46 million was granted in 1989.
10. World Bank, *World Debt Tables, 1993-94*, Washington DC, p. 383. The outstanding debt had increased by more than 400 per cent since 1980 (from US$150.3 million in 1980 to $804.3 million in 1992).
11. See Myriam Gervais, "Etude de la pratique des ajustements au Niger et au Rwanda", *Labour, Capital and Society*, Vol. 26. No. 1, 1993, p. 36.
12. This figure is a conservative estimate. Economist Intelligence Unit, *Country Profile, Rwanda/Burundi 1993/1994*, London, 1994, p. 10.
13. In 1993, a third devaluation of the order of 30 per cent had been recommended by the World Bank as a means of eliminating the debts of the *Fonds d'égalisation.*
14. The International Committee of the Red Cross (ICRC) had estimated in 1993 that more than a million people were affected by famine, *Marchés tropicaux*, 2 April 1993, p. 898. A FAO communiqué released in March 1994 pointed to a 33 per cent decline in food production in 1993. See *Marchés tropicaux*, 25 March 1994, p. 594.

15. There has been no official communiqué or press report confirming or denying the channelling of balance-of-payments aid towards military expenditure. According to the Washington-based Human Rights Watch, Egypt agreed with Kigali to supply US$6 million worth of military equipment. The deal with South Africa was for US$5.9 million. See *Marchés tropicaux*, 28 January 1994, p. 173.
16. See *New African*, June 1994, p. 15. See also the interview with Colette Braeckman on France's military aid in *Archipel*, No. 9, July 1994, p. 1.
17. See *Marchés tropicaux*, 26 February 1992, p. 569.
18. See *Marchés tropicaux*, 8 October 1993, p. 2492.

PART III

South and South-East Asia

Chapter 6

India: The IMF's "Indirect Rule"

Indirect rule in India has a long history: the Rajputs and princely states had a fair degree of autonomy in relation to the British colonial government. In contrast under the IMF-World Bank tutelage, the Union Minister of Finance reports directly to 1818 H Street N W, Washington DC, bypassing parliament and the democratic process. The Union budget text, formally written by Indian bureaucrats in Delhi, has become a repetitious and redundant document. Its main clauses are included in the loan agreements signed with the World Bank and the IMF.

Introduction

THE IMF bail-out to the minority Congress government of Prime Minister P. V. Narasimha Rao in 1991 did not, at first glance, point towards a major economic breakdown and disintegration of civil society comparable to that which had occurred in many debt-stricken countries in Latin America and Eastern Europe undergoing IMF "shock treatment". While India did not experience hyperinflation nor the collapse of its foreign exchange market, the social impact in a country of 900 million people was devastating: in India, the IMF programme initiated in July 1991 directly affected the livelihood of several hundred million people. There was evidence of widespread chronic starvation and social destitution which resulted directly from the macro-economic measures.

In India, the IMF-World Bank programme was set in motion with the fall of the Janata Dal government of V. P. Singh in 1990, and the assassination of Rajiv Gandhi during the election campaign in Tamil Nadu in 1991. The government was obliged to airlift some 47 tons of gold to the vaults of the Bank of England for "safe custody" to satisfy the requirements of international creditors.[1] The IMF agreement implemented shortly thereafter was to provide at best a short breathing-space: with a debt of more than US$80 billion, the IMF and World Bank loans (already earmarked to pay back international creditors) barely provided the cash required to fund six months of debt servicing.

The IMF's "economic surgery" under the 1991 New Economic Policy required the Indian government to cut spending in social programmes and infrastructure, eliminate state subsidies and price support programmes (including food subsidies) and sell off the more profitable public enterprises at "a good price" to the large business houses and foreign capital. Other reform measures included the closing down of a large number of so-called"sick public enterprises", the liberalisation of trade, the free entry of foreign capital, as well as major reforms in banking, financial institutions and the tax structure.

The IMF loan agreement together with the World Bank structural adjustment loan (SAL) signed in December 1991 (of which the contents and conditions were a closely guarded state secret) were intended to "help India" alleviate its balance-of-payments difficulties, reduce the fiscal deficit and relieve inflationary pressures. The IMF-World Bank package, however, accomplished exactly the opposite results: it pushed the economy into a stagflation (the price of rice increased by more than 50 per cent in the months following the 1991 economic measures) and heightened the balance-of-payments crisis (as a result of the increased cost of imported raw materials and the influx of imports in support of luxury consumption). Moreover, trade liberalisation, combined with the compression of internal purchasing power and the free entry of foreign capital, pushed a large number of domestic producers into bankruptcy.

A National Renewal Fund (NRF) was created in July 1991. This "social safety net" devised by World Bank advisors and targeted towards so-called "vulnerable groups" did not provide adequate compensation to an estimated 4 to 8 million public- and private-sector workers (out of a total organised labour force of 26 million) who were to be laid off as a result of the programme. The NRF was intended to buy out trade-union opposition. In the textile industry, approximately one third of the workers were to be laid off. A large share of the automobile and engineering industry was to be phased out with the entry of foreign capital and the establishment of joint ventures. The G-7 countries were anxious to "export their recession"; Western and Japanese transnationals were eager to capture a part of India's domestic market as well as obtain – with the help of the GATT rules on intellectual property rights – the abrogation of India's 1970 Patent Law. This would enable them to register product patents in manufacturing as well as in agriculture (through plant breeders' rights) thereby virtually gaining control over a large portion of the Indian economy.

It should be noted that the "exit policies" as such did not address in a meaningful way the serious problems of bureaucracy and mismanagement of public-sector enterprises as well as the necessity to modernise Indian industry. While the IMF programme denied India the possibility of an autonomous national capitalist development (its "hidden agenda"), the reforms, nonetheless, received the firm backing of India's largest business houses (in a fragile alliance with the upper-caste landlord lobby). The Tatas and the Birlas identify increasingly with foreign capital and the global market economy rather than with the "national interest". The tendency is towards increased concentration of ownership. Preferential credit to small and medium-sized enterprises is eliminated and the big business families in partnership with foreign capital are rapidly entering into a variety of areas previously preserved for small-scale industry (i.e. small-scale industrial units).

The so-called "exit policy" proposed by the government and the IMF was viewed by the large industrial corporations as "an opportunity to change the labour laws and to get rid of our workers. For us it is more profitable to sub-contract with small factories which employ casual and unorganised labour".[2] Bata, the multinational shoe manufacturer, pays its unionised factory workers 80 rupees a day (US$3). With the reforms of the labour laws, it would be able to lay off its workers and subcontract with independent cobblers at no more than 25 rupees a day (approximately $1). In the jute industry, in small engineering, in the garment industry, the large corporate monopolies tend to subcontract thereby reducing their modern-sector labour force.

Crushing the Rural and Urban Poor

Instead of extending the labour laws to protect casual and seasonal workers, the IMF programme proposed "to help the poor" by scrapping the labour laws altogether because "these laws favour the labour aristocracy" and "discriminate against" the non-unionised sectors of the labour force. Neither the government nor the IMF had addressed the broader social impact of the New Economic Policy on farm-workers, artisans and small enterprises.

In India, more than 70 per cent of rural households are small marginal farmers or landless farm workers, representing a population of over 400 million people. In irrigated areas, agricultural workers are employed for 200 days a year, and in rain-fed farming for approximately 100 days. The phasing-out of fertiliser subsidies (an explicit condition of the IMF agreement) and the increase in the prices of farm inputs and fuel was pushing a large number of small and medium-sized farmers into bankruptcy. The price of chemical fertiliser shot up by 40 per cent in the immediate aftermath of the 1991 New Economic Policy.

In turn, millions of landless farm workers belonging to the scheduled and backward castes – already well below the official poverty line – were being crushed by Finance Minister Manmohan Singh's New Economic Policy. These are "the untouchables of economic policy". For the upper-caste élites, the Harijans are people who really do not matter. The impact of the IMF's "economic medicine" on these sectors of the labour force was carefully overlooked. For the IMF and the government, there were no "exit policies" for the unorganised sectors. In the words of the Finance Minister Manmohan Singh: "the cottage industries have no problems because the wages will go down".[3]

In Tamil Nadu, for instance, the minimum wage for farmworkers set by the state government was 15 rupees a day (US$0.57) in 1992. Labour legislation, however, was not enforced and actual wages paid to farm workers were (with the exception of the harvest period), substantially lower than the minimum daily wage: for paddy transplanting, for instance, workers were paid between 3 and 5 rupees a day; in heavy construction work, men received 10 to 15 rupees a day and women 8 to 10 rupees.[4] With perhaps the exception of the states of Kerala and West Bengal, minimum wage legislation has largely been ineffective in protecting the rights of farm workers.

On the Hyderabad-Bangalore national highway, one can observe the child labourers of the Dhone limestone mines transport heavy loads in bamboo baskets up a flight of some 60 steps where the limestone is emptied into tall brick kilns. Both adult workers and children are paid 9.50 rupees a day; there have been no wage increases since the July 1991 Union Budget: "we have to work here regardless of poisonous fumes, heat and dust. The wages are higher than on the farms..."[5]

"Eliminating the Poor" through Starvation Deaths

In the post-independence period, starvation deaths were limited largely to peripheral tribal areas (e.g. in Tripura or Nagaland). This is no longer the case, there is evidence that famine has become widespread since the adoption of the New Economic Policy in 1991. A study on starvation deaths among handloom weavers in a relatively prosperous rural community in Andhra Pradesh which occurred in the months following the implementation of the 1991 New Economic Policy enables us to pinpoint the transmission mechanism underlying the IMF-sponsored programme: with the devaluation and the lifting of controls on cotton-yarn exports, the jump in the domestic price of cotton yarn led to a collapse in the *pacham* (24 metres) rate paid to the weaver by the middle-man (through the putting-out system).

> Radhakrishnamurthy and his wife were able to weave between three and four *pachams* a month bringing home the meagre income of 300-400 rupees for a family of six, then came the Union Budget of 24 July 1991, the price of cotton yarn jumped and the burden was passed on to the weaver. Radhakrishnamurthy's family income declined to 240-320 rupees a month.[6]

Radhakrishnamurthy of Gollapalli village in Guntur district died of starvation on 4 September, 1991. Between 30 August and 10 November 1991, at least 73 starvation deaths were reported in only two districts of Andhra Pradesh. The IMF-World Bank programme, rather than "eliminating poverty" as claimed by the then World Bank president Lewis Preston, actually contributed to "eliminating the poor". Combined with a 50 per cent rise in the price of rice (which resulted from the devaluation and the removal of food and fertiliser subsidies), the real earnings of handloom workers declined by more than 60 per cent in the six-month period after the adoption of the IMF programme in 1991.[7] There are 3.5 million handlooms throughout India supporting a population of some 17 million people.

A similar situation prevails in most small-scale rural and urban cottage industries which operate through the putting-out system. For instance, there are in India more than a million diamond cutters supporting a population of nearly five million people. The large diamond export houses based in Bombay import rough diamonds from South Africa, and subcontract the work through middle-men to rural workshops in Maharashtra. Seven out of 10 diamonds sold in Western Europe and the US are cut in India. Whereas in the rich countries diamonds are said to be "a girl's best friend", in India poverty is the necessary input into this profitable export activity: in the words of a major diamond exporter:

> Making jewellery is cheap labour,...[food prices have gone up] but we have not increased the rupee payments to village workers. With the devaluation, our dollar labour costs go down, we are more competitive, we pass on some of the benefits to our overseas customers...[8]

The IMF Supports Caste Exploitation

The IMF-World Bank programme recommended the repeal of minimum wage legislation as well as the deindexation of earnings. The proposed "liberalisation" of the labour market contributed to reinforcing despotic social relations thereby providing, in practice, a greater legitimacy to caste exploitation, semi-slavery and child labour. Under World Bank guidelines, the tendency was towards dispossession (through the formal removal of land ceilings) as well as the expropriation of communal village lands by feudal landlords and kulaks. The liberalisation of banking (e.g. by doing away with the rural credit cooperatives) contributed to strengthening the village money-lender.[9]

The IMF programme converted itself into an instrument of "economic genocide": several hundred million people (farm-workers, artisans, small traders, etc.) were surviving on per capita incomes substantially lower than 50 cents a day (with domestic prices, in the logic of the IMF measures, moving up to world levels).[10] An increase in the price of rice and wheat of more than 50 per cent (in the year following the July 1991 New Economic Policy) combined with a decline in the average number of days worked in both rain-fed and irrigated agriculture was pushing large sectors of the rural population into "chronic starvation", a process without precedent on this scale since the great famines in Bengal in the early 1940s.[11] In contrast, the drop in internal consumption of food had been matched by an increase in rice exports. In the words of Tata Exports:

> ...the devaluation was very good for us; together with the lifting of quantitative restrictions on rice exports, we expect to increase our sales of rice to the world market by 60 per cent.[12]

Poverty Supports Exports to the Rich Countries

The IMF-World Bank reforms feed on the poverty of the people and on the contraction of the internal market. While India's population is substantially larger than that of all OECD countries combined (approximately 750 million), the economic reforms entail a major redirection of the Indian economy towards exports. In the logic of the structural adjustment programme, the only viable market is that of the rich countries. The IMF programme compresses internal consumption and reorients India's productive system towards the international market. Poverty is an input on the supply side: labour costs in dollars are low, internal purchasing power is low. For instance, following the 1991 IMF-sponsored measures, the sale of cloth in India fell to 8 metres per capita per annum (16 metres in 1965, 10 metres in 1985), barely sufficient for a saree and a blouse.

Towards Political Collapse

With active secessionist movements in Kashmir, Punjab and Assam, disturbances in Amritsar and an uncertain truce along the "Line of Control" with Pakistan, the IMF's economic medicine has contributed to polarising further Indian society as well potentially creating the pre-conditions for the political break-up of the Indian union. The austerity measures imposed by the IMF have exacerbated tensions between the union and the state governments. More generally, the economic programme has contributed to embittering religious and ethnic strife.

In the aftermath of the reforms, the Congress Party remained deeply divided on economic policy with several cabinet ministers coming out openly against the IMF package. Moreover, the rise in food prices has weakened Congress' grass-root support, while its *rapprochement* with Israel since the Gulf War (in part as a result of US pressures) has tarnished its image as a secular party, leading to a strengthening of the Muslim League.

Both Hindu as well as Islamic fundamentalism feed on the poverty of the masses. The major opposition party, the Hindu Bharatiya Janata Party (BJP) had rhetorically condemned the government's "open-door" policy. Invoking Mahatma Gandhi's *swadeshi* (self-reliance) the Rashtriya Swayam Sevak Sangh (RSS) (the BJP's parent fundamentalist movement) called for a massive boycott of foreign goods. In turn, the National Front (NF) and the Leftist Front (LF), led by the Communist Party of India (Marxist), feared that if the minority Congress government were to fall, the BJP would take over. In 1996, with the defeat of Congress in parliamentary elections, the BJP formed a government.

The IMF's Indirect Rule

The Washington-based international bureaucracy has installed in India "a parallel government" which builds upon these internal social, religious and ethnic divisions ("divide and rule"). Since the Emergency Period in the mid-1970s, and more forcefully since Indira Gandhi's return to power in 1980, former IMF and World Bank employees have moved into key advisory positions in central government ministries. Not surprisingly, the IMF feels that:

> ...it has on the whole been easy to negotiate with Indian officials...compared to other Third World countries, where you see a lot of grim faces at the bargaining table. Economic thinking has largely been in the same direction, their attitude has been most conciliatory.[13]

A quarterly monitoring system was set up under the close guard of the IMF. Under this computerised system located in the Ministry of Finance, IMF and World Bank officials have access to key macroeconomic data no later than six weeks after the end of the quarter. In the words of the IMF liaison officer in Delhi: "We take the monitoring very seriously, we scrutinise all the information we get,... we are very careful that they [the government] do not cheat". Some 40 key economic variables are subject to quarterly verification by the IMF:

> We have also included in the agreement ten "structural benchmarks", these are not explicit conditions of the loan agreement, they pertain to broad areas of structural reform which we would like the government to address [in future loan negotiations].[14]

Despite precise targets for the fiscal deficit (contained in the loan agreements), the IMF's main objective was, however, to enforce the process of fiscal collapse and establish a system whereby the government is in a strait-jacket and no longer controls the main instruments of fiscal and monetary policy. These conditions forestalled virtually from the outset the possibility of economic growth. The IMF did not, however, quibble over numbers. In fact, the "structural benchmarks" rather than the quantitative targets are what really matters. Conformity to things which are understood by both sides but which are not necessarily stated as explicit conditions in the loan agreement is what counts: "the government must give us 'signals' that they are moving in the right direction..."[15]

Within the framework of the government's "relationship" to the Washington-based institutions, key government policy documents were drafted directly by the IMF and the World Bank on behalf of the Union Ministry of Finance. In this regard, the Indian press was careful to point out (with a touch of humour) that the Memorandum on Economic Policies of 27 August, 1991 (a key document in the government's initial agreement with the IMF), together with the covering letter addressed to the IMF Managing Director Mr Michel Camdessus, was drafted in "American script" (most probably by Washington-based officials) against the habitual British construction, style and spelling used by Indian bureaucrats:[16] "Yes sir, there are awful mistakes of grammar, spelling and syntax. But I did not type it, sir. It came from the World Bank for your signature".[17] A few days prior to the 29 February, 1992 Union Budget speech in the Lok Sabha, it became apparent that the main budget proposals had not only been "leaked" by the minister of finance in a letter to World Bank president Lewis Preston, but more importantly that the budget was already an integral part of the conditionalities contained in the structural adjustment loan agreement signed with the World Bank in December 1991.[18]

Endnotes

1. See M. K. Pandhe, *Surrender of India's Sovereignty and Self-Reliance*, Progressive Printers, New Delhi, 1991, p. 2.
2. Interview in Bombay with a major industrialist, January 1992.
3. Interview with Finance Minister Manmohan Singh, New Delhi, January 1992.
4. Interviews with leaders of farm-workers' organisations in Tamil Nadu, February 1992.
5. See "Around a Kiln, the Child Labourers of Dhone", *Frontline*, 13 March 1992, p. 52.
6. See the excellent study of K. Nagaraj *et al.*, "Starvation Deaths in Andhra Pradesh", *Frontline*, 6 December, 1991, p. 48.
7. Ibid.
8. Interview with a major diamond export house in Bombay, January 1992.
9. The Narasimhan Commission Report, *India: Financial Sector Report,* is a near "photocopy" of World Bank proposals; see S. Sanhar's scrutiny of the Narasimhan Report in *Indian Express*, 8 December, 1991.
10. For a majority of the rural and urban population, household income (with five to six family members) is less than R1,000 a month, – i.e. a per capita income of less than R7 a day (less than US30 cents).
11. According to the National Nutrition Monitoring Bureau (NNMB), the diet and nutrition surveys conducted between 1977 and 1989 would indicate some improvement in "severe" malnutrition among children. While abject poverty according to these figures had declined in India, the levels of average poverty have remained very high. See "Starvation Deaths and Chronic Deprivation", *Frontline*, 6 December, 1991, p. 81. Chronic starvation is defined as "a situation in which the subjects subsist on diets which are very deficient in energy for a long period of time", *Frontline*, 6 December 1991, p. 79.

12. Interview with Tata Exports in Bombay, January 1992.
13. Interview with the IMF liaison officer in Delhi, January 1992.
14. Ibid.
15. Ibid.
16. See Praful Bidwani, *Times of India*, 18 December, 1991.
17. See Laxman (the famous cartoonist) in *Times of India*, reproduced in *Structural Adjustment, Who Really Pays*, Public Interest Research Group, New Delhi, March 1992, p. 44.
18. *Economic Times*, 28 February 1992, p. 1.

Chapter 7

Bangladesh: Under the Tutelage of the "Aid" Consortium

The 1975 Military Coup

THE military coup of August 1975 led to the assassination of President Mujibur Rahman and the installation of a military junta. The authors of the coup had been assisted by key individuals within the Bangladesh National Security Intelligence and the CIA office at the American Embassy in Dhaka.[1] In the months which preceded the assassination plot, the US State Department had already established a framework for "stable political transition" to be carried out in the aftermath of the military take-over.

Washington's initiative had been firmly endorsed by the Bretton Woods institutions: less than a year before the assassination of Sheik Mujib, Dhaka's international creditors had demanded the formation of an "aid consortium" under the custody of the World Bank. Whereas the "structural adjustment" programme had not yet been launched officially, the Bangladesh economic package of the mid-1970s contained most of its essential ingredients. In many respects, Bangladesh was "a laboratory test-case", a country in which the IMF "economic medicine" could be experimented with on a trial basis (prior to the debt crisis of the early 1980s). An economic stabilisation programme had been established: devaluation and price liberalisation contributed to exacerbating a situation of famine which had broken out in several regions of the country.

In the aftermath of Sheik Mujib's overthrow and assassination, continued US military aid to Bangladesh was conditional upon the country's abiding by the IMF's policy prescriptions. The US State Department justified its aid programme to the new military regime on the grounds that the government's foreign policy was "pragmatic and nonaligned". The United States was to support this non-alignment and help Bangladesh in its economic development.[2]

The Establishment of a Parallel Government

Bangladesh has been under continuous supervision by the international donor community since the accession of General Ziaur Rahman to the presidency in 1975 (in turn assassinated in 1981) as well as during the reign of General Hussein Mahommed Ershad (1982-90).[3] The state apparatus was firmly under the control of the IFIs and "aid agencies" in collusion with the dominant clique of the military. Since its inauguration, the "aid consortium" has met annually in Paris. The Dhaka government is usually invited to send observers to this meeting.

The IMF had established a liaison office on the fourth floor of the Central Bank, World Bank advisors were present in most of the ministries. The Asian Development Bank controlled by Japan also played an important role in the shaping of macro-economic policy. A monthly working meeting held under the auspices of the World Bank Dhaka office enabled the various donors and agencies to "coordinate" efficiently (outside the ministries) the key elements of government economic policy.

In 1990, mounting opposition to the military dictatorship as well as the resignation of General Hussein Mahommed Ershad, accused of graft and corruption, was conducive to the formation of a provisional government and the holding of parliamentary elections. The transition towards "parliamentary democracy" under the government of Mrs Khaleda Zia, the widow of President General Ziaur Rahman, was not conducive, however, to a major shift in the structure of state institutions. Continuity has in many respects been maintained: many of General Ershad's former cronies were appointed to key positions in the new "civilian" government.

Establishing a Bogus Democracy

The IMF-sponsored economic reforms contributed to reinforcing a "rentier economy" controlled by the national élites and largely dependent on foreign trade and the recycling of aid money. With the restoration of "parliamentary democracy", powerful individuals within the military had strengthened their business interests.[4] The government party, the Bangladesh National Party (BNP), was under the protection of the dominant clique of the military.

With the restoration of formal democracy in 1991, the daughter of assassinated president Mujib Rahman Sheik Hasina Wajed of the Awami League Party became the leader of the opposition. With public opinion focusing on the rivalry in parliament between the "widow" and the "orphan", the dealings of local power groups, including members of the military, with the "aid agencies" and donors passed virtually unnoticed. The donor community had become, in the name of "good governance", the defender of a bogus democratic facade controlled by the armed forces and allied closely to the fundamentalist movement Jamaat-i-islami. In some respects, Begum Zia had become a more compliant "political puppet" than the deposed military dictator General Ershad.

Supervising the Allocation of State Funds

The"aid consortium" had taken control of Bangladesh's public finances. This process, however, did not consist solely in imposing fiscal and monetary austerity: the donors supervised directly the allocation of funds and the setting of development priorities. According to a World Bank advisor:

> We do not want to establish an agreement for each investment project, what we want is to impose discipline. Do we like the list of projects? Which projects should be retained, are there "dogs" in the list?[5]

Moreover, under the clauses of the Public Resources Management Credit (1992), the World Bank gained control over the entire budgetary process including the distribution of public expenditure between line ministries and the structure of operational expenditures in each of the ministries:

> Of course we cannot write the budget for them! The negotiations in this regard are complex. We nonetheless make sure they're moving in the right direction (...) Our people work with the guys in the ministries and show them how to prepare budgets.[6]

The aid consortium also controlled the reforms of the banking system implemented under the government of Mrs Khaleda Zia. Lay-offs were ordered, parastatal enterprises were closed down. Fiscal austerity prevented the government from mobilising internal resources. Moreover, for most public investment projects the "aid consortium" required a system of international tender. Large international construction and engineering companies took over the process of domestic capital formation to the detriment of local-level enterprises.

Undermining the Rural Economy

The IMF also imposed the elimination of subsidies to agriculture, a process which contributed as of the early 1980s to the bankruptcy of small and medium-sized farmers. The result was a marked increase in the number of landless farmers who were driven into marginal lands affected by recurrent flooding. Moreover, the liberalisation of agricultural credit not only contributed to the fragmentation of land-holdings (already under considerable stress as a result of demographic pressures), but also to the reinforcement of traditional usury and the role of the village money lender.

As a result of the absence of credit to small farmers, the owners of irrigation equipment reinforced their position as a new "waterlord" rentier class. These developments did not lead, however, to the "modernisation" of agriculture (e.g. as in the Punjab) based on the formation of a class of rich farmer-entrepreneurs. In other words, the structural adjustment programme thwarted the development of capitalist farming from the outset. In addition to the neglect of agricultural infrastructure, the Bretton Woods institutions required the liberalisation of trade and the deregulation of grain markets. These policies contributed to the stagnation of food agriculture for the domestic market.

A blatant example of restructuring imposed by the IMF pertains to the jute industry. In spite of the collapse of world prices, jute was one of Bangladesh's main earners of foreign exchange in competition with synthetic substitutes produced by the large textile multinationals. Unfair competition?... The IMF required as a condition attached to its soft loan under the enhanced structural adjustment facility (ESAF) the closing down of one third of the jute industry (including public and private enterprises) and the firing of some 35,000 workers.[7] Whereas the latter were to receive severance payments, the IMF had neglected to take into account the impact of the restructuring programme on some three million rural households (18 million people) which depended on jute cultivation for their survival.

Dumping US Grain Surpluses

The deregulation of the grain market was also used to support (under the disguise of "US Food Aid") the dumping of American grain surpluses. The "Food for Work" programmes under the auspices of USAID were used to "finance" village-level public works projects through payments of grain (instead of money wages) to impoverished peasants thereby destabilising local-level grain markets.

It is worth noting that US grain sales on the local market served two related purposes. First, heavily subsidised US grain was allowed to compete directly with locally produced food staples thereby undermining the development of local producers. Second, US grain sales on the local market were used to generate "counterpart funds". The latter were in turn channelled into development projects controlled by USAID, – i.e. which by their very nature maintained Bangladesh's dependency on imported grain. For instance, counterpart funds generated from grain sales (under PL 480) were used in the early 1990s to finance the Bangladesh Agricultural Research Institute. Under this project, USAID determined the areas of priority research to be funded.

Undermining Food Self-Sufficiency

There is evidence that food self-sufficiency in Bangladesh could indeed have been achieved through the extension of arable lands under irrigation as well as through a comprehensive agrarian reform.[8] Moreover, a recent study suggested that the risks of flooding could be reduced significantly through the development of appropriate infrastructure.

The structural adjustment programme constituted, however, the main obstacle to achieving these objectives. First it obstructed the development of an independent agricultural policy; second it deliberately placed a lid (through the Public Investment Programme [PIP] under World Bank supervision) on state investment in agriculture. This "programmed" stagnation of food agriculture also served the interests of US grain producers. Fiscal austerity imposed by the "aid consortium" prevented the mobilisation of domestic resources in support of the rural economy.

The Fate of Local Industry

The war of independence had resulted in the demise of the industrial sector developed since 1947 and the massive exodus of entrepreneurs and professionals.[9] Moreover, the economic impact of the war was all the more devastating because no "breathing space" was provided to Bangladesh by the "aid consortium" to reconstruct its war-torn economy and develop its human resources.

The structural adjustment programme adopted in several stages since 1974 provided a final lethal blow to the country's industrial sector. The macro-economic framework imposed by the Bretton Woods institutions contributed to undermining the existing industrial structure while at the same time preventing the development of new areas of industrial activity geared towards the internal market.

Moreover, with a fragmented agricultural system and the virtual absence of rural manufacturing, non-agricultural employment opportunities in Bangladesh's countryside were more or less non-existent. Urban-based industry was limited largely to the export garment sector which relied heavily on cheap labour from rural areas. According to the IMF resident representative in Dhaka, the only viable industries are those using abundant supplies of cheap labour for the export sector:

> What do you want to protect in this country? There is nothing to protect. They want permanent protection but they mainly have a comparative advantage in the labour-intensive industries.[10]

From the IMF's perspective, the garment industry was to constitute the main source of urban employment. There are some 300,000 garment workers most of whom are young girls. Sixteen per cent of this labour force are children between the ages of 10 and 14. Most of the workers come from impoverished rural areas.[11] Production in the factories is marked by compulsory overtime and despotic management: wages including overtime (1992) are of the order of US$20 a month. In 1992 a public gathering of garment workers was brutally repressed by the security forces. According to the government, the demands of the workers constituted a threat to the balance of payments.

The Recycling of Aid Money

Whereas many aid and non-governmental organisations are involved in meaningful projects at the grass-roots level, several of the "poverty alleviation schemes", rather than helping the poor, constitute an important source of income for urban professionals and bureaucrats. Through the various local executing agencies based in Dhaka, the local élites had become development brokers and intermediaries acting on behalf of the international donor community. The funds earmarked for the rural poor often contributed to the enrichment of military officers and bureaucrats. This "aid money" was then recyled into commercial and real-estate investments including office buildings, luxury condominiums, etc...

"The Social Dimensions of Adjustment"

With a population of over 130 million inhabitants, Bangladesh is among the world's poorest countries. Per capita income is of the order of US$170 per annum (1992). Annual expenditures on health in 1992 were of the order of $1.50 per capita (of which less than 25 cents per capita was spent on essential pharmaceuticals).[12] With the exception of family planning, social expenditures were considered to be excessive: in 1992-93, the Bangladesh "aid consortium" required the government to implement a further round of "cost-effective" cuts in social-sector budgets.

Undernourishment was also characterised by a high prevalence of Vitamin-A deficiency (resulting from a diet made up almost exclusively of cereals). Many children and adults particularly in rural areas had become blind as a result of Vitamin-A deficiency.

A situation of chronic starvation prevailed in several regions of the country. The Bangladesh "aid consortium" meeting in Paris in 1992 urged the government of Mrs Khaleda Zia to speed up the implementation of the reforms as a means of "combating poverty". The government of Bangladesh was advised (in conformity with World Bank president Lewis Preston's new guidelines) that donor support would only be granted to countries "which make a serious effort in the area of poverty reduction".

In 1991, 140,000 people died as a result of the flood which swept the country (most of whom were landless peasants driven into areas affected by recurrent flooding). Ten million people (almost ten per cent of the population) were left homeless.[13] Not accounted, however, in these "official" statistics, were those who died of famine in the aftermath of the disaster. While the various relief agencies and donors underscored the detrimental role of climatic factors, the 1991 famine was aggravated as a result of the IMF-supported macro-economic policy. First, the ceilings on public investment in agriculture and flood prevention imposed by the donor since the 1970s had been conducive to the stagnation of agriculture. Second, the devaluation implemented shortly after the 1991 flood, spurred on a 50 per cent increase in the retail price of rice in the year which followed the disaster. And this famine was all the more serious because a large share of the emergency relief provided by the donors had been appropriated by the privileged urban élites.

Endnotes

1. According to the study of Lawrence Lifschutz, *Bangladesh, the Unfinished Revolution,* Zed Press, London, 1979, part 2.
2. According to a report of the US State Department published in 1978, quoted in Lawrence Lifschultz, op. cit., p. 109.
3. General Ziaur Rahman becomes head of state as Commander in Chief of the Armed Forces in 1975 during the period of martial law. He was subsequently elected president in 1978.
4. Interview with the leader of an opposition party in Dhaka, February 1992.
5. Interview with a World Bank advisor in Dhaka, 1992.
6. Ibid.
7. Many of the smaller jute enterprises were pushed into bankruptcy as a result of the liberalisation of credit.
8. See Mosharaf Hussein, A. T. M. Aminul Islam and Sanat Kumar Saha, *Floods in Bangladesh, Recurrent Disaster and People's Survival,* Universities' Research Centre, Dhaka, 1987.

9. See Rehman Sobhan, *The Development of the Private Sector in Bangladesh: a Review of the Evolution and Outcome of State Policy*, Research report no: 124, Bangladesh Institute of Development Studies, pp. 4-5.
10. Interview with the resident representative of the IMF, Dhaka, 1992.
11. Seventy per cent of the garment workers are female, 74 per cent are from rural areas, child labour represents respectively 16 and 8 per cent of the female and male workers. See Salma Choudhuri and Pratima Paul-Majumder, *The Conditions of Garment Workers in Bangladesh, An Appraisal*, Bangladesh Institute of Development Studies, Dhaka, 1991.
12. See World Bank, *Staff Appraisal Report, Bangladesh, Fourth Population and Health Project*, Washington DC, 1991.
13. See Gerard Viratelle, "Drames naturels, drames sociaux au Bangladesh", *Le Monde diplomatique*, Paris, June 1991, pp. 6-7.

Chapter 8

The Post-War Economic Destruction of Vietnam

THE social consequences of structural adjustment applied in Vietnam since the mid-1980s are devastating. Health clinics and hospitals have closed down, local-level famines have erupted, affecting up to a quarter of the country's population, and three quarters of a million children have dropped out from the school system. There has been a resurgence of infectious diseases with a tripling of recorded malaria deaths during the first four years of the reforms. Five thousand (out of a total of 12,000) state enterprises have been driven into bankruptcy, more than a million workers and some 200,000 public employees, including tens of thousands of teachers and health workers, have been laid off.

A secret agreement reached in Paris in 1993, which in many regards was tantamount to forcing Vietnam "to compensate Washington" for the costs of the war, required Hanoi to recognise the debts of the defunct Saigon regime of General Thieu as a condition for the granting of fresh credit and the lifting of the US embargo.

The achievements of past struggles and the aspirations of an entire nation are undone and erased almost "with the stroke of the pen". No orange or steel-pellet bombs, no napalm, no toxic chemicals: a new phase of economic and social (rather than physical) destruction has unfolded. The seemingly "neutral" and "scientific" tools of macro-economic policy (under the guidance of the Bretton Woods institutions) constitute, in the aftermath of the Vietnam War, an equally "effective" and formally "non-violent" "instrument of recolonisation" and impoverishment affecting the livelihood of millions of people.

Rewriting the History of the War

In 1940, the Vichy government had appointed Admiral Jean Decoux as governor-general to negotiate the terms of Indochina's integration into Japan's "Greater East Asia Co-Prosperity Sphere" while formally retaining France's colonial territories under the mandate of the Vichy administration. The Viet Minh Front, which had led the resistance movement against the Vichy regime and Japanese occupation forces, received Washington's assent as of 1944, with weapons and financial support provided through the Office of Strategic Services (OSS), the predecessor of today's Central Intelligence Agency (CIA). September 2, 1945: at the Declaration of Independence on Ba Dinh Square in Hanoi proclaiming the founding of the Democratic Republic of Vietnam, American OSS agents were present at the side of Ho Chi Minh. Almost 30 years of history separate this event from the equally momentous surrender of General Duong Vanh Minh in Saigon's Independence Hall on 30 April 1975, marking the end of the Vietnam War and the opening of the period of national reconstruction.

The devastation left by the war created from the outset of the post-war era an atmosphere of helplessness and policy inertia. The subsequent outbreak of the Cambodian civil war – fuelled by Washington's covert support to Pol Pot's forces after 1979 – and China's invasion on the northern border further thwarted the reconstruction of the civilian economy. With reunification, two divergent socio-economic systems were united: the reforms in the South were enforced narrowly following central committee guidelines, with little discernment of the social forces at work: small-scale trade in Ho Chi Minh City was suppressed while a hasty process of collectivisation was carried out in the Mekong River Delta with strong opposition from the middle peasantry. Political repression affected not only those sectors of society which had ties to the Saigon regime but also many of those who had opposed General Thieu.

In turn, the international environment had changed: the transformations of the global market system and the breakdown of the Soviet bloc (which was Vietnam's main trading partner) backlashed, creating a situation of disarray in the national economy. The Communist Party was unable to formulate a coherent programme of economic reconstruction. Profound divisions and shifts within the Communist Party leadership unfolded from the early 1980s.

Today, after more than 50 years of struggle against foreign occupation, the history of the Vietnam War is being cautiously rewritten: neoliberalism constitutes (with the technical support of the Bretton Woods institutions) the Communist's Party's official doctrine. Bureaucrats and intellectuals are called upon unreservedly to support the new dogma in the name of socialism. With the adoption in 1986 of "*Renovation*" ("*Doi moi*"), references to America's brutal role in the war are increasingly considered improper. The Communist Party leadership has recently underscored the "historic role" of the United States in "liberating" Vietnam from Japanese occupation forces in 1945. In turn, the symbols of the US period have gradually returned to the streets of Saigon. At the "Museum of American War Crimes", now renamed "Exhibition House of Aggression War Crimes", a model light fighter-jet used by the US Air Force in bombing-raids can be purchased at the souvenir kiosk with an encoated Coca-cola logo on its fuselage, alongside a vast selection of manuals on foreign investment and macro-economic reform. Not a single text on the history of the war is in sight. Outside the museum, the frenzy of an incipient consumer economy is in sharp contrast with the squalor of beggars, street children and cyclo-drivers, many of whom were war veterans in the liberation of Saigon in 1975.

The New Vietnam War

The stylised image portrayed by much of the Western media is that the free-market mechanism has propelled Vietnam into the status of a prospective "Asian tiger". Nothing could be further from the truth: the economic reforms launched in 1986 under the guidance of the Bretton Woods institutions have, in the war's brutal aftermath, initiated a new historical phase of economic and social devastation. Macro-economic reform has led to the impoverishment of the Vietnamese people striking simultaneously at all sectors of economic activity.

The first step in 1984-85 (prior to the formal launching of "*Doi moi*" by the Sixth Party Congress) consisted in crushing the Vietnamese currency: inflation and the "dollarisation" of domestic prices were engineered by repeated devaluations reminiscent of the spectacular tumble of the piastre in 1973 under the Saigon regime, in the year following the Paris agreement and the formal "withdrawal" of American combat troops.[1] Today Vietnam is once again inundated with US dollar notes, which have largely replaced the Vietnamese dong as a "store of value". Whereas the IMF closely monitors monetary emissions by Vietnam's Central Bank, the US Federal Reserve Bank has in a de facto sense taken over the responsibility of issuing currency (i.e. a massive credit operation in its own right) for America's former wartime enemy. The delusion of "economic progress" and prosperity narrowly portrayed in the Western press is based on the rapid growth of small yet highly visible "pockets" of Western-style consumerism, concentrated largely in Saigon and Hanoi. The harsh economic and social realities are otherwise: soaring food prices, local-level famines, massive lay-offs of urban workers and civil servants and the destruction of Vietnam's social programmes.[2]

Reimbursing the "Bad Debts" of the Saigon Regime

Vietnam never received war reparations payments, yet Hanoi was compelled as a condition for the "normalisation" of economic relations and the lifting of the US embargo in February 1994 to "foot the bill" of the multilateral debts incurred by the US-backed Saigon regime. At the donor conference held in Paris in November 1993, a total of US$1.86 billion of loans and "aid" money was generously pledged in support of Vietnam's market reforms, yet immediately after the conference another (separate) meeting was held, this time "behind closed doors", with the Paris Club of official creditors.[3] On the agenda: the rescheduling of the "bad debts" incurred by the Saigon regime prior to 1975. Who gives the green light to whom? The IMF gave its stamp of approval to Vietnam's economic reforms prior to the Paris donor conference. However it was ultimately the results of the meetings with the Paris Club which were decisive in providing the "green light to Washington". And it was only after the formal lifting of the embargo that multilateral and bilateral disbursements were allowed to proceed.

The reimbursement of arrears of US$140 million (owed by Saigon) to the IMF was also demanded as a condition for the resumption of credit. To this effect, Japan and France (Vietnam's former colonial masters of the Vichy period) formed a so-called "friends of Vietnam" committee to "lend to Hanoi" the money needed "to reimburse the

IMF". By fully recognising the legitimacy of these debts, Hanoi had in effect accepted to repay loans which had been utilised to support the US war effort. Ironically, these negotiations were undertaken with the participation of a former minister of finance (and acting prime minister) in the military government of General Duong Vanh Minh which had been installed by the US military mission in 1963 in the aftermath of the assassination of President Ngo Dinh Diem and his younger brother. Dr Nguyen Xian Oanh (a prominent economist who also happened to be a former staff member of the IMF) occupied the position of economic advisor to Prime Minister Vo Van Kiet. (Oanh had worked closely with Kiet since the early 1980s when the latter was Communist Party Secretary in Ho Chi Minh City).[4]

Destroying the National Economy

Through the seemingly innocuous mechanism of the "free" market (and without the need for warfare and physical destruction), the reforms had contributed to a massive demobilisation of productive capacity: more than 5,000 out of 12,300 state-owned enterprises (SOEs) had by 1994 been closed down or steered into bankruptcy. This process was further exacerbated as a result of the collapse of trade with the countries of the former Soviet bloc. Rules on the liquidation of state enterprises were adopted in 1990, leading to a further "down-sizing" of the industrial base through the restructuring of the remaining enterprises.[5] More than a million workers and some 136,000 public employees (of which the majority were health workers and teachers) had been laid off by the end of 1992.[6] The government's target under "decision no: 111" was to lay off another 100,000 employees by the end of 1994, reducing the size of the civil service by 20 per cent. Moreover, with the withdrawal of Vietnamese troops from Cambodia, an estimated 500,000 soldiers had been demobilised and 250,000 "guest workers" had returned from Eastern Europe and the Middle East with few prospects for employment.[7]

According to World Bank data, the growth in private-sector employment was insufficient to accommodate the new entrants into the labour force. With soaring prices, the real earnings of "those who remain employed" had dropped to abysmally low levels: unable to subsist on government salaries of US$15 a month, a variety of "survival activities" including frequent "moonlighting" by state employees had unfolded, leading to high rates of absenteeism and the de facto paralysis of the entire administrative apparatus. With the exception of joint-venture enterprises, where the recommended minimum wage had been set at $30-35 a month (1994) (it is not enforced), there is no minimum wage legislation nor are there any guidelines pertaining to the indexation of wages. "The Party's free market policy is that the labour market should also be free."[8]

Whereas many of the SOEs were grossly "inefficient" and "uncompetitive" by Western standards, their demise had been engineered through the deliberate manipulation of market forces: the restructuring of state banking and financial institutions (including the elimination of the commune-level credit cooperatives) was conducive to the "freeze" of all medium- and long-term credit to domestic producers. Short-term credit was available at an interest rate of 35 per cent per annum (1994). Moreover, the state was not permitted under the terms of its agreement with the IMF to provide budget support either to the state-owned economy or to an incipient private sector.

The demise of the state economy had also been engineered as a result of a highly discriminatory tax system: whereas SOEs continued to pay (in a situation where all subsidies and state credits had been removed) the 40-50 per cent profit-withholding tax inherited from the system of central planning, foreign investors (including all joint ventures) enjoyed generous exemptions and tax holidays. Moreover, the profit-withholding tax was no longer collected on a regular basis from private-sector enterprises.[9]

The reforms' "hidden agenda" was to destabilise Vietnam's industrial base: heavy industry, oil and gas, natural resources and mining, cement and steel production were to be reorganised and taken over by foreign capital with the Japanese conglomerates playing a decisive and dominant role. The most valuable state assets were to be transferred to joint-venture companies. No concern was expressed by the leadership to reinforce and preserve its industrial base, or to develop for that matter a capitalist economy owned and controlled by "nationals"... The prevailing view within the "donor community" was that a "downsizing" of the state economy was required "to make room" for the spontaneous development of a Vietnamese private sector. State investment was said to "crowd out" private capital formation. The reforms not only demobilised the state economy, they also prevented a transition towards national capitalism.

Moreover, the relative weakness of Vietnam's business groups combined with the freeze on credit and the virtual absence of state support contributed to thwart the development of a domestic private-sector economy. While various token incentives had been offered to returning Viet Kieu ("overseas Vietnamese"), much of the "Vietnamese diaspora", including the refugees of the Vietnam War and the "Boat People", had little in terms of financial resources or savings. With some exceptions, their activities were largely concentrated in family-owned and medium-sized enterprises in the commercial and services economy.[10]

A blatant example of "economic engineering" set in motion by the market reforms concerns the fate of Vietnam's steel industry. Nearly eight million tons of bombs together with a bounty of abandoned military hardware had provided Vietnam's heavy industry with an ample supply of scrap metal. Irony of history, America's only tangible "contribution" to post-war reconstruction had been revoked: with the "open-door policy", large quantities of scrap metal were being freely "re-exported" (at prices substantially below world-market values). Whereas production at Vietnam's five major steel mills was stalled due to the shortage of raw materials (not to mention a legal ban on the import of scrap metal by state enterprises), a Japanese conglomerate made up of the Kyoei, Mitsui and Itochu corporations had established in 1994 a modern joint-venture steel plant in Ba-Ria Vung Tau province which imports the scrap metal (at world-market prices) "back" into Vietnam.

Excluding Domestic Producers from their Own Market

Through the deliberate manipulation of market forces, domestic producers were being literally "excluded from their own market" even in areas where they were considered to have "a comparative advantage". Tariff barriers were removed and much of Vietnam's light manufacturing industry was displaced by a massive influx of imported consumer goods. Since 1986, a large share of Vietnam's meagre foreign exchange earnings had been allocated to the import of consumer goods, creating a vacuum in the availability of capital equipment for domestic industry. The reforms allowed SOEs involved in the export trade freely to use their hard-currency earnings to import consumer goods. A network had been established between the managers of SOEs involved in the import-export business, local-level bureaucrats and private merchants. Hard-currency earnings were squandered and large amounts of money were appropriated. With the market reforms, many of the SOEs escaped state control and became involved in a variety of illicit activities. With the lifting of state budget support and the freeze on credit, productive activities were abandoned.

In the new areas of light manufacturing and industrial processing promoted as a result of the "open door", the internal market is "off limits" to Vietnamese companies. Cheap-labour garment producers, involved in joint ventures or subcontracting agreements with foreign capital, will usually export their entire output. In contrast, the domestic Vietnamese market is supplied with imported second-hand garments and factory rejects from Hong Kong, leading also to the demise of tailors and small producers in the informal economy. (The price of used garments purchased in the developed countries is US$80 a ton.)

Thwarting the Channels of Internal Trade

The reforms promoted the "economic Balkanisation" of the regions each of which is separately integrated into the world market: the deregulation of the transport industry led to skyrocketing freight prices. State transport companies were also driven into bankruptcy with a large share of the transport industry taken over by joint-venture capital.

Moreover, with the freeze on budget transfers from the central to the provincial and municipal governments recommended by the World Bank, provincial and local authorities became increasingly "free" to establish their own investment and trading relations with foreign companies to the detriment of internal trade. The provinces were negotiating numerous investment and trade agreements including the granting of land to foreign investors as well as concessions which allowed foreign capital (in a completely unregulated environment) to plunder Vietnam's forest resources. In the context of the budget crisis, these various agreements often constituted the only means of covering central and provincial government expenditures, including the salaries of state officials.

Moreover, in a situation where the salaries of public employees are exceedingly low (US$15 to 30 a month), foreign cooperation and joint-venture linkages inevitably constitute a means for obtaining "salary supplements" in the form of consulting fees, expense accounts, travel allowances, etc. The latter – invariably disbursed in hard currency – enable the foreign donors and contractors to secure the allegiance of professional cadres and local-level officials. The state is bankrupt and unable (under the clauses of its agreements with the creditors) to remunerate its civil servants. Foreign contractors and "aid agencies" not only appropriate human capital in research institutes and government departments, they become the main source of income for senior and middle-level bureaucrats involved in the management of foreign trade and investment.

The Disintegration of the State's Public Finances

The reforms have pushed the state's public finances into a straitjacket. The Central Bank is not allowed to expand the money supply or issue currency without IMF approval. Neither is it allowed to grant credit or finance the SOEs. The latter are in turn precipitated into bankruptcy as a result of the freeze on credit and state funding. In turn the bankruptcy of the state enterprises was conducive to the collapse of state tax revenues which backlashed on the state's public finances.

A similar situation existed with regard to the state banks. The latter had been affected by the decline of dong deposits by the population (who preferred to hold their savings in the form of hoards in dollar notes), not to mention the lifting of state subsidies, strict reserve requirements and high withholding taxes. In turn, the contraction of credit as well as increased loan default by SOEs was pushing the state banks into receivership to the advantage of the numerous foreign and joint-venture banks operating in Vietnam. In 1994, more than 10,000 out of the 12,300 enterprises were heavily indebted to the state banks.

The state enterprises were not, however, allowed to approach foreign banks directly for credit. On the other hand, the foreign banks had access to this lucrative short-term credit market by providing collateral loans to Vietnamese state banks.

Collapse of State Capital Formation

The reforms contributed to triggering an impressive collapse of public investment. From 1985 to 1993, the share of government capital expenditure in GDP declined by 63 per cent, from 8.2 to 3.1 per cent. In agriculture and forestry the decline (90 per cent) was even more dramatic, – i.e. from 1.0 to 0.1 per cent of GDP. In industry and construction, capital expenditure fell from 2.7 to 0.1 per cent of GDP (a decline of 96 per cent).[11]

New rules pertaining to the levels of recurrent and investment expenditure had been established under the policy-based loan agreements negotiated with the Bretton Woods institutions. Precise ceilings were placed on all categories of expenditure, public employees were laid off, allocations to health and education were frozen, etc. The underlying objective was to reduce the budget deficit. In other words, the state was no longer permitted to mobilise its own resources for the building of public infrastructure, roads or hospitals, etc. – i.e. the creditors not only became the "brokers" of all major public investment projects, they also decided in the context of the "Public Investment Programme" (PIP) (established under the technical auspices of the World Bank) on what type of public infrastructure was best suited to Vietnam, and what should or should not be funded by the "donor community". Needless to say, the process of funding public investment created debt which in turn reinforced the grip of the creditors on economic policy.

This supervision applied not only to the *amount of public investment*, it affected the precise composition of public expenditure and the setting of investment priorities by the creditors. It also required divestiture and privatisation of most SOEs involved in infrastructure and strategic sectors of the economy. In turn, the loans pledged at the Paris Donor Conference in November 1993 required a system of international tender (and "competitive bidding") which allocated the entire execution of all public-works projects to international construction and engineering firms. The latter in turn skimmed off large amounts of money (which Vietnam will ultimately have to repay) into a variety of consulting and management fees. In turn, Vietnamese companies (whether public or private) were excluded from the tendering process although much of the actual construction work was undertaken by local companies (using Vietnamese labour at very low wages) in separate sub-contracting deals reached with the transnationals.

Reintegrating the Japanese Empire

The tendency is towards the reintegration of Vietnam into the Japanese sphere of influence, a situation reminiscent of World War II when Vietnam was part of Japan's "Great East Asia Co-Prosperity Sphere". This dominant position of Japanese capital was brought about through control over more than 80 per cent of the loans for investment projects and infrastructure. These loans channelled through Japan's Overseas Economic Cooperation Fund (OECF) as well as through the Asian Development Bank (ADB) supported the expansion of the large Japanese trading companies and transnationals.

With the lifting of the US embargo in February 1994, American capital scrambled to restore its position in a highly profitable investment and trading arena dominated by Japan (and to a lesser extent by the European Union). The Japanese have a "head lead" not only in key investments, they also control much of the long-term credit to Vietnam. Confrontations between Washington and Tokyo are likely to unfold as American transnationals attempt to restore the position they held in South Vietnam (e.g. in offshore oil) prior to 1975. Other important players are the Koreans, and the Chinese from Taiwan and Hong Kong. A clear demarcation prevails, however: the latter tend to concentrate in manufacturing and export processing whereas the large infrastructural, oil and gas and natural resources projects are in the hands of Japanese and European conglomerates.

It is worth noting that Japan also controls a large share of the loans used to finance consumer imports. This consumer frenzy of Japanese brand products is now largely sustained on borrowed money fuelled by the infusion of hundreds of millions of dollars of so-called "quick disbursing loans" pledged by Japan and the multilateral banks (including the ADB, the World Bank and the IMF).[12] These loans (which in the official jargon are said to constitute "balance-of-payments aid") are earmarked explicitly for commodity imports. Administered by Vietnam's Central Bank, the disbursements under these loans are allocated in the form of foreign-exchange quotas to thousands of state enterprises involved in the import trade. This process accelerates the deluge of consumer goods while contributing to swelling the external debt. With the exception of a small number of larger state corporations (and those involved in the import trade), the reforms have contributed to demobilising entire sectors of the national economy: the only means for a national enterprise to "survive" is to enter the lucrative import business or to establish a "joint-venture" in which the "foreign partner" has access to credit (in hard currency) and control over technology, pricing and the remittance of profits. Moreover, the entire international trading system is prone (from the lower echelons to top state officials) to corruption and bribery by foreign contractors.

Vietnam's economic crisis did not signify, however, a concurrent decline in the "recorded" rate of GDP growth. The latter has increased largely as a result of the rapid redirection of the economy towards foreign trade (development of oil and gas, natural resources, export of staple commodities and cheap-labour manufacturing). Despite the wave of bankruptcies and the compression of the internal market, there has been a significant growth in the new export-oriented joint ventures. In turn, the "artificial" inflow of imported goods was conducive to the enlargement of the commercial sector and its share of the GDP.

Economic growth was being fuelled by debt. The burden of debt servicing increased more than tenfold from 1986 to 1993. It was also boosted as a result of the government's agreement with the Paris Club in late 1993 to recognise the bad debts of the defunct Saigon regime.

The Outbreak of Famine

The adoption of a more flexible "farm contract system" among the reforms of 1981 in support of household production was broadly welcomed by the rural people. In contrast, however, the second wave of agricultural reforms adopted since 1986 has contributed to the impoverishment of large sectors of that same population. Under the guidance of the World Bank and the FAO, the authorities abrogated the policy of "local-level self-sufficiency in food" which was devised to prevent the development of regional food shortages. In the highland areas of central Vietnam, farmers were encouraged to specialise "according to their regional comparative advantage", namely to give up food farming and switch into "high-value" cash crops for export. Over-cropping of coffee, cassava, cashew-nuts and cotton, combined with the plummeting of world commodity prices and the high cost of imported farm inputs, was conducive to the outbreak of local-level famines.

Ironically, the process of "switching" into export crops also resulted in a net decline in foreign-exchange earnings because large shipments of agricultural commodities were sold by the state trading companies to international contractors at substantial financial losses:

> We mobilise farmers to produce cassava and cotton, but they cannot export at a profit because the international price has gone down... What happens is that the state trading companies are obliged to export the coffee or the cassava at a loss. They manage, however, to compensate for these losses because they use the foreign-exchange proceeds to import consumer goods. They also make large profits through price mark-ups on imported fertiliser.[13]

In other words, the state export corporations, while showing a book-value profit, were in fact contributing to generating debt (in foreign exchange) by routinely selling staple commodities below their world-market price. In many of the food-deficit areas, export crops by farmers (who had abandoned food farming) remained unsold due to the situation of oversupply which characterised the world market. The result was famine because the farmers could neither sell the industrial cash crops nor produce their own food.

A similar situation prevailed with regard to the SOEs involved in the rice trade. The latter preferred to export at a financial loss rather than sell in the domestic market. With the complete deregulation of the grain market and sales in the hands of private merchants, domestic prices soared particularly in the food-deficit areas. Whereas rice was being exported below world-market prices, severe food shortages had unfolded in regions where paddy production had been abandoned as a result of the policy of "regional specialisation". In 1994, for instance, the authorities acknowledged the existence of a famine in Lai Cai province on the border with China affecting more than 50,000 people. Whereas food shortages had built up in Lai Cai over a five-month period (without any emergency relief being provided), two million tons of rice remained unsold in the Mekong Delta as a result of the collapse of the state-owned rice-trading companies.

Famine was not limited to the food-deficit areas. It was affecting all major regions, including the urban areas and the "food-surplus economy" of the Mekong Delta. In the latter region, 25.3 per cent of the adult population had a daily energy intake below 1,800 calories.[14] In the cities, the devaluation of the dong together with the elimination of subsidies and price controls had led to soaring prices of rice and other food staples. Deindexation of salaried earnings and massive urban unemployment (resulting from the retrenchment of civil servants and workers in SOEs) had also resulted in lower levels of food intake and a deterioration in the nutritional status of children in urban areas.

Child Malnutrition

The deregulation of the grain market had triggered famine and a high incidence of child malnutrition. Despite the increased "availability" of staple foods as suggested by FAO data, a nutrition survey confirmed an abrupt overall deterioration in the nutritional status of both children and adults. The adult mean energy intake (per capita/per day) for the country was 1,861 calories with 25 per cent of the adult population below 1,800 calories (1987-90) indicating a situation of extreme undernourishment.[15] In 9 per cent of the sample households, energy intake by adults was less than 1,500 calories. Recorded energy intakes for young children under six were on average 827 calories per capita.

The situation with regard to child malnutrition was acknowledged by the World Bank:

> Vietnam has a higher proportion of underweight and stunted children [of the order of 50 per cent] than in any other country in South and Southeast Asia with the exception of Bangladesh... The magnitude of stunting and wasting among children certainly appears to have increased significantly... it is also possible that the worsening macro-economic crisis in the 1984-86 period may have contributed to the deterioration in nutritional status.[16]

It is also worth noting (according to the survey) that Vitamin-A deficiency which causes blindness (resulting from a diet composed almost exclusively of cereals) is widespread among children in all regions of the country except Hanoi and the southeast. This situation compares to that of Bangladesh (see Chapter 7).

The deregulation of the grain market (under World Bank guidance) allowed easy access to the world market (although at very low commodity prices) while disrupting the channels of internal trade and triggering local-level famines.[17] This pattern was candidly acknowledged by the World Bank:

> Of course since private sector flows typically respond to price incentives, the problem of food availability in the food deficit areas will not disappear overnight, since consumers in these areas do not have the purchasing power to bid up the price paid for foodgrains from the surplus regions. In fact at present it is financially more rewarding to export rice outside Vietnam than to transfer it to the deficit regions within the country. Indeed as private sector grain trade expands, the availability of food in the deficit regions may initially decline before it improves.[18]

Into the Net of International Agribusiness

The general direction of the government's grain policy largely coincided with the interests of international agribusiness: a switch out of paddy into a variety of crops (citrus trees, hybrid maize, cashew-nuts, etc.) was being encouraged even in regions (e.g. Mekong Delta) which were favourable to paddy cultivation. In Dong Nai province in the south, for instance, farmers were encouraged to move out of paddy, hybrid maize seedlings were purchased from an international grain conglomerate with short-term loans (at 2.5 per cent per month) financed by the State Agricultural Bank. The harvested maize was then "purchased back" by Proconco, a French agro-industrial joint venture exporting as well as selling animal feed in the domestic market to produce meat products for Taiwan and Hong Kong.[19] Short-term credit was available only for designated commercial crops with loan periods (less than 180 days) shorter than those required to complete the entire cycle of agricultural production and marketing of the commodity.

Vietnam as a Major Exporter of Rice

An impressive increase in paddy production took place between 1987-89 and 1992 which enabled Vietnam to move from a position of net importer to that of an exporter of rice. This tendency was sustained without an increase in the land areas allocated to paddy. It was largely the result of a shift into new varieties as well as increased use of chemical fertiliser and pesticides entailing substantially higher costs to the small farmer. The government had moved out of supplying farm inputs; the SOEs producing pesticides had collapsed. Increasingly a large share of farm inputs were being imported:

> Our productivity has gone up but our income has not gone up, we must pay for the new seed varieties, insecticide and fertiliser. Transport costs have increased. If the costs continue to rise, we will not be able to continue farm activities; off-farm employment including handicrafts and labour in the city are essential; farming does not provide enough money to survive.[20]

Largely centred in the Mekong Delta this expanded paddy output (and the corresponding surge in exports) had also been conducive to increased land concentration. In the Red River delta, small farmers were paying royalties to the International Rice Research Institute (IRRI) (supported by the World Bank and the Rockefeller Foundation) for a new variety of paddy which was being reproduced in local nurseries. Agricultural research institutes whose funds had been cut off by the state had entered the lucrative business of seed development and production.[21]

The expansion in paddy production seems, however, to have reached a peak: the withdrawal of state support in the provision of irrigation infrastructure, water conservancy and maintenance, since 1987, will affect future output patterns. Large-scale irrigation and drainage have been neglected: the World Bank recommends cost recovery and the commercialisation of water resources while nonetheless acknowledging that "farmers outside the Mekong Delta are too poor to bear increased rates [irrigation charges] at this time".[22] The risk of recurrent flooding and drought has also increased as a result of the collapse of state enterprises responsible for routine operation and maintenance. A similar situation exists in agricultural support and extension services:

> Provision of agricultural support services – the supply of fertiliser, seed, credit, pest control, veterinary services, machinery services, research and extension advice, was until the late 1980s a predominantly governmental function... This system, while still functioning on paper, has now largely collapsed in reality due to the restoration of a family-based farming system, increasing real budgetary shortfalls, and civil service salary rates devalued to almost nothing by inflation. Those support services involving a marketable product or service have been semi-privatised with some success, and the remainder are hardly functioning. In the support service bureaucracy, a large number of employees survive on moonlighting activities, while some 8,000 graduates of the agro-technical schools reportedly are "unemployed".[23]

The Concentration of Land

The tendency is towards a major crisis in production, increased social polarisation in the countryside and a greater concentration of land ownership: large sectors of the rural population in the Red River and Mekong delta areas are being driven off the land; famines have also occurred in the rice-surplus regions. The Land Law passed in the National Assembly in October 1993 had been drafted with the support of the World Bank's Legal Department. Legal experts and World Bank seminars were organised to focus on the implications of the Land Law:

> The foreign experts brought in by the World Bank think that the Land Law is suitable to our particular conditions: if farmers lack capital or resources they can "transfer" the land

> or they can move to the cities or work for "an advanced household"... The lack of land is not the cause of poverty, the poor lack knowledge, experience and have limited education, the poor also have too many children.[24]

Under the law, farmland (under a formal system of long-term leases) can be freely "transferred" (i.e. sold) and mortgaged as "enforceable collateral" (officially only with a state banking institution but in practice also with private money-lenders). The land can then be "transferred" or sold if there is loan default.

The consequence has been the re-emergence (particularly in the south) of usury and land tenancy, forcing the peasant economy back to the struggles for land and credit waged at the end of the French colonial period. In the south, land concentration is already fairly advanced, marked by the development of medium-sized plantations (including numerous joint-venture with foreign capital). Many state farms had been transformed into joint-venture plantations using both permanent and seasonal workers. Landless farmers, who constitute an increasingly large share of the rural population, are confined to seeking employment in the cities or as seasonal wage labourers in commercial plantations operated by rich farmers or joint ventures. Rural wages in the Red River delta were of the order of 50 cents a day (1994). While land forfeiture of small farmers in north Vietnam is still at an incipient level, the Land Law opens the way for the appropriation of large tracts of agricultural land by urban merchants and money-lenders.

It is worth mentioning that the agricultural policies of the defunct Saigon regime of General Thieu are resurfacing. In the south, land titles granted by US "aid" programmes in 1973 as a means of "pacifying" rural areas are fully recognised by the authorities. In contrast, thousands of peasants who left their villages to fight alongside the liberation forces are without formal claims to agricultural land. We will recall that the US land-distribution programme was implemented in the aftermath of the 1973 Paris agreement during the last years of the Thieu regime. This period of so-called "Vietnamisation" of the war coincided with the formal withdrawal of American combat troops and the propping up of the Saigon government with massive amounts of US "aid". According to the Ministry of Agriculture, the United States wartime programme is a useful "model": "Our present policy is to emulate the US land-distribution programme of that period, although we lack sufficient financial resources."

The Destruction of Education

Perhaps the most dramatic impact of the reforms has been in the areas of health and education. Universal education and literacy was a key objective of the struggle against French colonial rule.

From 1954 (following the defeat of the French at Dien Bien Phu) to 1972, primary- and secondary-school enrolment in North Vietnam had increased sevenfold (from 700,000 to nearly five million). After reunification in 1975, a literacy campaign was implemented in the south. According to UNESCO figures, the rates of literacy (90 per cent) and school enrolment were among the highest in South-East Asia.

The reforms have deliberately and consciously destroyed the educational system by massively compressing the educational budget, depressing teachers' salaries and "commercialising" secondary, vocational and higher education through the exaction of tuition fees. The movement is towards the transformation of education into a commodity. In the official jargon of the UN agencies, this requires:

> ...consumers of [educational] services to pay increased amounts, encouraging institutions to become self-financing, and by using incentives to privatise delivery of education and training where appropriate.[25]

Virtually repealing all previous achievements, including the struggle against illiteracy carried out since 1945, the reforms have engineered an unprecedented collapse in school enrolment with a high drop-out rate observed in the final years of primary school. The obligation to pay tuition fees is now entrenched in the constitution which was carefully redrafted in 1992. According to official data, the proportion of graduates from primary education who entered the four-year lower-secondary education programme declined from 92 per cent in 1986/87 (prior to the inauguration of the tuition fees) to 72 per cent in 1989/90, a drop of more than half a million students. Similarly some 231,000 students out of a total of 922,000 dropped out of the upper-secondary education programme. In other words, *a total of nearly three quarters of a million children were pushed out of the secondary-school system during the first three years of the reforms* (despite an increase of more than 7 per cent in the population of school age). While recent enrolment data is unavailable, there is no evidence that this trend has been reversed.[26] The available data of the 1980s suggests a drop-out rate of 0.8 per cent per annum in primary education with total enrolment increasing but substantially behind the growth in the population of school age. The structure of underfunding will trigger a speedy erosion of primary education in the years ahead.

The state allocated (1994) an average of US$3 to 4 per annum per child at the primary-school level. In the Red River delta region, the cost to parents of school materials and books (previously financed by the government) was in 1994 equivalent to 100 kg. of paddy per child per annum (a significant fraction of total household consumption).

"Concern" was, nonetheless, expressed by the government and "the donors" that with a rapidly declining enrolment rate, "unit costs have increased" and there is now "an oversupply of teachers".[27] With a "down-sized" school system, consideration should be given "to quality rather than quantity" requiring (according to "the donors") the lay-off of surplus teachers. All echelons of the educational system are affected by this process: state-supported pre-primary crèches are being phased out, and will henceforth be run as commercial undertakings.

Cost recovery was also enforced for universities and all centres of higher learning. Institutes of applied research were called upon to recover their costs by commercialising the products of their research: "Universities and research institutes are so poorly funded that their survival depends on generating independent sources of income". The state covered only 25 per cent of total salaries of research and other operating expenditures of major research institutes.[28] Research establishments were, nonetheless, granted a preferential rate of interest on short-term credit (1.8 per cent per month instead of 2.3 per cent).

In vocational and technical education, including the teachers' training colleges, a freeze on enrolment (with precise "ceilings") was established under guidelines agreed with external donor agencies. The result: a major curtailment in the supply of human capital and qualified professionals.

In the above context, financial control and supervision of most research and training institutes is in the hands of external donor agencies which selectively fund salary supplements in foreign exchange, research contracts, etc. while also dictating the orientations for research and the development of academic curricula.

Collapse of the Health System

In health, the most immediate impact of the reforms was the collapse of the district hospitals and commune-level health centres. Until 1989, health units provided medical consultations as well as essential drugs free of charge to the population. The disintegration of health clinics in the south is on the whole more advanced where the health infrastructure had been developed after reunification in 1975. With the reforms, a system of user fees was introduced. Cost recovery and the free-market sale of drugs were applied. The consumption of essential drugs (through the system of public distribution) declined by 89 per cent pushing Vietnam's pharmaceutical and medical supply industry into bankruptcy.[29]

By 1989, the domestic production of pharmaceuticals had declined by 98.5 per cent in relation to its 1980 level with a large number of drug companies closing down. With the complete deregulation of the pharmaceutical industry, including the liberalisation of drug prices, imported drugs (now sold exclusively in the "free" market at exceedingly high prices) have now largely displaced domestic brands. A considerably "down-sized" yet highly profitable commercial market has unfolded for the large pharmaceutical transnationals. The average annual consumption of pharmaceuticals purchased in the "free" market is of the order of US$1 per annum (1993) which even the World Bank considers to be too low.[30] The impact on the levels of health of the population are dramatic.

The government (under the guidance of the "donor community") also discontinued budget support to the provision of medical equipment and maintenance, leading to the virtual paralysis of the entire public-health system. Real salaries of medical personnel and working conditions declined dramatically: the monthly wage of medical doctors in a district hospital was as low as US$15 a month (1994). With the tumble in state salaries and the emergence of a small sector of private practice, tens of thousands of doctors and health workers abandoned the public-health sector. A survey conducted in 1991 confirmed that most of the commune-level health centres had become inoperative: with an average staff of five health workers per centre, the number of patients had dropped to less than six a day (slightly more than one patient per health worker per day).[31] Since the reforms, there has also been a marked downturn in student admissions to the country's main medical schools which are currently suffering from a massive curtailment of their operating budgets.

The Resurgence of Infectious Diseases

The resurgence of a number of infectious diseases including malaria, tuberculosis and diarrhoea was acknowledged by the Ministry of Health and the donors. A WHO study confirmed that the number of malaria deaths increased threefold in the first four years of the reforms alongside the collapse of curative health and soaring prices of anti-malarial drugs. What is striking in this data is that the number of malaria deaths increased at a faster rate than the growth in reported cases of malaria suggesting that the collapse in curative health services played a decisive role in triggering an increase in (malaria) mortality.[32] These tendencies are amply confirmed by commune-level data:

> The state of health used to be much better, previously there was an annual check-up for tuberculosis, now there are no drugs to treat malaria, the farmers have no money to go to the district hospital, they cannot afford the user fees...[33]

The World Bank has acknowledged the collapse of the health system (the underlying macro-economic "causes", however, were not mentioned):

> [d]espite its impressive performance in the past, the Vietnamese health sector is currently languishing...there is a severe shortage of drugs, medical supplies and medical equipment and the government health clinics are vastly underutilised. The shortage of funds to the health sector is so acute that it is unclear where the grass-roots facilities are going to find the inputs to continue functioning in the future.[34]

Whereas the World Bank conceded that the communicable disease control programmes for diarrhoea, malaria and acute respiratory infections "have [in the past] been among the most successful of health interventions in Vietnam", the proposed "solutions" consisted of the "commercialisation" (i.e. commodification) of public health as well as the massive lay-off of surplus doctors and health workers. The World Bank proposed that the wages of health workers should be increased within the same budgetary envelope: "an increase in the wages of government health workers will almost necessarily have to be offset by a major reduction in the number of health workers..."[35]

The reforms brutally dismantle the social sectors, undoing the efforts and struggles of the Vietnamese people during nearly 40 years, reversing the fulfilment of past progress. There is a consistent and coherent pattern: the deterioration in health and nutrition (in the years immediately following the reforms) is similar (and so is the chronology) with that observed in school enrolment. In the aftermath of a brutal and criminal war, the world community must take cognisance of the "deadly" impact of macro-economic policy, applied to a former wartime enemy.

Endnotes

1. The devaluations of 1984-85 under the advice of the IMF were conducive to a tenfold collapse of the Vietnam dong, largely of the same magnitude as that which occurred in South Vietnam in 1973. The dong was worth US$0.10 at the official exchange rate in 1984; one year later it was worth US$0.01.
2. The reforms have triggered a collapse in the standard of living in many ways comparable to that which occurred in South Vietnam under the defunct regime of General Thieu. An eightfold increase in the price of rice was recorded between 1973 and 1974 after the US "withdrawal" of combat troops.
3. For a breakdown and composition of the international aid and loans pledged at the donor conference, see *Vietnam Today*, Singapore, Vol. 2, Issue 6, 1994, p. 58.
4. Interview with Dr Nguyen Xian Oanh in Ho Chi Minh City, April 1994.
5. From mid-1991 to mid-1992, some 4,000 enterprises ceased operations with some 1,259 being liquidated. Some of the enterprises which ceased

operating were merged with other state enterprises. See World Bank, *Viet Nam, Transition to Market Economy*, Washington DC, 1993, p. 61.

6. In the sector of SOEs, decision no: 176 passed in 1989 was conducive to 975,000 workers (36 per cent of labour force) being laid off between 1987 and 1992. The growth in private-sector employment has not been sufficient to accommodate new entrants into the labour market. See World Bank, *Viet Nam, Transition to Market Economy*, pp. 65-6, see also Table 1.3, p. 233.
7. Ibid., p. 65. See also Socialist Republic of Vietnam, *Vietnam: A Development Perspective* (main document prepared for the Paris Donor Conference), Hanoi, September 1993, p. 28.
8. Interview conducted with state officials in Hanoi, April 1994.
9. See World Bank, *Viet Nam, Transition to Market Economy*, p. 47.
10. In contrast to the "overseas Chinese", the Vietnamese diaspora cannot be considered as constituting an "economic élite".
11. See World Bank, *Viet Nam, Transition to Market Economy*, p. 246. It is worth noting that the statistics in current and constant dong are considered to be unreliable.
12. At the November 1993 Paris Donor Conference, over US$1.8 billion of multilateral and bilateral credit was pledged.
13. Interview with the Ministry of Agriculture and Food Industry (MAFI), Hanoi, April 1994.
14. See World Bank, *Vietnam, Population, Health and Nutrition Review*, Washington DC, 1993, Table 3.6, p. 47.
15. The percentage of children under five suffering from malnutrition is estimated at 45 per cent according to the weight for age criterion and 56.5 per cent according to height for age. Ibid., pp. 38-46 and 62.
16. See World Bank, *Viet Nam, Transition to Market Economy*, p. 182.
17. The policy of local food self-sufficiency had been dictated by the deficiencies of the internal rail and road transport network, destroyed during the war.
18. World Bank, *Vietnam, Population, Health and Nutrition Sector Review*, p. 42.
19. Interviews conducted in Dong Nai Province as well as with members of the Agricultural Research Institute, Ho Chi Minh, April 1994.
20. Interviews with farmers in Da Ton Commune, Gia Lam district near Hanoi, April 1994.
21. World Bank, *Viet Nam, Transition to Market Economy*, p. 144.
22. Ibid., p. 141.
23. Ibid., p. 143.

24. Interview with the Ministry of Agriculture and Food Industry (MAFI), Hanoi, April 1994.
25. See Ministry of Education, UNDP, UNESCO (National Project Education Sector Review and Human Resources Sector Analysis), *Vietnam Education and Human Resources Analysis*, Vol. 1, Hanoi, 1992, p. 39.
26. Ministry of Education, UNDP, UNESCO, op. cit. p. 65.
27. Ibid., p. 60.
28. World Bank, *Viet Nam, Transition to Market Economy*, p. 145.
29. Figures of the Ministry of Health quoted in World Bank, *Vietnam: Population, Health and Nutrition Sector Review*, Table 4.6, p. 159.
30. Ibid., p. 89.
31. Ibid., p. 86.
32. Ibid., Table 4.2, p. 154.
33. Interview conducted in Phung Thuong Commune, Phue Tho district, Hay Tay Province, North Vietnam.
34. World Bank, *Viet Nam, Transition to Market Economy*, p. 169.
35. Ibid., p. 171.

PART IV

Latin America

Chapter 9

Debt and "Democracy" in Brazil

POLITICAL scandal during the presidency of Fernando Collor de Mello played a significant role in the restructuring of the Brazilian State. This first"democratically elected" presidency marked the demise of military dictatorship, as well as the transition towards a new "authoritarian democracy" under the direct control of the creditors and the Washington-based international financial institutions.

A few weeks after the Rio Earth Summit in June 1992, a congressional inquiry confirmed that President Collor was personally involved, through his front-man and former campaign manager P. C. Farias, in a multi-million extortion racket involving the use of public funds. The money from the kick-back operation (involving government contracts to construction companies) had been channelled into "phantom bank accounts" or was diverted to pay for the personal expenses of the president's household including his wife Rosane's wardrobe. Public opinion had its eye riveted on the political scandal and the disgrace of the president: the viewing figures for the televised congressional hearings were higher than those of the Olympic Games.

Meanwhile "backstage" ("removed from the public eye"), another much larger multi-billion dollar deal was being negotiated between Collor's minister of finance and Brazil's international creditors: these negotiations unfolded from June to September of 1992, "behind closed doors" coinciding chronologically with the impeachment process. Government ministers resigned and declared publicly their lack of support for the president. The "internationally respected" minister of finance Mr Marcilio Marques Moreira stood firm ensuring the necessary liaison with the IMF and the commercial creditors. The weakening of the state combined with instability on the Sao Paulo stock exchange and capital flight also served to put further pressure on the government. The negotiations with the commercial banks were announced by

President Collor in June 1992 at the outset of the scandal.[1] A preliminary agreement on the "restructuring" formula (under the Brady Plan) of US$44 billion owed to international banks was disclosed shortly before Collor's impeachment by the senate on 29 September 1992. It was a sell-out: Brazil's burden of debt servicing would increase substantially as a result of the deal.[2]

The campaign to impeach the president had usefully distracted public attention from the real social issues: the large majority of the population had been impoverished as a result of the "Plan Collor" launched in March 1990 by the controversial minister of economy and finance Ms Zelia Cardoso de Mello, followed by the more orthodox yet equally damaging economic therapy of her successor Marcilio Marques Moreira: unemployment was widespread, real wages had collapsed, social programmes had been crushed.

The devaluation of the cruzeiro had been imposed by the creditors, inflation was running at more than 20 per cent a month largely as a result of the IMF's "anti-inflation programme". A hike in real interest rates imposed on Brazil in 1991 by the IMF,[3] had contributed to fuelling the internal debt as well as attracting large amounts of "hot" and "dirty" money into Brazil's banking system. Tremendous profits were made by some 300 large financial and industrial enterprises. These groups were largely responsible for "a profit-led inflation", the share of capital in GDP increased from 45 per cent in 1980 to 66 per cent in the early 1990s. "Democracy" had secured for the economic élites (in alliance with the international creditors) what the nationalist military regimes were not capable of achieving fully.

The IMF's "hidden agenda" consisted of supporting the creditors while at the same time weakening the central state. Ninety billion dollars in interest payments had already been paid during the 1980s, almost as much as the total debt itself (US$120 billion). Collecting the debt, however, was not the main objective. Brazil's international creditors wanted to ensure that the country would remain indebted well into the future and that the national economy and the state would be restructured to their advantage through the continued pillage of natural resources and the environment, the consolidation of the cheap-labour export economy and the taking over of the most profitable state enterprises by foreign capital.

State assets would be privatised in exchange for debt, labour costs would be depressed as a result of the deindexation of wages and the firing of workers. Inflation was directly engineered by the macroeconomic reforms. Poverty was not only "the result" of the reforms, it was also "an explicit condition" of the agreement with the IMF.

Brazil's Debt Saga: Act I: Plan Collor

Who are the "characters" in Brazil's "debt saga"?

The "Plan Collor" initiated in 1990 was an unusual "cocktail" combining an interventionist monetary policy with IMF-style privatisation, trade liberalisation and a floating exchange rate. A US$31 billion budget deficit was to be eliminated, 360,000 federal employees were to be fired, six ministries were abolished. Introduced in March 1990 shortly after the presidential inauguration, the Plan Collor was in many respects a continuation of the "Plan Verao" adopted in 1989 under the Sarney government. The target of 360,000 employees was not met because the government lay-offs did not receive congressional approval. Only 14,000 were laid off with severance pay. Many of them were rehired under Itamar Franco's presidency.

Savings accounts were frozen by Finance Minister Ms Zelia Cardoso de Mello in a naive monetarist attempt to control inflation: "Inflation is a tiger, we must kill the tiger". Instead, the measures largely "killed economic activity", unemployment grew to record levels and small businesses were crippled due to the freeze on bank deposits, leading to at least 200,000 lay-offs in 1990 alone. Organised labour responded to the Plan Collor in September 1990 with a strike, regrouping more than one million workers. In the words of economist Paulo Singer: "the shock was cruel, monstrous and unnecessary".

The "hidden agenda" of the Plan Collor consisted in curtailing public expenditure and cutting wages so as to release the money required to service the external and internal debts. The formula for repayment of Brazil's external debt, however, was still tainted by former-President Sarney's 1989 nationalist stance regarding the debt, – i.e."a partial moratorium" (much to the dislike of the international banks) limiting debt servicing to 30 per cent of total interest payments.

The IMF had provided its "stamp of approval" to the "Plan Collor", yet a US$2 billion stand-by loan approved in September 1990 was still on hold. In the words of IMF Managing Director Mr Michel

Camdessus: "before asking approval of the [IMF] executive council, I must be sure that the negotiations with the banks are moving in the right direction and that their results will be satisfactory".[4]

A few weeks later, the government reopened debt talks with the international creditors. Mr Jorio Dauster, Collor's chief debt negotiator, argued unconvincingly that "debt payments must be limited to Brazil's ability to pay".[5] The advisory group of 22 commercial banks led by Citicorp retaliated by vetoing the IMF loan agreement and by instructing the multilateral banks not to grant "new money" to Brazil.[6] This veto was officially sanctioned by the G7 at a meeting in Washington. In turn, the United States Treasury directed the World Bank and the Inter-American Development Bank (IDB) to postpone all new loans to Brazil. The IMF, also responding to precise directives from the commercial banks and the US administration, postponed its mission to Brasilia. The IMF was a mere "financial bureaucracy" responsible for carrying out economic policy reform in indebted countries on behalf of the creditors.

The Brazilian government was caught in a vicious circle: the granting of "fresh money" from the IMF needed to repay the commercial banks was being blocked by the advisory group representing those same commercial banks, an impossible situation. The government had satisfied all the conditions laid down by the IMF, yet Brazil was still on the blacklist. And failure to meet the demands of the commercial creditors could easily become a pretext for further reprisals and blacklisting. Tension was mounting. Ms Zelia Cardoso de Mello, Brazil's finance minister, angrily accused the G7 at the Inter-American Development Bank meetings in Nagoya, Japan in April 1991 of using unfair political pressure in blocking multilateral credit to Brazil.[7]

Act II: Conforming to "The Washington Consensus"

The Nagoya meetings marked an important turning point. "Nationalist rhetoric" and recrimination against the international financial community were regarded as untimely and improper. Zelia Cardoso was fired in early May. A new economic team "more in line" with the "Washington Consensus" was set up. The appointment of Marcilio Marques Moreira as minister of economy and finance, was welcomed by the US administration and the international financial institutions (IFIs)[8]. While ambassador in Washington, Marques Moreira had developed a close personal relationship with the IMF's Michel Camdessus, and with David Mulford, under-secretary of the US Treasury. Zelia Cardoso's debt negotiator Jorio Dauster was also dismissed and replaced by Pedro Malan, an advisor to the Inter-American Development Bank and a former World-Bank executive director. Malan's association for more than ten years with the Washington scene as well as Marques Moreira's personal ties were significant factors in the evolution of Brazil's debt negotiations in the second part of Collor's presidency.

In June 1991, the IMF sent a new mission to Brasilia headed by José Fajgenbaum. The IMF had withdrawn its "stamp of approval" on the instructions of the advisory group headed by Citicorp. New negotiations on macro-economic reform had to be initiated. José Fajgenbaum speaking on behalf of the IMF mission stated that if Brazil wanted to reach a new loan agreement with the IMF "structural economic reforms implying amendments to the Constitution were required".[9] There was uproar in the parliament, with the IMF accused of "intromission in the internal affairs of the state". President Collor requested the IMF to replace Fajgenbaum as head of mission "with a more qualified individual". "A populist victory for President Collor" in his battle with the IMF, said the *New York Times*.[10]

While the incident was identified as "an unfortunate misunderstanding", Fajgenbaum's statement was very much in line with established IMF practice.[11] The IMF was demanding the adoption of "*a much stronger economic medicine*" to allow a larger share of state revenues to be redirected towards servicing the debt with the commercial banks. Yet several clauses of the 1988 Constitution stood in the way of achieving these objectives. The IMF was fully aware that the budget targets could not be met without a massive firing of public-sector employees. And yet the latter required an amendment to a clause of the 1988 Constitution guaranteeing security of employment to federal civil servants. Also at issue was the financing formula (entrenched in the constitution) of state- and municipal-level programmes from federal government sources. This formula limited the ability of the federal government to slash social expenditures and shift revenue towards debt servicing.[12] From the standpoint of the IMF and the commercial banks, the amendment of the constitution was imperative.

The clauses of the state pension plan (*A Previdencia Social*) included in the 1988 Constitution were also considered a barrier to the servicing of the federal government's debt. The privatisation of state enterprises in strategic sectors of the economy (e.g. petroleum and telecommunications) also required a constitutional revision.

The second round of negotiations with the IMF was completed in late 1991: Michel Camdessus gave his approval to a new agreement after consultations with President Bush's Secretary of the Treasury Nicholas Brady and Under-Secretary David Mulford.[13] The second Letter of Intent prepared by Marcilio Marques Moreira was handed personally by President Collor de Mello to Michel Camdessus at a breakfast meeting held during the Latin-American Summit in Cartagena, Colombia in December (Remember, the first one signed by Zelia Cardoso in September 1990 had been torn up).

This new loan agreement (US$2 billion), however, was to commit the Brazilian government over a period of 20 months to a far more destructive set of economic reforms.[14] The fiscal adjustment was particularly brutal: 65 per cent of current expenditures were already earmarked for debt servicing and the IMF was demanding further cuts in social spending.

The agreement was signed on the explicit (unwritten) understanding that the Brazilian authorities would resume negotiations with the Paris Club and reach a satisfactory agreement with the commercial banks on debt-servicing arrears. In the words of Marcilio Marques Moreira the deal on the commercial debt represented "a new chapter full of opportunities. This is the 'new Brazil' reinserting itself into the international community in a dynamic, competitive and sovereign way".[15]

Act III: In the Aftermath of Collor's Impeachment

Act III of the debt saga commenced with the inauguration of Itamar Franco as acting president.[16] A clumsy beginning: the new president promised to increase real wages, bring down the prices of public utilities and modify the privatisation programme without realising that his hands were tied as a result of the agreement signed a year earlier with the IMF. Despite an impressive Congressional majority based on a coalition of parties extending from left to right (led by the former head of the Communist Party), Itamar Franco's cabinet failed to receive the immediate assent of the Washington institutions.

Franco's populist statements displeased both the creditors and the national élites. The IMF had decided to be much tougher on the new government: three ministers of finance were appointed during the first seven months of Itamar Franco's presidency, none of them receiving a friendly endorsement from the IMF. In the meantime, the IMF had sent in its auditors to monitor economic progress under the loan agreement: the quarterly targets for the budget deficit had not been met (and could not be met without amendments to the constitution). Even though the tax-reform legislation had been passed through Congress as required by the IMF, the programme was considered to be "no longer on course". The disbursements under the stand-by loan were discontinued, Brazil was "back on the blacklist" and negotiations with the IMF on economic reform were once again back to square one.

At another breakfast meeting, this time in Washington in February 1993, with Itamar's second minister of finance, Paulo Haddad, Michel Camdessus insisted upon the development of a new economic programme to be submitted for IMF approval within a 60-day period. Moreover, it was also made clear by the IMF that a stand-by loan would not be granted prior to the formal signing of the final agreement with the commercial banks, and that it was therefore necessary to synchronise the deadline dates set respectively for policy reform and debt restructuring.[17]

No time was lost. A few weeks later, an IMF mission had arrived in Brasilia headed by the same notorious José Fajgenbaum, who two years earlier had hinted of the need for constitutional reform. Continuity in personnel on the IMF side... Not on the Brazilian side! Paulo Haddad was no longer in charge. Upon arrival of the mission, the ministry's economic team was in a state of disarray; the economy and finance portfolio had been switched a few days earlier. Itamar Franco's third minister of finance Mr Eliseu Resende, would go to Washington to meet Camdessus in late April. He was dismissed in May.[18]

Act IV: A Marxist Sociologist as Finance Minister

A new phase of the "debt saga" was initiated with the appointment of Fernando Henrique Cardoso, a prominent intellectual and marxist sociologist, as minister of finance. The business community, somewhat apprehensive at first, was soon reassured: despite his leftist writings (*inter alia* on "social classes under peripheral capitalism"), the new minister pledged relentless support to the tenets of neoliberalism: "forget everything I have written...", he said at a meeting with leading bankers and industrialists. A few years earlier Cardoso had been nominated "intellectual of the year" for his critical analysis of social classes in Brazil.

By July 1993, President Itamar Franco had virtually abdicated from exercising any real political power, having fully entrusted the conduct of the economic reforms to his new minister. As a former opposition senator, the finance minister understood that passage of the IMF reforms would require the manipulation of civil society as well as the mustering of support in the legislature. Public opinion was led to believe that the proposed deindexation of wages was the only means "of combating inflation". In June 1993, Cardoso announced budget cuts of 50 per cent in education, health and regional development while pointing to the need for revisions to the constitution at the upcoming sessions of Congress. Under Cardoso's wages' proposal – which received Congressional approval – wages could decline (in real terms) by as much as 31 per cent, representing an estimated "savings" of US$11 billion for the public purse (and for the creditors!).[19]

Act V: Rescheduling the Commercial Debt[20]

The debt saga reached its final stage in April 1994. An agreement was sealed in New York on the "restructuring" of US$49 billion of commercial debt under the Brady Plan. The deal had been carefully negotiated by Cardoso and Citibank Corp Vice-Chairman Mr William Rhodes who was acting on behalf of some 750 international creditor banks.

In contrast to previous rounds of negotiations, precise deadline dates had been set for the safe passage of major pieces of "prescribed" legislation including amendments to the 1988 Constitution. The IMF had been entrusted with the bureaucratic task of enforcing and carefully monitoring the legislative process on behalf of the commercial banks. However, despite Finance Minister Cardoso's efforts to manipulate civil society, muster political support and jostle the various reforms through a "sovereign" parliament, time had been running out. The 16 March deadline for the signing of a "Letter of Intent" with the IMF could not be met. A tight schedule, the so-called "notification deadline" for a deal with the commercial banks' steering committee, had been set for 17 March.

While the 15 April agreement was formally reached against established practice (which requires prior approval of an IMF standby loan as collateral for the debt restructuring programme), the economic reforms were, nonetheless, considered "to be on track". IMF Managing Director Michel Camdessus stated that he was impressed with steps already taken and promised to cooperate closely with the government. In turn, Cardoso (who in the meantime had become presidential candidate) stated that the "IMF's promise of further cooperation" (once key elements of the economic programme were in place) should be enough for the debt restructuring deal to go ahead. Despite "unfortunate delays" in the parliamentary process, the main condition – requiring a massive release of state financial resources in favour of the creditors – had been met: the legislature had approved the IMF's fiscal reforms, including the creation of a "Social Emergency Fund" (SEF), (on the World-Bank model). The vote in Congress (requiring a constitutional amendment) obliged the government to slash the federal budget (including public investment) by 43 per cent while redirecting state revenue towards debt servicing.

The measures imposed by the creditors constituted a final lethal blow to Brazil's social programmes, already in an advanced stage of decay as a result of successive "shock therapies". The SEF was "financed from the budget cuts" (implying transfers of funds to the SEF) through the concurrent phasing out of regular government programmes and the massive dismissal of government employees. Its inauguration represented an important political landmark: sovereignty in social policy was foregone, henceforth budgets and organisational structures would be monitored directly by the Washington-based Bretton Woods institutions acting on behalf of the international creditor banks. The collapse and destruction of the state's social programmes and the phasing out of part of the government pension plan (*Previdencia Social*) were "pre-conditions" for the signing of the agreement. Moreover, the reforms also engineered a squeeze of real wages by establishing "a salary ceiling" in the public sector,[21] as well as the "switching" of all wage contracts into a new currency unit, the URV (or "real").[22] The latter reform, requiring a separate piece of legislation, had been worked out well in advance (in high-level meetings behind closed doors) in close consultation with the Washington-based bureaucracy: Winston Fritsch, Brazil's secretary of state in charge of economic policy, had inadvertently leaked to the press in October 1993 that he would "deliver to the IMF, the skeleton of a plan of deindexation".[23]

The IMF's "economic therapy" had also redefined in a fundamental way the relationship between the central and regional governments entrenched in the 1988 Constitution. The proposed "model" of fiscal reform was in this regard analogous to that imposed by the international creditors on the Yugoslav Federation in 1990 (see Chapter 13): federal transfers to state and municipal governments earmarked for health, education and housing were frozen, the regions were to become "fiscally autonomous" and the savings accruing to the federal Treasury were to be redirected towards interest payments.

But the IMF had also pointed to the need for constitutional amendments which would allow for the speedy privatisation of Petrobras and Telebras, the petroleum and telecommunications parastatals.

Cardoso had "performed much better" than his predecessors in the finance portfolio under the Collor presidency. "Success" in carrying out the IMF programme was rewarded. The minister of finance was elected president in the 1994 elections supported by a massive multi-million-dollar media campaign as well as an (unwritten) agreement by the country's major business interests not to increase prices during the election campaign. The introduction of the new currency by Cardoso while he was minister of finance had engineered the deindexation of wages. Yet the remarkably low rates of inflation in the months preceding his election as president were instrumental in providing support to Cardoso's candidacy, particularly among the poorest sections of the population which survived on the fringe of the labour market.[24]

Continuity with the authoritarian democratic regime established under Fernando Collor de Mello had been ensured. In the words of a senior executive of one of Brazil's largest creditor banks:

> Collor had a double personality, he was very committed to economic reform, he acted as a catalyst in implementing what the Brazilian people wanted..., his second cabinet under Finance Minister Marcilio Marques Moreira was the best, today [1993] Fernando Henrique Cardoso is doing the right thing at a lesser speed,... To reach the deficit targets set by the IMF, the Congress must accept the US$6 billion budget cut, another US$6 billion will have to come from the Constitutional revision, essentially through the lay-off of public employees... What we would need in Brazil is a "soft Pinochet government", preferably civilian, something like Fujimori, the military is not an option...

Act VI, Epilogue: The Management of Poverty at Minimal Cost to the Creditors

Macro-economic policy had accelerated the "expulsion" of landless peasants from the countryside leading to the formation of a nomadic migrant labour force moving from one metropolitan area to another. In the cities, an entirely new "layer of urban poverty" (socially distinct from that which characterised the *favelas*) had unfolded: thousands of salaried workers and white-collar employees hitherto occupying middle- and lower-class residential areas had been evicted, socially marginalised and often "excluded" from the slum areas.

The SEF set up by Fernando Henrique Cardoso in 1994 required a "social engineering" approach, a policy framework for "managing poverty" and attenuating social unrest at minimal cost to the creditors. So-called "targeted programmes" earmarked "to help the poor" combined with "cost recovery" and the "privatisation" of health and educational services were said to constitute "a more efficient" way of delivering social programmes. Concurrently, the National Institute of Social Security (INSS) was to become increasingly "self-financing" by substantially raising its premium contributions from both urban and rural workers.[25] The state which withdraws many programmes under the jurisdiction of line ministries will henceforth be managed by the organisations of civil society under the umbrella of the SEF. The latter will also finance "a social safety net" (in the form of severance payments) earmarked for public-sector workers laid off as a result of the constitutional reform process.

The establishment of the SEF was carried out "in the name of poverty alleviation". The "Citizens' campaign against famine" initiated after Collor's impeachment in the Senate in 1992 provided the government of Itamar Franco with the necessary ideological backbone as well as a populist mouthpiece. The campaign had lost its original momentum as a broad democratic grass-roots movement directed against the policies of the state. Although the campaign was officially non-partisan, both the opposition Workers Party (PT) and the government were involved. A deal had also been struck between the leader of the campaign Dr Herbert de Souza ("Betinho") and Mr Alcyr Calliari, president of the Bank of Brazil. The Bank of Brazil (a powerful financial arm of the central state), was entrusted with setting up local campaign committees throughout the country. More than two thirds of these grass-roots committees were controlled by employees of the Bank of Brazil.[26] In turn, the powerful business tycoon Roberto Marinho who controls the "Globo" television network offered to grant free Hollywood-style commercials to the campaign during prime TV time.

Poverty and famine were portrayed in a stylised tabloid form in the Brazilian press; with funding in the hands of the financial élites, no pervasive linkage was made between the IMF's "economic medicine" and the occurrence of famine. As the economic crisis deepened, the "Citizens' campaign" served the "useful" purpose of diverting attention from the real policy issues; it sought a broad national consensus, avoided controversy and refrained from directly indicting either the government or Brazil's privileged social élites.

The campaign against famine also served another related function: the main "poverty indicators" put forth by the campaign were based on the "estimates" of the government's official "economic think tank", the Institute of Applied Economic Research (IPEA), now entrusted with supportive "research" on famine and poverty. Grossly manipulated and falsified, IPEA's "estimates" suggested that a mere 21 per cent of the Brazilian population was situated below the "critical poverty" line.[27] Double standards: 32 million people in Brazil against 35.7 million in the United States (according to the definition of the US government).

In other words, the campaign portrayed poverty as pertaining essentially to a "social minority" thereby vindicating the World Bank's framework of "selective targeting in favour of the poor". It not only distorted but tacitly denied the obvious (amply confirmed by official statistics), namely that most sectors of society including the middle classes were being impoverished as a result of the economic reforms adopted since the outset of the Collor government.[28]

The SEF officially sanctioned the withdrawal of the state from the social sectors (a process which was already ongoing), and "the management of poverty" (at the micro-social level) by separate and parallel organisational structures. Since the outset of the Collor government, various non-governmental organisations (NGOs) funded by international "aid programmes" had gradually taken over many of the functions of the municipal governments whose funds had been frozen as a result of the structural adjustment programme.

Small-scale production and handicraft projects, sub-contracting for export processing firms, community-based training and employment programmes, etc. were set up under the umbrella of the "social safety net". A meagre survival to local-level communities was ensured while at the same time containing the risk of social upheaval. An example of "micro-level management of poverty" is in Pirambu, a sprawling slum area of 250,000 inhabitants in the Northeastern city of Fortaleza. Pirambu had been "carved up", each slice of the urban space was under the supervision of a separate international aid organisation or NGO. In the Couto Fernandes neighbourhood of Pirambu, the German Aid Agency GTZ supported the establishment of a model of "community management".[29]

This "micro-democracy" installed under the watchful eye of the "donor community" also served the purpose of subduing the development of independent grass-roots social movements. German funding financed the salaries of the expatriate experts whereas the investment funds earmarked for small-scale manufacturing were to be "self-financed" through a "revolving fund" managed by the local community.

The "management of poverty" in rural areas served the same broad objectives: to subdue the peasant movement on behalf of Brazil's powerful land-owning class while ensuring a meagre survival to millions of landless peasants uprooted and displaced by large-scale agri-business. In the northeastern Sertâo, for instance, a region affected by recurrent drought, a minimum works programme (*frentes de trabalho*) provided employment (at US$14 a month) to some 1.2 million landless farm workers (1993).[30] The latter, however, were often hired by the large landowners at the expense of the federal government. The distribution of US grain surpluses financed under Public Law 480 (Washington's food aid programme-PL 480) to impoverished farmers (through government and relief agencies) also served the related purpose of weakening local-level food agriculture and uprooting the small peasantry. The food distribution programmes were adopted in the name of the "Citizens' Campaign against Famine".

The expropriation of peasant lands was an integral part of the IMF-World Bank structural adjustment programme. In this context, the National Institute for Colonisation and Agrarian Reform (INCRA) among several government agencies was in charge of "the rural safety net" through token land distribution programmes and the development of cooperatives for the "*posseiros*" (landless farmers). These schemes were invariably established in marginal or semi-arid lands which do not encroach upon the interests of the land-owning class. In the states of Para, Amazonas and Maranhao, several international donors including the World Bank and the Japanese Aid Agency (JICA) had contributed to financing (through INCRA) so-called "areas of colonisation".[31] The latter served largely as "labour reserves" for large-scale plantations. It is also worth mentioning that the proposed constitutional amendments implied the *de facto* derogation of customary land rights of the indigenous people, a process which was already underway with the transformation (under the jurisdiction of INCRA) of the "Indian reserves" in the Amazon into areas of settlement for plantation workers.[32]

Consolidating a Parallel Government

The IMF-sponsored reforms had contributed to social polarisation and the impoverishment of all sectors of the population including the middle classes. Moreover, as the federal fiscal structure breaks down, there is the added risk of regional Balkanisation: instability within the military, routine violation of fundamental human rights, urban and rural violence, an increasingly vocal secessionist movement in the south.

Since the presidency of Fernando Collor de Mello, a *de facto* "parallel government" reporting regularly to Washington has developed. Under the presidency of Fernando Henrique Cardoso (1994-99), the creditors are in control of the state bureaucracy, of its politicians. The state is bankrupt and its assets are being impounded under the privatisation programme.

Endnotes

1. The Senate provided its approval to the debt restructuring formula in December 1992.
2. Interest payments to international creditors had been limited to 30 per cent in a partial moratorium negotiated with the commercial banks in 1989 under the government of Joseph Sarney. Under the restructuring plan, interest payments would increase to 50 per cent.
3. Contained in the Letter of Intent to the IMF of December 1991.
4. Quoted in *Jornal do Brasil*, 21 September 1990.
5. See Simon Fisher and Stephen Fidler, "Friction likely as Brazil reopens Debt Talks", *Financial Times*, London, 10 October 1990.
6. Prior to the payment of debt-servicing arrears amounting to some US$8 billion.
7. See Christina Lamb, "Brazil Issues Angry Protest at Suspension of Development Loans", *Financial Times*, London, 4 April 1991.
8. See Luiz Carlos Bresser Pereira, "O FMI e as carrocas", *Folha de São Paulo*, 27 July 1991, pp. 1-3.
9. In an interview with the *Jornal do Brasil*, quoted in *Estado de São Paulo*, 23 June 1991. See also "Missão do FMI adota discurso moderado", *Folha de São Paulo*, 19 June 1991.
10. See *O Globo*, 27 June 1991.
11. See *Folha de São Paulo*, 19 July 1991.
12. The right to strike is also entrenched in the 1988 Constitution.
13. See José Meirelles Passos, "FMI e EUA apoiam programa brasilieira", *O Globo*, 7 December 1991.
14. The Letter of Intent was appproved by the IMF in January 1992. See also, "Carta ao FMI preve 'aperto brutal' em 92", *Folha de São Paulo*, 6 December 1991.
15. Quoted in Stephen Fidler and Christina Lamb, "Brazil sets out Accord on 44 billion Debt", *Financial Times*, London, 7 July 1992.

16. Itamar Franco was appointed acting president pending a court decision on the Senate impeachment vote.
17. Pedro Malan (the debt negotiator appointed under Collor) confirmed in March from his Washington office that 802 banks, including Chase Manhattan and Lloyds Bank, had already approved the debt-restructuring formula. Yet, in practice, the veto of the advisory committee on the granting of multilateral loans to Brazil was still in effect. See Fernando Rodrigues, "Bancos aderem ao acordo da divida externa", *Folha de São Paulo*, 16 March 1993.
18. See Claudia Sofatle, "Missão do FMI volta sem acordo", *Gazeta Mercantil*, 17 March 1993.
19. *Financial Times*, 20 August 1993. The US$11 billion are the "savings" for the state in relation to a congressional wage-adjustment proposal which provided for a 100 per cent cost-of-living adjustment to salaried workers. This proposal, adopted by the Congress in July, was vetoed by the government. Cardoso's wages proposal was meant to constitute a compromise solution. See also *Folha de São Paulo*, 30 July 1993.
20. The latter part of this chapter was written in collaboration with Micheline Ladouceur.
21. The "salary ceiling" is established in the context of Provisional Measure no: 382. *O Globo*, 8 December 1993, pp. 2-11.
22. Initially operating as an accounting unit.
23. Quoted in *Folha de São Paolo*, 3 March 1994, pp. 1-10.
24. Interview with Minister of Finance Fernando Henrique Cardoso, Brasilia, August 1993.
25. In accordance with the clauses of provisional measure no: 381; see *O Globo*, 8 December 1993, pp. 2-11.
26. See *Veja*, Rio de Janeiro, December 1993.
27. See Instituto de Pesquisa Econômica Aplicada (IPEA), *O Mapa da Fome II: Informações sobre a Indîgencia por Municipios da Federação*, Brasilia, 1993.
28. Eighty per cent of the labour force had earnings below US$300 a month in 1991 according to the Brazilian Institute of Geography and Statistics (IBGE).
29. Interviews conducted in Pirambu, Fortaleza, July 1993.
30. Interviews with rural farm workers in the region of Monsenhor Tabosa, Ceara, July 1993.
31. Celia Maria Correa Linhares and Maristela de Paula Andrade, "A Açao Oficial e os Conflitos Agrarios no Maranãho", *Desenvolvimento e Cidadania*, No. 4. São Luis de Maranhão, 1992.
32. See *Panewa*, Porto Velho, Vol. VI, No. 18, November-December 1993 and Vol. VII, No. 19, January 1994.

Chapter 10

IMF Shock Treatment in Peru

THE August 8, 1990 "Fujishock" named after President Alberto Fujimori was announced in a message to the nation by Prime Minister Juan Hurtado Miller: "Our major objectives are to curtail the fiscal deficit and eliminate price distortions"...: from one day to the next, the price of fuel increased by 31 times (2,968 per cent) and the price of bread increased by more than twelve times (1,150 per cent). In the true "spirit of Anglo-Saxon liberalism", these prices were "fixed" through presidential decree rather than by the"free" market (a form of "planned liberalism"). The Fujishock was intended to crush hyperinflation: this was achieved, however, through a 446 per cent increase in food prices in a single month! Inflation during the first year of the Cambio 90 government had "fallen" to a modest 2,172 per cent.

Many countries in Latin America had experienced "shock treatment" yet the extent of "economic engineering" in Peru was unprecedented. The social consequences were devastating: whereas an agricultural worker in Peru's northern provinces was (in August 1990) receiving US$7.50 a month (the equivalent of the price of a hamburger and a soft drink), consumer prices in Lima were higher than in New York.[1] Real earnings declined by 60 per cent in the course of August 1990; by mid-1991 the level of real earnings was less than 15 per cent of their 1974 value (a decline of more than 85 per cent). The average earnings of government employees had declined by 63 per cent during the first year of the Fujimori government and by 92 per cent in relation to 1980 (see Table 10.3).[2] On the IMF blacklist since the mid-1980s, Peru had been "rewarded" for President Alan Garcia's (1985-90) rhetorical stance to limit debt-servicing payments to 10 per cent of export earnings.

Table 10.1: The Impact of the August 1990 Shock Treatment on Consumer Prices

Lima Metropolitan Area, August 1990		
Percentage Increase	**INEI**	**Cuanto**
Food and beverages	446.2	288.2
Transport and communication	571.4	1428.0
Health and medical services	702.7	648.3
Rent, fuel and electricity	421.8	1035.0
Consumer price index	397.0	411.9

Source: Instituto Navoual de Estadistica (INEI), Anuario estadistico, 1991, *Cuanto* , Peru en Numeros, chapter 21, Lima, 1991.

Historical Background

Peru's first macro-economic stabilisation programme was initiated in the mid-1970s after the 1975 *coup d'état* directed against the populist military government of General Velasco Alvarado. The economic reforms had been carried out by the military junta under General Morales Bermudez, Velasco's successor, as a condition for the re-scheduling of Peru's external debt with the commercial banks and the official creditors. These reforms had been directly negotiated with the creditor banks without the involvement of the IMF. In 1978, a second "economic package" was put in motion this time in the context of a formal agreement with the IMF.

These earlier economic reforms adopted prior to the formal launching of the structural adjustment programme in the early 1980s had been modelled on those applied in Chile (under General Pinochet and the Chicago Boys in 1973). The conditionality clauses were on balance less stringent and coherent in comparison to the policy-based loan agreements under the structural adjustment programmes initiated in the early 1980s.

The macro-economic reforms of the mid- to late 1970s, nonetheless, were instrumental in initiating in Peru an historical process of impoverishment: successive currency devaluations unleashed an inflationary spiral, real purchasing power in the modern urban sector declined by approximately 35 per cent from 1974 to 1978 (Table 10.3). This compression of real wages (and labour costs) was not conducive, however, to enhancing Peru's export potential as claimed by the Bretton Woods institutions.

With the accession of President Fernando Belaunde Terry in 1980, macro-economic policy became more cohesive. Those policies firmly supported by the IMF contributed to weakening the state and the system of state enterprises established under the government of General Velasco Alvarado. Generous exploration and exploitation contracts were granted to foreign capital (e.g. in petroleum to Occidental). Reduced tariff barriers also contributed to undermining key sectors of the national economy. The state's participation in the banking sector was curtailed and the influx of foreign capital into commercial banking was encouraged, as was the establishment of subsidiaries of a number of international banks including Chase, Commerzbank, Manufacturer's Hannover and Bank of Tokyo.[3]

This IMF-supported programme was implemented by the Belaunde government at the very outset of the debt crisis: a bonanza of imported consumer goods resulting from the liberalisation of trade coincided (chronologically) with the collapse of export revenues and the decline in the terms of trade (1981-82). The combination of these two factors contributed to exacerbating the balance of payments crisis, resulting in a decline of GDP of the order of 12 per cent in 1982 and a rate of inflation of more than 100 per cent in 1983.

From 1980 to 1983, the levels of infant malnutrition increased dramatically. In 1985, estimated food consumption had fallen by 25 per cent in relation to its 1975 level. In the course of Belaunde's five-year presidential term (1980-85), real earnings at the minimum wage (*remuneración minima vital*) declined by more than 45 per cent. All categories of the labour force were affected: the average decline of real earnings for blue- and white-collar workers was respectively of 39.5 and 20.0 per cent (see Table 10.3).

In the 10-year period from the end of the Velasco government

Table 10.2: The Impact of the August 1990 Shock Treatment on Consumer Prices

Lima Metropolitan Area, August 1990

(Intis)

	Before 3 August 1990	After 9 August 1990	Percentage Increase
Commodity			
Kerosene (gal)	19	608	3100
Gasoline (84oct)(gal.)	22	675	2968
Propane gas (924 lbs.)	41	1120	2632
Bread (36 gr/unit)	2	25	1150
Beans (kg.)	240	2800	1067
White Potatoes (kg.)	40	300	650
Flour (kg)	220	1500	531
Milk (litre)	60	290	383
Spaghetti (kg)	180	775	331
Vegetable oil (litre)	220	850	236
Rice (grade A)(kg)	94	310	230
Powdered Milk (410 gr)	100	330	230
Eggs (kg)	170	540	218
Chicken (kg)	213	600	182

Source: *Cuanto*, Vol. 2, No. 19, August 1990, p. 5.

Table 10.3: Index of Real Wages (1974-1991)

(1974=100)*

Year	Minimum Legal Income	White-Collar Private Sector	Blue-Collar Private Sector	Wages in Govt Sector
1974	100.0	100.0	100.0	
1975	93.1	100.6	88.3	
1976	85.6	83.3	95.1	
1977	75.3	72.4	79.2	
1978	58.4	62.2	71.3	
1979	63.6	56.9	70.9	
1980	79.9	61.1	75.0	
1981	67.9	62.1	73.5	100.0
1982	62.2	67.0	74.4	91.7
1983	64.6	57.4	61.6	66.3
1984	49.7	59.6	52.5	58.2
1985	43.5	48.8	45.4	46.4
1986	45.1	61.0	60.8	48.4
1987	49.0	63.9	65.6	59.2
1988	41.5	44.2	41.3	53.5
1989	25.1	36.3	37.6	35.3
1990	21.4	18.7	20.1	18.8
July	20.9	13.8	16.2	21.1
August		7.5	8.3	8.9
September	19.4	11.1	12.9	8.6
December[1/]	13.8	14.6	16.3	6.1
1991				
April	15.3	15.7	19.4	8.6
May	14.1			7.8

Source: Estimated from official data of INEI, *Anuario estadis*tico, 1991., Cuanto, *Peru en Numeros*, 1991, ch. 21 and *Cuanto Suplemento*, No. 13, July 1991.

*: the base year of the index for Government Sector Wages is 1981.

[1]/Includes *gratificación.*

The private sector categories include white-collar and blue-collar earnings in private sector employment in the Lima Metropolitan Area.

Since 1963, the Minimum Legal Income was equal to the reference unit (*unidad de referencia*). From June 1984 to August 1990 it was equivalent to the reference unit plus additional bonus payments. From August 1990, the government abolished the Minimum Legal Income *(Ingreso Minimo Legal)* and replaced it by the so-called *Remuneración Minima Vital.*

(The category General Government includes earnings in the central and regional governments and decentralised public institutions.)

(1975) to the end of Belaunde's term of office (1985), the minimum wage had declined (according to official data) by 58.2 per cent, the average wage by 55.0 per cent (blue collar workers) and the average earnings of middle-income white-collar workers by 51.7 per cent.

The APRA's Non Orthodox Economic Policy (1985-87)

The Acción Popular government of President Fernando Belaunde Terry had been discredited. In the 1985 election campaign, the opposition American Popular Revolutionary Alliance (APRA) (a populist party founded in the 1920s) had presented an "alternative economic programme". In overt confrontation with the Bretton Woods institutions, the newly-elected APRA government of President Alan Garcia put forth its so-called "Economic Emergency Plan" (*Plan Economico de Emergencia*) in July 1985. This programme went directly against the IMF's usual economic prescriptions.

At the outset of Alan Garcia's presidency, the annual rate of inflation was in excess of 225 per cent. The government's programme consisted of reactivating consumer demand. A price freeze on essential consumer goods and public services was implemented. Interest rates were brought down and the exchange rate was "stabilised". The economy had been stagnating under the Belaunde government and operating with a considerable amount of excess capacity. It was therefore possible for the APRA government to reactivate economic activity "on the demand-side" without creating undue inflationary pressures on production costs.[4]

President Alan Garcia had committed himself during the election campaign to paying higher producer prices to farmers with a view to reactivating production and bringing about a redistribution of income in favour of the rural areas. During the first year of operation of the economic package, there was (according to World Bank estimates) an improvement of 75 per cent of the rural-urban terms of trade and a significant short-term growth of agricultural production.[5]

In the urban economy, the authorities decreed increases in wages and salaries somewhat in excess of inflation. A temporary employment programme was established, an expansionary fiscal policy was adopted and credit was characterised by negative real interest rates. Various tax incentives and subsidies were devised in support of this reactivation of aggregate demand. These exemptions, however, largely benefited the national economic and financial élites. The state's tax base as well its international foreign exchange reserve position were consequently weakened.

The APRA's Debt-Negotiating Strategy

Upon assuming office, President Garcia declared a moratorium on the payment of debt-servicing obligations. The latter were not to exceed ten per cent of export earnings. Peru was immediately put on the blacklist by the international financial community. The inflow of fresh money was frozen; the international commercial banks cut off their support to Peru in 1985. By 1986 no new commercial loans were granted. Official agencies and OECD governments also substantially curtailed their levels of disbursements to Peru.[6]

Despite the moratorium, the Peruvian external debt increased dramatically – on average by 9 per cent per annum during the APRA government.[7] In terms of net flows of capital, President Garcia's rhetorical stance on debt-servicing did not serve its purpose: actual debt-servicing payments were on average of the order of 20 per cent of export earnings during the 1985-89 period. With the freeze on new loans, not to mention capital flight to offshore bank accounts, the 1985-89 period was marked by a massive outflow of real resources.[8]

The Economic Programme Enters a Deadlock

During the first 18 months of the APRA government, there was significant growth of GDP. Inflation was brought down largely as a result of the system of "price freezes", the dollarisation process of the national economy was reduced and levels of consumption increased markedly.

But the programme could not be sustained beyond the short run. Whereas economic growth had been supported by an expansionary fiscal policy, the tax base remained extremely fragile. Indirect taxes had been reduced, there was massive tax evasion and the various subsidies and exemptions to large corporations were "funded" through deficit financing and an expansion of the money supply. The system was prone to corruption and speculation. The structure of multiple exchange rates (*mercado unico de cambios*), theoretically intended as an instrument of income redistribution, ultimately benefited the wealthiest segment of Peruvian society.[9]

In 1988, the level of foreign-exchange reserves plummeted to minus US$252 million.[10] While levels of purchasing power had expanded, a large portion of the country's foreign-exchange earnings had been appropriated by the economic élites in the form of subsidies and tax exemptions. The state had implemented a standard Keynesian "counter-cyclical" policy in support of aggregate demand without tackling more fundamental structural issues. While these measures exhibited some minimal level of technical coherence under conditions of extreme stagnation and underutilisation of industrial capacity, they were unable to sustain the economic recovery beyond the short term.

In practice, the APRA government had supported vested economic interests through the manipulation of its various regulatory policy instruments. The economic model had been defined in narrow technical terms supported by populist rhetoric: the APRA did not have the required social basis, nor the political will, let alone the grass-roots support to implement substantive and sustainable economic and social reforms in such areas as tax reform, regionalisation, reactivation of agriculture and support to small-scale productive units of the informal economy.

Beyond its populist rhetoric, the APRA government was unwilling to take actions which encroached directly upon the vested interests of the economic elites. In 1987, the proposed nationalisation of the banking sector (which did not even concur with a politically defined mandate), announced rhetorically with a view to "democratising credit", was easily circumvented by the commercial banks and financial institutions in a drawn-out legal battle which led ultimately to the abandonment of the nationalisation project. The intent marked the end of the APRA's "populist honeymoon" with the financial élites. It created divisions within the APRA, discredited the government and generated an aura of economic uncertainty and mistrust on the part of the business sector which, according to some observers, unleashed the hyperinflationary process of 1988-90. The economic élites had "declared war on the government".

Similarly, in tackling the issue of ownership rights, in 1990 the APRA government presented the issue demagogically at the level of formal "registration" (*registro predial)* of ownership rights which would enable, for instance, units of the rural economy (*parceleros*) and informal economy to accede to formal ownership. The question of concentration of ownership of real assets and wealth-formation by the privileged classes was carefully avoided.

De Facto "Shock Treatment" (1988-90)

The growth in real purchasing power achieved in 1985 and 1986 was short-lived. Economic activity started to slow down by the beginning of 1987. Expansion was replaced by contraction: the movement of real earnings was reversed in a matter of months. Between December 1987 and October 1988, real earnings plummeted by 50 to 60 per cent, the wages of public employees declined by two-thirds.[11] By mid-1988, real wages were 20 per cent below their 1985 level.

In July 1988, the government initiated a new emergency plan and in September a more "orthodox" anti-inflationary programme was introduced. The September 1988 package contained most of the essential ingredients of the standard IMF programme without the neoliberal ideology and the support of international creditors.

In many respects, the September 1988 package set the pace for the economic shock measures to be adopted by the Fujimori government in August 1990. The economic package included all the essential elements: devaluation and unification of the exchange rate, the enactment of price increases of public services and gasoline, substantial cuts in government expenditure and the introduction of cost recovery for most public enterprises. The package also implied the deindexation of wages and salaries.

Failure of the APRA's Non-orthodox Economic Package

The failure of the non-orthodox economic package under President Alan Garcia does not vindicate the neoliberal framework. The economic programme was politically ambivalent from the outset. The APRA failed to take a stance with regard to the regulation of profit margins and the setting of prices by powerful commercial and agro-industrial interests. Keynesian instruments were adopted mechanically without addressing fundamental structural issues. To succeed, the programme required a positive influx of foreign exchange. Exactly the opposite occurred: the net outflow of resources continued unabated. The international creditors maintained their grip on Peru's balance of payments.

The Restoration of IMF Rule

During the 1990 election campaign, Alberto Fujimori had confronted his opponent author Mario Vargas Llosa of the Democratic Front Coalition (Fredemo). Vargas Llosa had proposed "economic shock treatment" as a solution to Peru's economic crisis. Fujimori's party, Cambio 90, had rejected the neoliberal recipe promising an economic programme which would lead to "stabilisation without recession" combining a solution to hyperinflation while protecting workers' purchasing power.[12]

An expansionary economic policy had been envisaged by Fujimori in the months preceding his inauguration as president on the 28 July 1990. This programme, however, had been defined in narrow technical terms (debated within a closed circle of professional and academic economists) without focusing on the political process required to carry it out. The programme had been defined as a technical "solution" to the economic crisis in isolation from the broader political debate and without the participation of representative organisations of civil society in its formulation.

On the plane to Washington to meet IMF Managing Director Michel Camdessus, the president-elect is reported to have stated thoughtfully to his principal economic advisor: "if the economic shock were to work, the Peruvian people would no doubt forgive me...". Strong internal and external political pressures were being exercised on the president-elect to abandon the "alternative programme" in favour of an orthodox IMF-sponsored package. Upon his return from Washington and Tokyo, from his meetings with Peru's international creditors, the president-elect had become an unbending supporter of "strong economic medicine". Yet this shift in policy direction was known only within his immediate political entourage: nothing was revealed to the Peruvian people who had voted against Fredemo's "economic shock treatment".

Divisions developed within the economic advisory team and the president-elect developed close links with another group of economists firmly committed to the "Washington Consensus" and the IMF package. His main economic advisors resigned shortly before his accession to the presidency, and a new economic stabilisation package – not markedly different from that proposed by Mario Vargas Llosa during the election campaign – was put together in a hurry with the technical support of the IMF and the World Bank.

The August 1990 IMF-Fujishock

The August 1990 shock treatment not only conformed to IMF prescriptions it went far beyond what was normally expected of an indebted country as a condition for the renegotiation of its external debt. Despite the high levels of critical poverty prevailing in the last months of the APRA government, a further "adjustment" in real earnings was considered necessary to "alleviate inflationary pressures". Peru's hyperinflation was said to be caused by "demand factors", requiring a further compression in wages and social expenditures, together with massive lay-offs of public-sector workers.

The spread of the cholera epidemic in 1991 – while largely attributable to poverty and the breakdown of the country's public health infrastructure since the Belaunde government – was also a result of the IMF-sponsored programme. With a thirty-fold increase in the price of cooking oil, people in Lima's "*pueblos jovenes*", including the "middle classes", were no longer able to afford to boil their water or cook their food.

The international publicity surrounding the outbreak of the cholera epidemic (approximately 200,000 declared cases and 2,000 registered deaths in a six-month period) overshadowed in the international press a more general process of social destruction: since the August 1990 Fujishock, tuberculosis had also reached epidemic proportions heightened by malnutrition and the breakdown of the government's vaccination programme. The collapse of the public-health infrastructure in the Selva region had led to a resurgence of malaria, dengue and leishmaniasis.[13] Public schools, universities and hospitals had been closed down as a result of an indefinite strike by teachers and health workers (their wages were an average US$45-70 a month [July 1991] – 40 times lower than in the US).

More than 83 per cent of the population (mid-1991 estimate) (including the middle class) did not meet minimum calorie and protein requirements. The recorded rate of child malnutrition at the national level was of the order of 38.5 per cent (the second highest in Latin America). One child in four in the Sierra died before the age of five. One child in six in Lima died before age five. The recorded total fertility rate was of the order of 4.8 (four live births per mother) which suggests that for the Sierra there was on average an incidence of at least one child death per family unit (see Table 10.4). Yet Fujimori had been commended by the international financial community for his successful economic policies.

The IMF-World Bank Tutelage

"Get a serious economic programme in place and we will help you". The implementation of what the IMF calls a "serious economic programme" (in the words of Mr Martin Hardy, head of the IMF mission which visited Peru in 1991) is usually a precondition for the granting of bridge-financing by an "international support group". There were no "promises" by the international financial institutions attached to the implementation of the August 1990 economic package. The latter was an "IMF Shadow Programme" (see Chapter 2) with no loan money attached to it. While there were no undue pressures from the IMF, it was made clear that Peru would remain on the "black list" as long as it did not conform to IMF economic prescriptions.

The economic package, however, was implemented by the Fujimori government prior to the signing of a loan agreement and "before" reaching an agreement on the rescheduling of Peru's external debt. Once the first set of measures had been adopted, there was little left to negotiate. Moreover, immediately after the August 1990 "economic stabilisation" phase, the Peruvian authorities initiated a number of major structural reforms ("phase two") in conformity with IMF-World Bank prescriptions.

The Fujimori government had expected that the "economic shock" of August 1990 would immediately lead the way to the formation of an International Support Group and the granting of a "rescue package". There was, however, reluctance on the part of the creditors to form a support group. Peru was faithfully paying all its current debt-servicing

Table 10.4 : Undernourishment, Malnutrition and Infant Mortality

1. Undernourishment (deficient calorie and protein intake according to WHO/FAO standards)	
at national level (1991)	in excess of 83% of population*
2. Infant malnutrition (1985-86)	
at national level	38.5 %
rural areas	57.6 %
urban areas	24.2 %
3. Infant mortality less than one year (1985-86)	
Lima	61.4%
Sierra***	130-134%
4. Child Mortality less than five (1985-86)**	
Lima	16.5 %
Sierra***	26.5 %
5. Life expectancy at birth (years) (1985-86)	
Lima	67.7
Sierra	47.6-49.0

* author's estimate based on household expenditure data.
** percentage of children who die before age five estimated from mortality rates by specific age groups (Ministry of Health).
***based on rates recorded in Huancavelica and Cusco.

Source: Ministry of Health and ENNIV.

obligations and macro-economic policy was in conformity with the IMF menu.[14] From the point of view of the international creditors, there was, therefore, no need to grant "favours" to Peru (as in the cases of Egypt or Poland).

It was of course difficult for the government to adopt an independent stance, – i.e. "negotiate with the IMF" when IMF and World Bank officials were sitting in the Ministry of Economics and Finance. These advisors to the government were directly on IMF and World Bank payrolls "on loan" to Peru.[15] One of the senior advisors to Minister of Economics and Finance Carlos Boloña was an IMF staff member directly on the IMF payroll.

The Granting of Fictitious Money

At the outset, the government's main objective was to be removed from the IMF blacklist by unconditionally accepting to reimburse Peru's debt arrears to the International Financial Institutions (IFIs). This objective was to be achieved through the negotiation of "new loans" from the IFIs earmarked "to pay back old debts". (For further details see Chapter 2).[16] Not one dollar of this money would actually enter Peru. These "new loans" were money which the IFIs were "giving to themselves", they unconditionally legitimised the external debt (without a write-down), and obliged Peru to start servicing its debt arrears immediately. The loans from the IFIs granted in 1991 would have to be repaid over a period of three to five years. As a direct result of these new loans, Peru's debt-servicing obligations more than doubled in 1991 (from US$60 million a month to over $150 million).

The Role of the Military

Peru conformed faithfully to Washington's model of "democratisation". Prior to his inauguration in July 1990, Fujimori retreated in the armed forces compound in Lima for daily discussions with the military high command. A "deal" was struck between the president-elect and the military and a major reorganisation of the armed forces was carried out. This unconditional support of the armed forces was required to repress civil dissent and enforce the IMF programme. A few days before the Fujishock, a state of emergency was declared in the whole country. On 8 August 1990, the military and security forces had carefully cornered the entire Lima downtown area with troops, anti-riot forces and armoured vehicles.

Under the veil of "parliamentary democracy", the military under Fujimori increasingly took on a more active role in "civilian" administration. The situation at the outset of the Fujimori government was in some regards comparable to that which had developed in the early 1970s in Uruguay under President Bordaberry where the military ruled under the formal disguise of a civilian government.

The Collapse of the State

The IMF austerity measures were conducive to the phasing out of government programmes: the reduction of health and educational expenditures and the collapse of civil administration in the regions, etc. This state of affairs also contributed to discrediting the central government to the benefit of the Shining Path insurgents (*Sendero luminoso*) directed against the state.

From its involvement in civilian politics during the 1960s and 1970s, Sendero had developed as a clandestine organisation during the Belaunde government. Sendero was able to control and establish a parallel administration in some regions of the Selva and Sierra. In certain parts of the country, the Peruvian state had lost control over normal functions of civilian government. The application of the IMF's economic surgery in 1990-91 contributed to exacerbating this situation.

The state was losing control over the national territory, and this applied not only to areas of the Sierra and the Selva. Increasingly the insurgency by Sendero had permeated the Lima Metropolitan Area. The "pacification programme" initiated during the Belaunde government (and continued during the APRA and Cambio 90 governments) implied the handing over of the functions of civilian administration in the southern-central Sierra to the armed forces. Instead of curtailing Sendero, however, this strategy – combined with the failures of economic and social policy – contributed to the advancement of the insurgency. Moreover, the state, through its military and police apparatus, had officially sanctioned indiscriminate arrests, arbitrary and extra-judicial executions and torture of "political prisoners", and the arrest of family members and presumed "sympathizers" (amply documented by Amnesty International). In other words, "counter-insurgency" was marked by the curtailment of civil liberties, particularly among the poorer segments of society.[17] In 1988, right-wing death squadrons appeared under the name "Comando Rodrigo Franco"; their targets were left-wing personalities and trade-union leaders.

Under Fujimori, repression of the Shining Path insurgency became a pretext for systematic harassment by the security forces of civilian opposition to the IMF programme. From the outset of the Cambio 90 government, the indiscriminate torture and execution of "suspects" was applied far more systematically. The strategy of assassination and intimidation of civilian opposition directed against trade union, peasant and student leaders emanated directly from the military high command. In the so-called "dirty war" (*la guerra sucia*) with the Shining Path, the official guideline (with regard to the treatment of suspects) was "Neither prisoners nor wounded" (*ni prisoneros, ni heridos*) (as contained in a secret military document leaked to the press in 1991).[18]

The Plight of the Rural Economy

The IMF programme had an immediate impact on the rural economy: with the exception of the illegal coca cultivation, there was a major contraction in agricultural production in the year which followed the August 1990 shock treatment.

The impoverishment of the rural population was worsened by the continued control of marketing and distribution channels by powerful agro-industrial monopolies. Domestic producers were displaced as a result of the import of cheap agricultural staples. The 1990 economic measures were conducive to immediate and abrupt hikes in the prices of fuel, farm inputs, fertilisers, and agricultural credit: in many rural areas in the Sierra, costs of production increased well in excess of the farmgate price. The result was the bankruptcy of the small independent farmer. In the Sierra, for instance, some 800,000 producers of wool and alpaca fibres, who are among the poorest segment of the rural population, were further impoverished as a result of the decline of the real price of wool and alpaca fibres in 1990-91.

The Concentration of Land

The privatisation of agricultural land was conducive to undermining the existing structure of the rural economy characterised by small-scale individual production (*parcelero*) and agricultural communities (*comunidades agricolas*). The 1991 Land Law required a minimum unit of ownership of ten hectares. Land concentration was thus encouraged, leading to the strengthening of medium-sized holdings and the consolidation of a middle peasantry. *Parceleros* pushed into bankruptcy as a result of the economic reforms were obliged to sell or give up their land.[19] This initial process of land concentration was, however, but a first step towards the restructuring of agricultural ownership. Agricultural credit was also reformed. Production units below ten hectares were no longer eligible for agricultural credit.

In turn, the middle peasantry became firmly subordinated to banking and commercial interests through the mortgaging of their newly acquired land titles. The legislation introduced in 1991 was conducive to land forfeiture by the *parcelero* and the purchase of large amounts of land by urban commercial interests.

Whereas the peasant communities of the Sierra were formally "protected" from the privatisation of land, the increased prices of fuel and transportation contributed to cutting them out of the market economy. Farmgate prices had been pushed below costs. Many peasant communities which had previously sold their agricultural surplus in local markets were forced to withdraw totally from commercial agriculture.

There was a de facto return to subsistence agriculture. Commercial farm inputs such as seeds, fertiliser, etc, were no longer applied; the tendency was towards the consolidation of "traditional agriculture" marked by a dramatic decline in the levels of productivity of both the *parceleros* and the peasant communities. The countryside became increasingly polarised. The peasant communities impoverished as a result of structural adjustment could no longer survive without outside sources of income. Increasingly the peasant communities became "reserves of labour" for commercial agriculture.

The Illegal Narco-economy

The August 1990 economic shock created the conditions for the further growth of the drug trade. The contraction of internal demand for food, coupled with the lifting of tariffs on imported food staples, contributed to a serious recession in agricultural production. Combined with the subsequent repeal of the Agrarian Reform, impoverished peasants from the Sierra migrated to the coca producing areas in the Alto Huallaga Valley. In the Sierra, coca-cultivation as a cash crop for export started to develop on a significant scale.

Peru is by far the largest world producer of coca leaf used to produce cocaine (more than 60 per cent of total world production, the second most important producer being Bolivia) (see Chapter 11). Both Peru and Bolivia are the direct producers, selling coca paste to the Colombian drug cartels which process it into cocaine powder. With the clamping down of the Medellin cartel, however, there was in the early 1990s a shift in the marketing and processing channels and the development within Peru of commercial intermediaries and an increased use of the Peruvian banking system as a safe financial haven for transferring funds in and out of the country. The weakening of the Medellin cartel and the development of the Cali cartel initially favoured a greater "autonomy" of both Peru and Bolivia in the drug trade.

Moreover, a large amount of dollar bills from the drug economy had been channelled into the informal foreign-exchange market on Lima street corners (*el mercado Ocoña*). Since the Belaunde government (1980-85), the Central Bank had used the Ocoña street market periodically to replenish its failing international reserves. In other words, Peru's ability to meet its debt-servicing obligations depends on the recycling of narco-dollars into the local foreign-exchange market. In 1991, it was estimated that the Central Bank purchased some 8 million dollars a day in the informal foreign-exchange market of which a large part was earmarked to service Peru's external debt.

With the freeze of wages and government expenditure (imposed by the IMF), monetary issues by the Central Bank had been dramatically curtailed. Ironically, this tight monetary policy – combined with the inundation of the Ocoña market with dollar bills brought into the country with the illegal cocaine trade – had been conducive, as of early

1991, to the tumble of the American dollar against the Peruvian currency much to the dismay of the IMF which had insisted on a "real devaluation" in support of the export sector.

Internal demand had been compressed but so had exports: as a result of the economic measures, all sectors of the national economy with the exception of the illegal coca production were marked by deep recession.

The Anti-Drug Agreement with Washington

"Coca eradication programmes" by Washington had invariably been combined with counterinsurgency and "pacification" programmes, with strong military and intelligence backing to the Peruvian military and the police from the United States military and the US Drug Enforcement Administration (DEA). The latter had established a military base in Santa Lucia in the Huallaga region.[20]

Rather than weakening Sendero in the Alto Huallaga, however, these military operations enabled Shining Path to gain some element of support among coca producers. It is worth noting that under Fujimori, the military had become increasingly involved in the marketing of coca paste and the laundering of drug money.

The Anti-Drug Agreement signed in May 1991 with the US had a direct bearing on macro-economic policy. In the words of a witness to the US Senate committee:

> The President's [George Bush] national drug control strategy ... says that [US] economic aid is conditioned on drug control performance and the existence of sound economic policies.[21]

Yet ironically these same "sound economic policies" had largely contributed to the rapid development of the narco-economy. In other words, the economic reforms had encouraged the migration of impoverished peasants to the coca-producing areas.

Moreover, the macro-economic policies adopted under Fujimori, including the privatisation of agricultural land and the reform of the system of agricultural credit, had virtually destroyed from the outset the possibility of "an alternative development" in the Alto Huallaga valley as envisaged in the Anti-Drug Agreement. The latter was based on the substitution of coca by alternative cash crops (tobacco, maize, etc). Yet as a result of the IMF-sponsored reforms (which were also included as "cross-conditionalities" in the Anti-Drug Agreement), commercial agriculture in the Huallaga region – with the exception of the illegal coca production – was no longer viable.

The illicit narcotics trade had been reinforced as a result of of the structural adjustment programme. The legal economy had been undermined: the process of "crop substitution" was from the "alternative crops" (e.g. tobacco, maize, etc.) into coca marked by a steady increase in the acreage allocated to the cultivation of coca leaf (see Table 10.5).[22]

US Military and Security Objectives

A large part of US support under the agreement had been granted in the form of military aid. In other words, debt conditionalities were also being used by the US to pursue military and security objectives in the Andean region under the formal umbrella of the Anti-Drug Pro-

Table10.5: Coca Production in the Alto Huallaga Region (1974-91)

Year	Area	Production in metric tons	Population
1974	16,700	12,200	7,000
1978	21,540	18,120	9,900
1982	50,600	47,000	23,500
1986	60,200	61,000	27,350
1991	90,000	84,750	50,000

Source: Cooperativa "Alto Huallaga", Uchiza, *Agronoticias*, No. 138, June 1991, p. 14.

gramme. The latter had also strengthened the Peruvian military in the Alto Huallaga and consequently its ability to "protect" the narco-economy.

It is worth mentioning in this regard that there is ample evidence that the United States Central Intelligence Agency (CIA) has used the "laundering" of drug money to fund its covert operations and support pro-US military and para-military groups throughout the World.[23]

If Washington had really been interested in a solution to the drug trade, it would not have obliged Peru to adopt an economic policy under IMF guidance which strengthened the position of the narco-traders in alliance with the military.

Whereas one arm of the American state was involved in bona fide drug eradication programmes, another arm was doing exactly the opposite. The laundering of "dirty money" was also being reinforced by the IMF-sponsored reforms of the banking system and the foreign-exchange regime, allowing for the "free" movement of money in and out of the country. This strengthening of the narco-economy, however, also served the interests of Peru's international creditors because it contributed to generating the dollar revenues required for Peru to meet its debt-servicing obligations.

In other words, macro-economic reform undermined the legal economy, reinforced illicit trade and contributed to the recycling of "dirty money" towards Peru's official and commercial creditors.

Endnotes

1. *Cuanto*, Lima, September 1990.
2. These estimates are based on official statistics, see *Peru en Numeros, 1991, Annuario estadistico*, chapter 21, Cuanto, Lima, 1991, and *Cuanto Suplemento*, No. 13, July 1991.
3. Carlos Malpica, *El poder economico en el Peru*, Vol. I, Mosca Azul Editores, Lima, 1989.
4. The expansion of farm output was achieved through the expansion of aggregate demand and necessary consumption (*consumo popular*) rather than through the readjustment of the preferential exchange rate applying to the imports of basic food staples and the elimination of the subsidies (which essentially supported the agro-industrial monopolies). This indi-

cated that the development of agriculture required the maintenance of urban consumer demand.

5. See World Bank, *Peru, Policies to Stop Hyperinflation and Initiate Economic Recovery*, Washington, 1989, p. 10.
6. See Drago Kisic and Veronica Ruiz de Castilla, *La Economia peruana en el contexto internacional,* CEPEI, Vol. 2, No. 1, January 1989, pp. 58-9.
7. *Peru Economico*, August 1990, p. 26.
8. Another important factor was the decision of the Aprista government to revoke the convertibility of the foreign-exchange deposit certificates. This measure was adopted without assessing the nature of the foreign-exchange market and its relationship to the narco-economy.
9. The abuses pertaining to the (subsidised) "dollar MUC" have been amply documented: requests for MUC dollar allotments for the purpose of importing commodities were submitted to the Central Bank, the imports were not undertaken (or receipts were falsified indicating a transaction for a larger amount and the money was then converted into bona fide foreign exchange or back into local currency at a considerable profit). See for instance "Quien volo con los MUC", *Oiga*, No. 468, Lima, 5 February 1990, pp. 18-19.
10. See Kisic and Ruiz, *op. cit*, p. 60.
11. See Fernando Rospigliosi, "Izquierdas y clases populares: democracia y subversion en el Peru", in Julio Cotler (editor), *Clases populares, crisis y democracia en America Latina*, Instituto de Estudios Peruanos, Lima, 1989, p. 127.
12. See "Plan de Gobierno de Cambio 90: una propuesta para el Peru", *Pagina Libre*, 21 May 1990, pp. 17-24.
13. Based on author's interviews of health workers conducted in Peru in July 1991.
14. For further details see "Peru, Situación economica", *Situación latinoamericana*, Vol. 1, No. 2, April 1991, pp. 122-8.
15. Their daily consulting incomes of US$500-700 a day (including a "daily subsistence allowance" of some US$130 a day) was only slightly less than Peru's annual per capita income.
16. The IMF loans were to be granted in the form of "an accumulation of rights" clause. Debt arrears were estimated (1991) at approximately US$14 billion of which US$2.3 billion were with the IFIs.
17. A report by Amnesty International confirmed that approximately 3,000 people had "disappeared" (*desaparecidos*) between 1982 and 1989 and another 3,000 had been executed "extrajudicially". Amnesty also pointed to the practice of illegal detention and torture by the security forces and

the absence of sanctions directed against members of the security forces involved in assassinations and torture. *Pagina Libre*, 17 March 1990, p. A2. Cf. also *La Republica*, 11 February, 1990, p. 14.

18. See the secret documents revealed by the journalist Cesar Hildebrandt in the TV series *En Persona*, July 1991, which led to the closing down of the programme and the curtailment of most public-affairs TV programmes.
19. See *Alerta Agraria*, June 1991, p. 2.
20. Several other US institutions operated out of the Santa Lucia Military Base: the NAS (an affiliate of the DEA) and CORAH (a US project geared towards coca-crop eradication).
21. United States Senate, Committee on Governmental Affairs, *Cocaine Production, Eradication and the Environment: Policy, Impact and Options*, Washington, August 1990, p. 51 (italics added).
22. In the San Martin region (in the coca-producing region), areas under cultivation in "alternative crops" such as maize, rice and cocoa supported by credits from the Banco Agrario declined by 97% between 1988/89 to 1990/91, from 101,100 to 6,730 hectares. For further details see *Revista Agronoticias*, No. 138, Lima, June 1991, p. 7.
23. For a review of alleged CIA support to drug laundering in Indochina and the Golden Triangle since the early 1950s see Alfred McCoy, *The Politics of Heroin in Southeast Asia*, New York, Harper and Row, 1972.

Chapter 11

Debt and the Illegal Drug Economy: The Case of Bolivia

THE Bolivian experience is regarded by the Bretton Woods institutions as a "successful" model of structural adjustment to be emulated by countries "who want to stabilise their economy and establish a sustained process of economic growth". It is also worth noting the similarity between the Bolivian and Peruvian adjustment processes. Both economies depend heavily on illegal coca exports as their major source of foreign exchange. In both countries the "recycling" of narco-dollars constitutes a means for servicing the external debt.

Bolivia's New Economic Policy

In September 1985, the MNR government of Victor Paz Estenssoro initiated an orthodox economic stabilisation package ("Decreto Supremo 21,060") geared towards "combating inflation" and "eliminating internal and external imbalances". The economic package contained all the essential ingredients of the IMF structural adjustment programme. The currency was devalued, the exchange rate was unified and a foreign-exchange auction (*bolsin*) was set up.

Government expenditure was curtailed and some 50,000 public employees were laid off. A tight monetary policy was adopted together with the elimination of price controls. The deindexation of wages and the "liberalisation" of the labour market were adopted. The package also included the liberalisation of trade involving substantial reductions in import tariffs.[1]

The stabilisation programme was followed by a reorganisation of the state mining industry, the closing down of unprofitable mines and the firing of some 23,000 workers.

The architect of the Bolivian economic adjustment package Gonzalo Sanchez de Losada (who became President of Bolivia in 1993) described the events which followed the adoption of the New Economic Policy or Nueva Politica Economica (NPE) in August 1985 as follows:

> ...Once we implemented the measures, we had a general strike, the country was paralysed for ten days in September 1985 (...) On the tenth day, the union leaders declared a Hunger Strike, that was their big mistake. It was then that we decided to declare a state of emergency. [President] Paz had hoped that the people would be of the opinion that the situation could not continue that way. So we captured the union leaders and deported them to the interior of the country. This disarticulated the labour movement. We closed down COMIBOL, the state mining consortium and fired 24,000 workers in addition to some 50,000 public employees fired at a national level. We eliminated job security.[2]

The policy was, nonetheless, "successful" in bringing inflation under control within a matter of months. Prior to the adoption of the September 1985 measures, the rate of inflation was running at approximately 24,000 per cent per annum. The objective of price stabilisation, however, was achieved through the "dollarisation" of prices (rather than as a result of the economic stabilisation measures): "since most prices were de facto indexed to the exchange rate, stabilisation of the latter implied an almost immediate stabilisation of the former".[3]

A debt-reduction scheme was negotiated. Under this scheme, official donors would finance the "buy back" of Bolivia's commercial debt at a substantial discount from the commercial banks. The debt buy-back was conditional upon the adoption of the IMF programme.

Economic and Social Impact

The stabilisation package was conducive to a significant decline in the levels of employment and real earnings. In turn, the contraction of salaried earnings backfired on the informal urban sector and the rural economy. Reduced levels of purchasing power, combined with the impact of trade liberalisation (and the influx of cheap food imports), contributed to undermining the peasant economy which relied heavily on the internal market. Similarly, the lifting of tariffs contributed to the displacement of the national manufacturing industry. Commercial imports flourished largely at the expense of domestic production.

The levels of earnings and government expenditure had already declined dramatically in the first part of the 1980s during the Siles-Zuazo government. Yet in the immediate aftermath of the 1985 economic reforms, real government expenditure (particularly in the areas of health and education) was trimmed by a further 15 per cent.[4] While wages in the modern sector had declined (according to official data) by only 20 per cent, the number of people employed had fallen to abysmally low levels. With the reduction in modern-sector employment, largely through dismissals, the collapse in earnings was substantially higher than 20 per cent.

Programmed Economic Stagnation

The IMF programme initiated in 1985 contributed to the stagnation of all major sectors of the national economy (mining, industry and agriculture) with the exception of the illegal coca economy and the urban services sector. This pattern is comparable to that observed in Peru under Fujimori (see Chapter 10).

Stagnation in the mining industry (made up largely of the state mining consortium COMIBOL and a small sector of privately operated mines) resulted from the closing down of "unprofitable mines" (and the firing of workers) and the collapse of the international tin market. The decline in the terms of trade further exacerbated the impact of the economic reforms.

Severance payments to redundant miners were invested in the acquisition of land in the coca-producing areas by workers who had been laid off to the extent that both capital and labour were redirected towards the coca economy. The NPE provided no other alternative source of employment for workers laid off by COMIBOL.

The manufacturing sector (mainly geared towards the internal market) was in part displaced (e.g. textiles and agro-industry) as a result of the liberalisation of imports. The decline in internal purchasing power and the surge of smuggling activities also played an important role in pushing small-scale manufacturing enterprises into bankruptcy.

The Impact on the Rural Economy

Bolivia's agriculture consists of three distinct sub-sectors:

a) the peasant economy (*economia campesina*) characterised by small-scale agriculture (*parceleros*) and peasant communities (*comunidades campesinas*) concentrated in the Andean valleys and the Altiplano (high-plateaux). The peasant economy is the product of the Agrarian Reform of the 1950s and the dismantling of the landed estates (*haciendas*). As in Peru, the highlands' peasant communities are characterised by a high incidence of critical poverty (97 per cent of the rural population is classified as "poor" and between 48 and 77 per cent as "critically poor" (*pobreza critica*).[5]
b) a sub-sector of commercial farming geared largely towards the export market and characterised by medium- to large-sized plantations, particularly in the new (lowland) areas of agricultural colonisation (*llanos orientales*) (e.g. in the area of Santa Cruz).
c) the production of coca both for processing into coca paste and export as well as for "traditional" sale in the domestic market.

The NPE contributed to undermining the peasant economy. Local grain markets were affected by the influx of cheap food imports (e.g. wheat) including food aid and smuggling from Argentina and Brazil. This influx depressed the real prices of domestically produced food staples. Real agricultural wholesale prices declined by 25.9 per cent in the three years following the adoption of the NPE in 1985.

The decline in the (real) farmgate price was also accompanied by a significant rise in the margins between retail and wholesale prices. A larger share of the surplus was being appropriated by merchants and intermediaries to the detriment of the direct agricultural producers. The dramatic increase in transport costs was also a major factor in compressing the revenues of the peasantry and increasing the gap between the farmgate price and the wholesale price.[6]

The 1985 IMF-sponsored programme did not – with the exception of soya beans (located largely in the lowland areas of commercial farming) – contribute to increasing the production of cash crops for exports. As in Peru, there was a shift out of traditional export crops into the illegal coca economy.

The Laundering of Dirty Money

The national economic élites including the commercial banks were tied into the illegal drug trade. Government monetary and foreign-exchange policy upheld the role of commercial banking in the laundering of coca dollars.

The liberalisation of the foreign-exchange market through the Dutch auction system (*bolsin*) was accompanied by measures which provided legitimacy to the laundering of narco-dollars in the domestic banking system. The secrecy of foreign-exchange transactions *(el secreto bancario)* was introduced, the development of dollar deposits and the repatriation of capital to the domestic banking system were encouraged. Abnormally high interest rates (5 per cent above LIBOR) contributed to attracting "hot money deposits" into Bolivia's commercial banks.

These deposits also included the earnings from the drug trade accruing to Bolivian intermediaries. The bank secrecy (*"no questions asked"*), the reforms of the foreign-exchange regime which allowed for the free movement of money in and out of the country combined with the high interest rates encouraged the deposit of narco-dollars in the Bolivian commercial banking sector.

The reforms of the banking system contributed to a significant decline in real productive investment. From 1986 to 1988, the lending interest rate (in US dollars) was between 20 and 25 per cent per annum and credit to agriculture and manufacturing had been frozen.[7]

"Eradication" of Coca Production

While the macro-economic framework directly supported the narco-economy and the laundering of dirty money, the government had also adopted legislation with the support of the US Drug Enforcement Administration (DEA) with a view to curbing coca production. In accordance with their mandate under the relevant legislation (*Ley del regimen de la coca*), the government had set up mobile rural surveillance units (UMOPAR, *Unidad Movil de Patrullaje Rural*) in the coca-producing areas. These units, however, were largely involved in repressive actions directed against the small coca producer (often in areas of traditional production). Their activities had little impact on the narco-trade and the various powerful interests involved in the commercialisation and export of coca paste. According to one report, it has been suggested that UMOPAR was controlled by the drug mafia.[8]

The Narco-State

The coca economy had been "protected" at the highest level by officials of the Bolivian government during the dictatorship of Garcia Meza (1980-82) which was commonly labelled in international circles as the "government of cocaine".[9] The structure of the state was not modified, however, as a result of the restoration of parliamentary democracy. Important financial and industrial interests continue to have direct links to the coca trade including the use of coca-revenues to finance investments in the modern economy.

Since the mid-1970s, the development of the urban-services economy geared towards the upper-income market was largely financed by the narco-economy. The recycling of narco-dollars into domestic capital formation had been conducive to the development of residential real estate, shopping centres, tourist and entertainment infrastructure, etc. This process had been reinforced as a result of the IMF-sponsored programme.

With the adoption of the NPE in 1985, the ruling MNR party abandoned its populist stance and shifted its political allegiance by combining forces with the rightist Nationalist Democratic Action Party (ADN) of former dictator General Hugo Banzer. (This represented a political turn-around since historically the MNR had depended on the support of organised labour.)

Banzer had allegedly been a key figure in the illegal coca trade since the mid-1970s and there was firm evidence that members of the ADN parliamentary caucus, together with senior officers of the military, were connected to the drug mafia.[10]

The MNR/ADN "Pact for Democracy" enabled the MNR government to carry out the various components of the NPE legislation in parliament including the deregulation of the labour market and the repression of the labour movement.

ADN retained its involvement in the government coalition with the accession of President Paz Zamora of the MIR (Revolutionary Left) in 1989. Paz Zamora was the second runner-up in the 1989 presidential race after Hugo Banzer and the MNR candidate Gonzalo Sanchez de Losada. Paz acceded in 1989 to the presidency in the context of a political arrangement with General Hugo Banzer. Whereas Paz Zamora occupied the presidential seat, General Banzer and the ADN controlled key cabinet appointments.

The ADN/MIR government coalition pursued the macro-economic policies initiated with the NPE in 1985 under the MNR. ADN and its leader Hugo Banzer have thus provided, in the two democratically elected civilian governments, both political continuity as well as the maintenance of a cohesive link between government policy and the interests of the illegal coca trade.

Endnotes

1. For further details see Juan Antonio Morales, *The Costs of the Bolivian Stabilisation Programme*, documento de trabajo, no: 01/89, Universidad Catolica Boliviana, 1989, La Paz, p. 4.
2. Interview with Gonzalo Sanchez de Lozada, minister of finance under the MNR government of Paz Estenssoro and architect of the Bolivian economic package, *Caretas*, No: 1094, Lima, 5 February, 1990, p. 87 (our translation).
3. Morales, op. cit., p. 6.
4. Morales, op. cit., p. 9a.
5. See Morales, op. cit., p. 6. See also Juan Antonio Morales, *Impacto de los ajustes estructurales en la agricultura campesina boliviana*, mimeo, Universidad Catolica Boliviana, 1989, La Paz.
6. See Morales, *The Costs of the Bolivian Stabilisation Programme,* pp. 24a-25a.
7. The borrowing rate was between 12 and 16 per cent with a spread between lending and borrowing rates of between 6.8 and 14.0 per cent. For further details see Morales, *The Costs of the Bolivian Stabilisation Programme,* p. 14, Table 7.

8. For details on the involvement of major political and social personalities in the narco-trade, see Amalia Barron, "Todos implicados en el narcotrafico", *Cambio 16*, Madrid, 8 August 1988.
9. See Henry Oporto Castro, "Bolivia: El complejo coca-cocaina" in Garcia Sayan (editor), *Coca, cocaina y narcotrafico*, Comision Andina de Juristas, Lima, 1989, p. 177.
10. See G. Lora, *Politica y burguesia narcotraficante*, Mi Kiosco, La Paz, 1988.

PART V

The Former Soviet Union and the Balkans

Chapter 12

The "Thirdworldisation" of the Russian Federation

Macro-Economic Reform in the Russian Federation Phase I: The January 1992 Shock Treatment

"IN Russia we are living in a post-war situation...", but there is no post-war reconstruction. "Communism" and the "Evil Empire" have been defeated yet the Cold War, although officially over, has not quite reached its climax: the heart of the Russian economy is the military-industrial complex and "the G-7 wants to break our high tech industries...the objective of the IMF economic programme is to weaken us" and prevent the development of a rival capitalist power.[1]

The IMF-style "shock treatment" initiated in January 1992 precluded from the outset a transition towards "national capitalism", – i.e. a national capitalist economy owned and controlled by a Russian entrepreneurial class and supported as in other major capitalist nations by the economic and social policies of the state. For the West, the enemy was not "socialism" but capitalism. How to tame and subdue the polar bear, how to take over the talent, the science, the technology, how to buy out the human capital, how to acquire the intellectual property rights? "If the West thinks that they can transform us into a cheap labour high technology export haven and pay our scientists US$40 a month, they are grossly mistaken, the people will rebel..."[2]

While narrowly promoting the interests of both Russia's merchants and the business mafias, the "economic medicine" was killing the patient, destroying the national economy and pushing the system of state enterprises into bankruptcy. Through the deliberate manipulation of market forces, the reforms had defined which sectors of economic activity would be allowed to survive. Official figures pointed to a decline of 27 per cent in industrial production during the first year of the reforms; the actual collapse of the Russian economy in 1992 was estimated by some economists to be of the order of 50 per cent.[3]

The IMF-Yeltsin reforms constitute an instrument of "Thirdworldisation"; they are a carbon copy of the structural adjustment programme imposed on debtor countries in Latin America and sub-Saharan Africa. Harvard economist Jeffrey Sachs, advisor to the Russian government, had applied in Russia the same "macro-economic surgery" as in Bolivia where he was economic advisor to the MNR government in 1985 (see Chapter 11). The IMF-World Bank programme adopted in the name of democracy constitutes a coherent programme of impoverishment of large sectors of the population. It was designed (in theory) to "stabilise" the economy, yet consumer prices in 1992 increased by more than one hundred times (9,900 per cent) as a direct result of the "anti-inflationary programme".[4] As in Third World "stabilisation programmes", the inflationary process was largely engineered through the "dollarisation" of domestic prices and the collapse of the national currency. The "price liberalisation programme" did not, however, resolve (as proposed by the IMF) the distorted structure of relative prices which existed under the Soviet system.

The price of bread increased (by more than a hundred times) from 13-18 kopeks in December 1991 (before the reforms) to over 20 roubles in October 1992; the price of a (domestically produced) television set rose from 800 roubles to 85,000 roubles. Wages, in contrast, increased approximately ten times, – i.e. real earnings had declined by more than 80 per cent and billions of roubles of life-long savings had been wiped out. Ordinary Russians were very bitter: "the government has stolen our money".[5] According to an IMF official, it was necessary to "sop up excess liquidity, purchasing power was too high...",[6] "the government opted for 'a maximum bang'" so as to eliminate household money holdings "at the beginning of the reform programme".[7] According to one World Bank advisor, these savings "were not real, they were only a perception because [under the Soviet system] they [the people] were not allowed to buy anything".[8] An economist of the Russian Academy of Science saw things differently:

> Under the Communist system, our standard of living was never very high. But everybody was employed and basic human needs and essential social services although second-

> rate by Western standards, were free and available. But now social conditions in Russia are similar to those in the Third World.[9]

Average earnings were below US$10 a month (1992-3), the minimum wage (1992) was of the order of US$3 a month, a university professor earned US$8, an office worker US$7, a qualified nurse in an urban clinic earned US$6.[10] With the prices of many consumer goods moving rapidly up to world-market levels, these rouble salaries were barely sufficient to buy food. A winter coat could be purchased for US$60, the equivalent of nine months pay.[11]

The collapse in the standard of living engineered as a result of macro-economic policy is without precedent in Russian history: "We had more to eat during the Second World War".

Under IMF-World Bank guidelines, social programmes are to become self-financing: schools, hospitals and kindergartens (not to mention state-supported programmes in sports, culture and the arts) were instructed to generate their own sources of revenue through the exaction of user fees.[12] Charges for surgery in hospitals were equivalent to two to six months earnings which only the "*nouveaux riches*" could afford. Not only hospitals but theatres and museums were driven into bankruptcy. The famous Taganka Theatre was dismantled in 1992, many small theatres no longer had the funds to pay their actors. The reforms were conducive to the collapse of the welfare state. Many of the achievements of the Soviet system in health, education, culture and the arts (broadly acknowledged by Western scholars) have been undone.[13]

Continuity with the *ancien régime* was nonetheless maintained. Under the masque of liberal democracy, the totalitarian state remained unscathed: a careful blend of Stalinism and the "free" market. From one day to the next, Yeltsin and his cronies had become fervent partisans of neoliberalism. One totalitarian dogma was replaced by another, social reality was distorted, official statistics on real earnings were falsified: the IMF claimed in late 1992, that the standard of living "had gone up" since the beginning of the economic reform programme.[14] The Russian Ministry of Economy maintained that "wages were growing faster than prices".[15] In 1992, the consumer price index computed with the technical support of the IMF, pointed to a 15.6 times increase in prices (1,660 per cent).[16] "But the people are not stupid, we simply do not believe them [the government]; we know that prices have gone up one hundred times"[17]

The Legacy of Perestroika

During the period of perestroika, buying at state-regulated prices and reselling in the free market combined with graft and corruption were the principal sources of wealth formation. These "shadow dealings" by former bureaucrats and party members became legalised in May 1988 with the Law on Cooperatives implemented under Mikhail Gorbachev.[18] This law allowed for the formation of private commercial enterprises and joint-stock companies which operated alongside the system of state enterprises. In many instances, these "cooperatives" were set up as private ventures by the managers of state enterprises. The latter would sell (at official prices) the output produced by their state enterprise to their privately owned "cooperatives" (i.e. to themselves) and then resell on the free market at a very large profit. In 1989, the "cooperatives" were allowed to create their own commercial banks, and undertake foreign-trade transactions. By retaining a dual price system, the 1987-89 enterprise reforms rather than encouraging bona fide capitalist entrepreneurship, supported personal enrichment, corruption and the development of a bogus "bazaar bourgeoisie".

Developing a Bazaar Bourgeoisie

In the former Soviet Union, "the secret of primitive accumulation" is based on the principle of "quick money": stealing from the state and buying at one price and re-selling at another. The birth of Russia's new "*biznesmany*", an offshoot of the Communist nomenclatura of the Brezhnev period, lies in the development of "apparatchik capitalism". "Adam bit the apple and original sin fell upon 'socialism'".[19]

Not surprisingly, the IMF programme had acquired unconditional political backing by the "Democrats", – i.e. the IMF reforms supported the narrow interests of this new merchant class. The Yeltsin government unequivocally upheld the interests of these "dollarised élites". Price liberalisation and the collapse of the rouble under IMF guidance advanced the enrichment of a small segment of the population. The dollar was handled on the Interbank currency auction; it was also freely transacted in street kiosks across the former Soviet Union. The reforms have meant that the rouble is no longer considered a safe "store of value", – i.e. the plunge of the national currency was further exacerbated because ordinary citizens prefered to hold their household savings in dollars: "people are willing to buy dollars at any price". [20]

Distorting Social Relations

The Cold War was a war without physical destruction. In its cruel aftermath, the instruments of macro-economic policy perform a decisive role in dismantling the economy of a defeated nation. The reforms are not intent (as claimed by the West) in building market capitalism and Western style socio-democracy but in neutralising a former enemy and forestalling the development of Russia as a major capitalist power. Also of significance is the extent to which the economic measures have contributed to destroying civil society and distorting fundamental social relations: the criminalisation of economic activity, the looting of state property, money laundering and capital flight are bolstered by the reforms. In turn, the privatisation programme (through the public auction of state enterprises) also favoured the transfer of a significant portion of state property to organised crime. The latter permeates the state apparatus and constitutes a powerful lobby broadly supportive of Yeltsin's macro-economic reforms. According to a recent estimate, half of Russia's commercial banks were by 1993 under the control of the local mafias, and half of the commercial real estate in central Moscow was in the hands of organised crime.[21]

Pillage of the Russian Economy

The collapse of the rouble was instrumental in the pillage of Russia's natural resources: oil, non-ferrous metals and strategic raw materials could be bought by Russian merchants in roubles from a state factory and resold in hard currency to traders from the European Community at ten times the price. Crude oil, for instance, was purchased at 5,200 roubles (US$17) a ton (1992), an export licence was acquired by bribing a corrupt official and the oil was resold on the world market at $150 a ton.[22] The profits of this transaction were deposited in offshore bank accounts or channelled towards luxury consumption (imports). Although officially illegal, capital flight and money laundering were facilitated by the deregulation of the foreign-exchange market and the reforms of the banking system. Capital flight was estimated to be running at over $1 billion a month during the first phase of the IMF reforms (1992).[23] There is evidence that prominent members of the political establishment had been transferring large amounts of money overseas.

Undermining Russian Capitalism

What role will "capitalist Russia" perform in the international division of labour during a period of global economic crisis? What will be the fate of Russian industry in a depressed global market? With plant closures in Europe and North America, "is there room for Russian capitalism" on the world market? Macro-economic policy under IMF guidance shapes Russia's relationship to the global economy. The reforms tend to support the free and unregulated export of primary goods including oil, strategic metals and food staples, while consumer goods including luxury cars, durables and processed food are freely imported for a small privileged market but there is no protection of domestic industry, nor are there any measures to rehabilitate the industrial sector or to transform domestic raw materials. Credit for the purchase of equipment is frozen, the deregulation of input prices (including oil, energy and freight prices) is pushing Russian industry into bankruptcy.

Moreover, the collapse in the standard of living has backlashed on industry and agriculture, – i.e. the dramatic increase in poverty does not favour the growth of the internal market. Ironically, from "an economy of shortage" under the Soviet system (marked by long queues), consumer demand has been compressed to such an extent that the population can barely afford to buy food.

In contrast, the enrichment of a small segment of the population has encouraged a dynamic market for luxury goods including long queues in front of the dollar stores in Moscow's fashionable Kuznetsky area. The *"nouveaux riches"* look down on domestically produced goods: Mercedes Benz, BMW, Paris *haute couture*, not to mention high-quality imported "Russian vodka" from the United States at

US$345 in a crystal bottle (four years of earnings of an average worker) are preferred. This "dynamic demand" by the upper-income groups is therefore largely diverted into consumer imports financed through the pillage of Russia's primary resources.

Acquiring State Property "at a Good Price"

The enormous profits accruing to the new commercial élites are also recycled into buying state property "at a good price" (or buying it from the managers and workers once it has gone through the government's privatisation scheme). Because the recorded book-value of state property (denominated in current roubles) was kept artificially low (and because the rouble was so cheap), state assets could be acquired for practically nothing.[24] A high-tech rocket production facility could be purchased for US$1 million. A downtown Moscow hotel could be acquired for less than the price of a Paris apartment. In October 1992, the Moscow City government put a large number of apartments on auction; bids were to start at three roubles.

While the former nomenclatura, the new commercial élites and the local mafias are the only people who have money (and who are in a position to acquire property), they have neither the skills nor the foresight to manage Russian industry. It is unlikely that they will play a strong and decisive role in rebuilding Russia's economy. As in many Third World countries, these "compradore" élites prosper largely through their relationship to foreign capital.

Moreover, the economic reforms favour the displacement of national producers (whether state or private) and the taking over of large sectors of the national economy by foreign capital through the formation of joint ventures. Marlboro and Philip Morris, the American tobacco giants, for instance, have already acquired control over state production facilities for sale in the domestic market; British Airways has gained access to domestic air-routes through Air Russia, a joint venture with Aeroflot.

Important sectors of light industry are being closed down and replaced by imports whereas the more profitable sectors of the Russian economy (including the high-tech enterprises of the military-industrial complex) are being taken over by joint ventures. Foreign capital, however, has adopted a wait-and-see attitude. The political situation is uncertain, the risks are great: "we need guarantees regarding the ownership of land, and the repatriation of profits in hard currency".[25] Many foreign enterprises prefer to enter "through the back door" with small investments. These often involve joint ventures or the purchase of domestic enterprises at a very low cost, largely to secure control over (highly qualified) cheap labour and factory space.

Weakening Russia's High-Tech Economy

Export processing is being developed in the high-tech areas. It constitutes a very lucrative business: Lockheed Missile and Space Corporation, Boeing and Rockwell International among others have their eye on the aerospace and aircraft industries. American and European high-tech firms (including defence contractors) can purchase the services of top Russian scientists in fibre optics, computer design, satellite technology, nuclear physics (to name but a few) for an average wage below US$100 a month, at least 50 times less that in Silicon Valley. There are 1.5 million scientists and engineers in the former Soviet Union representing a sizeable reserve of "cheap human capital".[26]

Macro-economic policy supports the interests of Western high-tech firms and military contractors because it weakens the former Soviet aerospace and high-tech industries and blocks Russia (as a capitalist power in its own right) from competing on the world market. The talent and scientific know-how can be bought up and the production facilities can either be taken over or closed down.

A large share of the military-industrial complex is under the jurisdiction of the Ministry of Defence. Carried out under its auspices, the various "conversion programmes" negotiated with NATO and Western defence ministries aim at dismantling that complex, including its civilian arm, and preventing Russia from becoming a potential rival in the world market. The conversion schemes purport physically to demobilise Russia's productive capabilities in the military, avionics and high-tech areas while facilitating the take-over and control by Western capital of Russia's knowledge base (intellectual property rights) and human capital, including her scientists, engineers and research institutes. AT&T Bell Laboratories, for instance, has acquired through a "joint venture" the services of an entire research laboratory at the General Physics Institute in Moscow. McDonnell

Douglas has signed a similar agreement with the Mechanical Research Institute.[27]

Under one particular conversion formula, military hardware and industrial assets were "transformed" into scrap metal which was sold on the world commodity market. The proceeds of these sales were then deposited into a fund (under the Ministry of Defence) which could be used for the imports of capital goods, the payment of debt-servicing obligations or investment in the privatisation programmes.

Taking Over Russia's Banking System

Since the 1992 reforms and the collapse of many state banks, some 2,000 commercial banks have sprung up in the former Soviet Union of which 500 are located in Moscow. With the breakdown of industry, only the strongest banks and those with ties to international banks will survive. This situation favours the penetration of the Russian banking system by foreign commercial banks and joint-venture banks.

Undermining the Rouble Zone

The IMF programme was also intent on abolishing the rouble zone and undermining trade between the former republics. The latter were encouraged from the outset to establish their own currencies and central banks with technical assistance provided by the IMF. This process supported "economic Balkanisation": with the collapse of the rouble zone, regional economic power serving the narrow interests of local tycoons and bureaucrats unfolded.

Bitter financial and trade disputes between Russia and the Ukraine have developed. Whereas trade is liberalised with the outside world, new "internal boundaries" were installed, impeding the movement of goods and people within the Commonwealth of Independent States.[28]

Phase II: The IMF Reforms Enter an Impasse

The IMF-sponsored reforms (under Prime Minister Yegor Gaidar) entered an impasse in late 1992. Opposition had built up in parliament as well as in the Central Bank. The IMF conceded that if the government were to meet the target for the fiscal deficit, up to 40 per cent of industrial plants might have been forced to close down. The president of the Central Bank, Mr. Gerashchenko with support from Arcady Volsky of the Civic Union Party, took the decision (against the advice of the IMF) to expand credit to the state enterprises, while at the same time cutting drastically expenditures in health, education and old-age pensions. The Civic Union had put forth an "alternative programme" in September 1992. Despite the subsequent replacement of Yegor Gaidar as prime minister in the parliamentary crisis of December 1992, the Civic Union's programme was never carried out.

The IMF had nonetheless agreed in late 1992 to the possibility of "the less orthodox" approach of the centrist Civic Union prior to Gaidar's dismissal. In the words of the IMF resident representative in Moscow: "the IMF is not married to Gaidar, he has a similar economic approach but we will work with his successor".

At the beginning of 1993, the relationship between the government and the parliament evolved towards open confrontation. Legislative control over the government's budgetary and monetary policy served to undermine the "smooth execution" of the IMF programme. The parliament had passed legislation which slowed down the privatisation of state industry, placed restrictions on foreign banks and limited the government's ability to slash subsidies and social expenditures as required by the IMF.[29]

Opposition to the reforms had largely emanated from within the ruling political élites, from the moderate centrist faction (which included former Yeltsin collaborators). While representing a minority within the parliament, the Civic Union (also involving the union of industrialists led by Arcady Volsky) favoured the development of national capitalism while maintaining a strong role for the central state. The main political actors in Yeltsin's confrontation with the parliament (e.g. Alexander Rutskoi and Ruslan Khasbulatov), therefore, cannot be categorised as "Communist hardliners".

The government was incapable of completely bypassing the legislature. Both houses of parliament were suspended by presidential decree on 21 September 1993.

Abolishing the Parliament in the Name of "Governance"

On 23 September, two days later, Mr. Michel Camdessus, the IMF managing director, hinted that the second tranche of a US$3 billion loan under the IMF's systemic transformation facility (STF) would not be forthcoming because "Russia had failed to meet its commitments" largely as a result of parliamentary encroachment. (The STF loan is similar in form to the structural adjustment loans negotiated with indebted Third World countries, see Chapter 2.)

President Clinton had stated at the Vancouver Summit in April 1993 that Western "aid" was tied to the implementation of "democratic reform". The conditions set by the IMF and the Western creditors, however, could only be met by suspending parliament altogether (a not unusual practice in many indebted Third World countries). The storming of the White House by élite troops and mortar artillery was thus largely intent on neutralising political dissent from within the ranks of the nomenclatura both in Moscow and the regions, and getting rid of individuals opposing IMF-style reform.

The G7 had endorsed President Yeltsin's decree abolishing both houses of parliament prior to its formal enactment and their embassies in Moscow had been briefed ahead of time. The presidential decree of 21 September was immediately followed by a wave of decrees designed to speed up the pace of economic reform and meet the conditionalities contained in the IMF loan agreement signed by the Russian government in May: credit was immediately tightened and interest rates raised, measures were adopted to increase the pace of privatisation and trade liberalisation. In the words of Minister of Finance Mr. Boris Fyodorov, now freed from parliamentary control: "we can bring in any budget that we like".[30]

The timing of President Yeltsin's decree was well chosen: Yeltsin's finance minister Boris Fyodorov was scheduled to report to the G7 meeting of finance ministers on 25 September, the foreign minister Mr. Andrei Kosyrev was in Washington meeting President Clinton, the IMF-World Bank annual meeting was scheduled to commence in Washington on the 28 September, and 1 October had been set as a deadline for a decision on the IMF's standby loan prior to the holding in Frankfurt of the meeting of the London Club of commercial bank creditors (chaired by the Deutsche Bank) on 8 October. And on

Table 12.1: Storming the Russian Parliament, A Macro-Economic Chronology September–October 1993

Date	Event
13 September	President Yeltsin calls back Yegor Gaidar into the government
20 September	G7 embassies are advised of the suspension of parliament.
21 September	Boris Yeltsin dissolves parliament and abrogates the constitution.
22 September	G7 messages of support to Boris Yeltsin.
23 September	Michel Camdessus, managing director of IMF, states that Russia's economic reforms are not on track.
	A wave of economic decrees is initiated by Yegor Gaidar.
24 September	Troops and riot police encircle the White House.
25 September	The finance minister Mr. Boris Fyodorov meets G7 finance ministers.
28 September	The annual meeting of the IMF and World Bank opens in Washington; Boris Fyodorov meets Michel Camdessus.
	IMF mission of economists is in Moscow to monitor progress of economic reforms.
1 October	Deadline date for decision by IMF regarding stand-by loan.
4 October	Storming of the White House.
4 October	Decision by the IMF (based on economists' mission report) to delay loan disbursements.
5 October	The US, the European Community and Japan support Yeltsin's decision to crush the parliamentary revolt.
	Massive purges of Yeltsin opponents begin in Moscow and the regions.
8 October	Meeting in Frankfurt of the London Club pertaining to the rescheduling of Russia's debt with the commercial banks.
12 October	Boris Yeltsin arrives in Tokyo.
14 October	Price of bread increases from 100 to 300 roubles.

Financial Times, September and October 1993, several issues.

12 October, President Yeltsin was to travel to Japan to initiate negotiations on the fate of four Kuril islands in exchange for debt relief and Japanese "aid".

Following the suspension of parliament, the G7 expressed "their very strong hope that the latest developments will help Russia achieve a decisive breakthrough on the path of market reforms".[31] The German minister of finance Mr. Theo Wagel said that "Russian leaders must make it clear that economic reforms would continue or they would lose international financial aid". Mr. Michel Camdessus expressed hope that political developments in Russia would contribute to "stepping up the process of economic reform".

Yet despite Western encouragement, the IMF was not yet prepared to grant Russia the "greenlight": Mr. Viktor Gerashchenko, the pro-Civic Union president of the Central Bank, was still formally in control of monetary policy; an IMF mission which travelled to Moscow in late September 1993 (during the heat of the parliamentary revolt), had advised Michel Camdessus that "plans already announced by the government for subsidy cuts and controls over credit were insufficient".[32]

The impact of the September 1993 economic decrees was almost immediate: the decision to further liberalise energy prices and to increase interest rates served the objective of rapidly pushing large sectors of Russian industry into bankruptcy. With the deregulation of Roskhlebprodukt, the state bread distribution company, in mid-October 1993, bread prices increased overnight by three to four times.[33] It is worth emphasising that this "second wave" of impoverishment of the Russian people was occurring in the aftermath of an estimated 86 per cent decline in real purchasing power in 1992![34] Since all subsidies were financed out of the state budget, the money saved could be redirected (as instructed by the IMF) towards the servicing of Russia's external debt.

The reform of the fiscal system proposed by Finance Minister Boris Fyodorov in the aftermath of the September 1993 coup followed the World Bank formula imposed on indebted Third World countries. It required "fiscal autonomy" for the republics and local governments by cutting the flow of revenue from Moscow to the regions and diverting the central state's financial resources towards the reimbursement of the creditors. The consequences of these reforms were fiscal collapse, economic and political Balkanisation, and enhanced control of Western and Japanese capital over the economies of Russia's regions.

"Western Aid" to Boris Yeltsin

By 1993, the reforms had led to the massive plunder of Russia's wealth resulting in a significant outflow of real resources: the balance of payments deficit for 1993 was of the order of US$40 billion, approximately the amount of "aid" ($43 billion) pledged by the G7 at its Tokyo Summit in 1993. Yet most of this Western "aid" was fictitious: it was largely in the form of loans (rather than grant aid) which served the "useful" purpose of enlarging Russia's external debt (of the order of $80 billion in 1993) and strengthening the grip of Western creditors over the Russian economy.

Russia was being handled by the creditors in much the same way as a Third World country: out of a total of US$43.4 billion which had been pledged in 1993 less than $3 billion was actually disbursed. Moreover, the agreement reached with the Paris Club regarding the rescheduling of Russia's official debt – while "generous" at first sight – in reality offered Moscow a very "short breathing space".[35] Only the debt incurred during the Soviet era was to be rescheduled;[36] the massive debts incurred by the Yeltsin government (ironically largely as a result of the economic reforms) were excluded from these negotiations.

With regard to bilateral pledges, President Clinton offered a meagre US$1.6 billion at the Vancouver Summit in 1993, $970 million was in the form of credits mainly for food purchases from US farmers and $630 million was arrears on Russian payments for US grain to be financed by tapping "The Food for Progress Programme" of the US Department of Agriculture, thus putting Russia on the same footing as countries in sub-Saharan Africa in receipt of US food aid under PL 480. Similarly the bulk of Japanese bilateral "aid" to Russia were funds earmarked for "insurance for Japanese companies" investing in Russia.[37]

Into the Strait-jacket of Debt-Servicing

The elimination of parliamentary opposition in September 1993 resulted in an immediate shift in Moscow's debt-negotiation strategy with the commercial banks. Again the timing was of critical importance. No "write-off" or "write-down" of Russia's commercial debt was requested by the Russian negotiating team at the Frankfurt meetings of the London Club held in early October 1993, only four days after the storming of the White House. Under the proposed deal, the date of reckoning would be temporarily postponed, US$24 out of US$38 billion of commercial debt would be rescheduled. All the conditions of the London Club were accepted by Moscow's negotiating team, with the exception of Russia's refusal to waive its "sovereign immunity to legal action". This waiver would have enabled the creditor banks to impound Russia's state enterprises and confiscate physical assets if debt-servicing obligations were not met. For the commercial banks, this clause was by no means a formality: with the collapse of Russia's economy, a balance of payments crisis, accumulated debt-servicing obligations due to the Paris Club, Russia was being pushed into a "technical moratorium", – i.e. a situation of *de facto* default.

The foreign creditors had also contemplated mechanisms for converting Russia's foreign-exchange reserves (at the Central Bank as well as dollar deposits in Russian commercial banks) into debt-servicing. They also had their eye on foreign-exchange holdings held by Russians in offshore bank accounts.

The IMF's economic medicine was not only devised to enforce debt-servicing obligations, it was also intent on "enlarging the debt". The reforms contributed to crippling the national economy thereby creating a greater dependency on external credit. In turn, debt default was paving the way towards a new critical phase in Moscow's relationship to the creditors. In the image of a subservient and compliant Third World regime, the Russian state was caught in the strait-jacket of debt and structural adjustment: state expenditures were brutally slashed to release state funds to reimburse the creditors.

The Collapse of Civil Society

As the crisis deepened, the population became increasingly isolated and vulnerable. "Democracy" had been formally installed but the new political parties, divorced from the masses, were largely heeding the interests of merchants and bureaucrats. The impact of the privatisation programme on employment was devastating: more than 50 per cent of industrial plants had been driven into bankruptcy by 1993.[38] Moreover, entire cities in the Urals and Siberia belonging to the military-industrial complex and dependent on state credits and procurements were in the process of being closed down. In 1994 (according to official figures), workers at some 33,000 indebted enterprises including state industrial corporations and collective farms were not receiving wages on a regular basis.[39]

The tendency was not solely towards continued impoverishment and massive unemployment. A much deeper fracturing of the fabric of Russian society was unfolding, including the destruction of its institutions and the possible break-up of the Russian Federation. G7 policy-makers should carefully assess the consequences of their actions in the interests of world peace. The global geopolitical and security risks are far-reaching; the continued adoption of the IMF economic package spells disaster for Russia and the West.

Endnotes

1. Interview with an economist of the Russian Academy of Science, Moscow, October 1992.
2. Ibid.
3. A 50 per cent decline in relation to the average of the previous three years. Interviews with several economists of the Russian Academy of Science, Moscow, September 1992.
4. Based on author's compilation of price increases over the period December 1991-October 1992 of some 27 essential consumer goods including food, transportation, clothing and consumer durables.
5. According to the government's official statement to the Russian Parliament, wages increased 11 times from January to September 1992.
6. Interview with the head of the IMF Resident Mission, Moscow, September 1992.

7. See World Bank, *Russian Economic Reform, Crossing the Threshold of Structural Reform*, Washington DC, 1992, p. 18.
8. Interview with a World Bank advisor, Moscow, October 1992.
9. Interview with an economist of the Russian Academy of Science, Moscow, September 1992.
10. Interview in a Moscow polyclinic, interviews with workers in different sectors of economic activity, Moscow and Rostow on the Don, September-October 1992. See also Jean-Jacques Marie, "Ecole et santé en ruines", *Le Monde diplomatique*, June 1992, p. 13.
11. The price and wage levels are those prevailing in September-October 1992. The exchange rate in September 1992 was of the order of 300 roubles to the dollar.
12. For further details see Jean Jacques Marie, op. cit.
13. There is a failure on the part of the Russian economic advisors to uncover the theoretical falsehoods of the IMF economic framework. There is no analysis on how the IMF policy package actually works, and little knowledge in the former Soviet Union of policy experiences in other countries, including sub-Saharan Africa, Latin America and Eastern Europe.
14. Interview with IMF official, Moscow, September 1992.
15. See *Delovoi Mir* (*Business World*), No. 34, 6 September 1992, p. 14.
16. During the first nine months of 1992.
17. Interview with ordinary Russian citizens, Rostov on the Don, October 1992.
18. See International Monetary Fund, World Bank, Organisation for Economic Cooperation and Development and European Bank for Reconstruction and Development, *A Study of the Soviet Economy*, Vol. 1, Paris, 1991, part II, chapter 2.
19. Paraphrase of "Adam bit the apple and thereupon sin fell on the human race" in Karl Marx "On Primitive Accumulation", *Capital* (book 1).
20. See "Rouble Plunges to New Low", *Moscow Times*, 2 October 1992, p. 1.
21. See Paul Klebnikov, "Stalin's Heirs", *Forbes*, 27 September 1993, pp. 124-34.
22. The government is said to have issued export licences in 1992 covering two times the recorded exports of crude petroleum.
23. According to estimates of the Washington-based International Institute of Banking.
24. It is estimated that with a purchase of US$1,000 of state property (according to the book value of the enterprise), one acquires real assets of a value of $300,000.

25. Interview with a Western commercial bank executive, Moscow, October 1992.
26. See Tim Beardsley, "Selling to Survive", *Scientific American*, February 1993, pp. 94-100.
27. Ibid.
28. With technical assistance from the World Bank, a uniform tariff on imports was designed for the Russian Federation.
29. The Central Bank was under the jurisdiction of parliament. In early September 1993, an agreement was reached whereby the Central Bank would be responsible to both the government and the parliament.
30. Quoted in *Financial Times*, 23 September 1993, p. 1.
31. Ibid., p. 1.
32. According to *Financial Times*, 5 October 1993.
33. See Leyla Boulton, "Russia's Breadwinners and Losers", *Financial Times*, 13 October 1993, p. 3.
34. Chris Doyle, *The Distributional Consequences of Russia's Transition*, Discussion Paper no. 839, Centre for Economic Policy Research, London, 1993. This estimate is consistent with the author's evaluation of price movements of basic consumer goods over the period December 1991–October 1992. Official statistics (which are grossly manipulated) acknowledge a 56 per cent collapse in purchasing power since mid-1991.
35. The amount eligible for restructuring pertained to the official debt contracted prior to January 1991 (US$17 billion). Two billion were due in 1993, 15 billion were rescheduled over 10 years with a five-year grace period.
36. Only debt incurred prior to the cut-off date (January 1991) was to be rescheduled; 15 out of $17 billion were rescheduled, $2 billion were due to the Paris Club in 1993.
37. See *The Wall Street Journal*, New York, 12 October 1993, p. A17. See also Allan Saunderson, "Legal Wrangle Holds Up Russian Debt Deal", *The European*, 14-17 October 1993, p. 38.
38. The World Bank has recommended to the government to "fracturise" large enterprises, that is to break them up into smaller entities.
39. See *Financial Times*, 1 August 1994, p. 1.

Chapter 13

Dismantling Former Yugoslavia, Recolonising Bosnia-Herzegovina

"Peace-making" and Macro-economic Policy

WESTERN public opinion has been misled: the plight of former Yugoslavia is presented as the outcome of an "aggressive nationalism", the inevitable result of deep-seated ethnic and religious tensions which have their roots in history.[1] The "Balkans' power-play" is the focal point, the global media has highlighted the clash of political personalities: "Tudjman and Milosevic are tearing Bosnia-Herzegovina to pieces".[2] Western mediation concluding with the Dayton Air-force Base Agreement in November 1995 was narrowly portrayed as the means to "restoring peace" in Bosnia-Herzegovina, while contributing under the hallmark of "the free market" to the rebuilding of the newly sovereign states.

The chronology of the numerous diplomatic initiatives is vividly portrayed, the precise agenda of United Nations' "peace-keeping" and humanitarian relief is spotlighted on TV screens across the globe. In this process, the economic and social causes of the civil war have been carefully concealed. The strategic interests of Germany and the US are not mentioned, the deep-seated economic crisis which preceded the civil war has long been forgotten. In the eyes of the global media, Western powers bear no responsibility for the impoverishment and destruction of a nation of 24 million people.

Yet the break-up of the Yugoslav federation bears a direct relationship to the programme of macro-economic restructuring imposed on the Belgrade government by its external creditors. This programme, adopted in several stages since 1980, contributed to triggering the collapse of the national economy, leading to the disintegration of the industrial sector and the piecemeal dismantling of the welfare state.

Secessionist tendencies feeding on social and ethnic divisions, gained impetus precisely during a period of brutal impoverishment of the Yugoslav population. The first phase of macro-economic reform initiated in 1980 shortly before the death of Marshal Tito "wreaked economic and political havoc.... Slower growth, the accumulation of foreign debt and especially the cost of servicing it as well as devaluation led to a fall in the standard of living of the average Yugoslav... The economic crisis threatened political stability... it also threatened to aggravate simmering ethnic tensions".[3] These reforms accompanied by the signing of debt-restructuring agreements with the official and commercial creditors also served to weaken the institutions of the federal state creating political divisions between Belgrade and the governments of the republics and autonomous provinces. "The Prime Minister Milka Planinc who was supposed to carry out the programme, had to promise the IMF an immediate increase of the discount rates and much more for the Reaganomics arsenal of measures...."[4]

Macro-economic Reform Supports Strategic Interests

The objectives of economic and "strategic restructuring" were carried out concurrently. The former was to reinforce the latter. Washington's intervention in this regard had been formalised in 1984 in a US National Security Decision Directive (NSDD 133) entitled "United States Policy towards Yugoslavia" labelled "SECRET SENSITIVE".[5] A censored version of this document was declassified in 1990; it largely conformed to a previous National Security Decision Directive (NSDD 54) issued in 1982 pertaining to Eastern Europe. The objectives contained in the latter document included "expanded efforts to promote a 'quiet revolution' to overthrow Communist governments and parties" while reintegrating the countries of Eastern Europe into a market-oriented economy.[6]

Despite Belgrade's political non-alignment and its extensive trading relations with the European Community and the US, the Reagan and Bush administrations were nonetheless intent upon dismantling Yugoslavia's "market socialism". Washington's strategic objective was to integrate the Balkans into the orbit of the "free market" system.

In 1983, a second economic stabilisation package was applied with support of the IMF, resulting in massive inflation. Combined with the impact of import liberalisation, the freeze on credit was conducive to an unprecedented collapse of investment. The growth of industrial production had averaged 7.1 per cent per annum during the 1966-79 period. Following the initial phase of macro-economic reform in 1980, industrial growth plummeted to 2.8 per cent in the 1980-87 period, plunging to zero in 1987-88 and to -10.6 per cent in 1990.[7]

In 1986, Branko Mikulic became prime minister. After an unsuccessful attempt to adopt an alternative "anti-recession policy", a more orthodox approach was launched under minister of finance Oscar Kovac.[8] In 1988, the so-called "May Anti-inflation Programme" was set in motion. In fact, this programme was conducive to speeding up rather than alleviating the inflationary process: "Everything went down the drain after the October uprising [1988] in Vojvodina and Montenegro. Slobodan Milosevic said at the YCLCC presidency session that interest rates are wearing out the economy. In a climate of total chaos, wages were deregulated".[9] Mr. Mikulic resigned a few months later.

The economic-reform measures reached their climax under the pro-US government of Mr. Ante Markovic. Prime Minister Markovic "continued with the same old promises of a 'positive policy' of support to manufacturers, while in actual fact he initiated the deregulation of the system. After the regulatory bindings had been released, the inflationary pressures which had accumulated over the years resulted in a wave of hyperinflation...".[10] Inflation had been engineered almost deliberately. Spurred on by price deregulation and the currency devaluations, the consumer price index increased by 2,700 per cent in 1989.

The federal premier travelled to Washington to meet President George Bush in the autumn of 1989 just prior to the collapse of the Berlin Wall. A "financial aid package" had been promised in exchange for sweeping economic reforms including a new devalued currency, the freeze of wages, the curtailment of government expenditure and the abrogation of the socially-owned enterprises under self-management.[11] The ground-work for the prime minister's mission had already been laid, many of the required reforms (including a major revamping of the foreign investment legislation) had already been put in place by the Belgrade nomenclatura with the assistance of Western advisors.

The Agreement with the IMF

The economic package was launched in January 1990 under an IMF Stand-by Arrangement (SBA) and a World Bank Structural Adjustment Loan (SAL II). The budget cuts requiring the redirection of federal revenues towards debt servicing were conducive to the suspension of transfer payments by Belgrade to the governments of the republics and autonomous provinces thereby fuelling the process of political balkanisation and secessionism. The government of Serbia rejected Markovic's austerity programme outright leading to a walk-out protest of some 650,000 Serbian workers directed against the federal government.[12] The Trade Union movement was united in this struggle: "worker resistance crossed ethnic lines, as Serbs, Croats, Bosnians and Slovenians mobilised (...) shoulder to shoulder with their fellow workers (...)".[13]

The agreement signed with the IMF required expenditure cuts equivalent to 5 per cent of GDP. While earnings had been eroded by inflation, the IMF had also ordered the freeze of wages at their mid-November 1989 level. Despite the pegging of the dinar to the deutschmark, prices continued to rise unabated. Real wages collapsed by 41 per cent in the first six months of 1990.[14] Inflation in 1990 was in excess of 70 per cent.[15] In January 1991, another devaluation of the dinar of 30 per cent was carried out, leading to another round of price increases. Inflation was running at 140 per cent in 1991 soaring to 937 per cent and 1,134 per cent respectively in 1992 and 1993.[16]

The January 1990 economic package also included the full convertibility of the dinar, the liberalisation of interest rates and further reductions in import quotas. The creditors were in control of monetary policy: the agreement signed with the IMF prevented the federal government from having access to credit from its own Central Bank (the National Bank of Yugoslavia). This condition virtually paralysed the budgetary process and crippled the ability of the federal state to finance its economic and social programmes. Moreover, the deregulation of commercial credit alongside the banking reforms was conducive to a further collapse of investment by the socially-owned enterprises.

The freeze of all transfer payments to the republics had created a situation of "de facto secession". The implementation of these conditions (contained in the agreement signed with the IMF) was also part of the debt rescheduling arrangements reached with the Paris and London clubs. The IMF-induced budgetary crisis had engineered the collapse of the federal fiscal structure. This situation acted in a sense as a *fait accompli*, prior to the formal declaration of secession by Croatia and Slovenia in June 1991. Political pressures on Belgrade by the European Community combined with the aspirations of Germany to draw the Balkans into its geo-political orbit had also encouraged the process of secession. Yet the economic and social conditions for the break-up of the federation resulting from ten years of "structural adjustment" had already been firmly implanted.

The 1989 Enterprise Reforms

The 1989 enterprise reforms adopted under Premier Ante Markovic played a central role in steering the industrial sector into bankruptcy. By 1990, the annual rate of growth of GDP had collapsed to -7.5 per cent.[17] In 1991, GDP declined by a further 15 per cent and industrial output collapsed by 21 per cent.[18] The restructuring programme demanded by Belgrade's creditors was intended to abrogate the system of socially-owned enterprises. The Enterprise Law of 1989 required abolishing the "Basic Organizations of Associated Labour (BOAL)". The latter were socially-owned productive units under self-management with the Workers' Council constituting the main decision-making body. The 1989 Enterprise Law required the transformation of the BOALs into private capitalist enterprises with the Worker's Council replaced by a so-called "Social Board" under the control of the enterprise's owners, including its creditors.[19] "The objective was to subject the Yugoslav economy to massive privatisation and the dismantling of the public sector. Who was to carry it out? The Communist Party bureaucracy, most notably its military and intelligence sector, was canvassed specifically and offered political and economic backing on the condition that wholesale scuttling of social protections for Yugoslavia's workforce was imposed...".[20]

Overhauling The Legal Framework

A number of supporting pieces of legislation were put in place in a hurry with the assistance of Western lawyers and consultants. The Financial Operations Act of 1989 was to play a crucial role in engineering the collapse of Yugoslavia's industrial sector, it was to provide for an "equitable" and so-called "transparent trigger mechanism" which would steer so-called "insolvent" enterprises in bankruptcy or liquidation. A related act entitled the Law on Compulsory Settlement, Bankruptcy and Liquidation was to safeguard "the rights of the creditors". The latter could call for the initiation of bankruptcy procedures enabling them to take over and/or liquidate the assets of debtor enterprises.[21]

The earlier 1988 Foreign Investment Law had allowed for unrestricted entry of foreign capital not only into industry but also into the banking, insurance and services' sectors. Prior to the enactment of the law, foreign investment was limited to joint ventures with the socially-owned enterprises.[22] In turn, the 1989 Law on the Circulation and Management of Social Capital and the 1990 Social Capital Law allowed for the divestiture of the socially-owned enterprises including their sale to foreign capital. The Social Capital Law also provided for the creation of "Restructuring and Recapitalisation Agencies" with a mandate to organise the "valuation" of enterprise assets prior to privatisation. As in Eastern Europe and the former Soviet Union, however, the valuation of assets was based on the recorded "book-value" expressed in local currency. This book-value tended to be unduly low thereby securing the sale of socially-owned assets at rock-bottom prices. Slovenia and Croatia had by 1990 already established their own draft privatisation laws.[23]

Also in 1989 and 1990, in separate pieces of legislation, a new Banking Law was enacted with a view to triggering the liquidation of the socially-owned "Associated Banks". More than half the country's banks were dismantled; the emphasis was on the formation of "independent profit-oriented institutions".[24] By 1990, the entire "three-tier banking system" consisting of the National Bank of Yugoslavia, the national banks of the eight republics and autonomous provinces and the commercial banks had been dismantled under the guidance of the World Bank. A World Bank Financial Sector Adjustment Loan was being negotiated in 1990. It was to be adopted by the Belgrade government in 1991.

A Federal Agency for Insurance and Bank Rehabilitation was established in June 1990 with a mandate to restructure and *"reprivatise"* restructured banks.[25] This process was to be undertaken over a five-year period. The development of non-banking financial intermediaries including brokerage firms, investment management firms and insurance companies was also to be promoted.

The Bankruptcy Programme

Industrial enterprises had been carefully categorised. Under the IMF-World Bank sponsored reforms, credit to the industrial sector had been frozen with a view to speeding up the bankruptcy process. So-called "exit mechanisms" had been established under the provisions of the 1989 Financial Operations Act.[26] The latter stipulated that if an enterprise were to remain insolvent for 30 days running, or for 30 days within a 45-day period, it must hold a meeting within the next 15 days with its creditors with a view to arriving at a settlement. This mechanism allowed creditors (including national and foreign banks) routinely to convert their loans into a controlling equity in the insolvent enterprise. Under the act, the government was not authorised to intervene. In case a settlement was not reached, bankruptcy procedures would be initiated in which case workers would not normally receive severance payments.[27]

In 1989, according to official sources, 248 firms were steered into bankruptcy or were liquidated, and 89,400 workers had been laid off.[28] During the first nine months of 1990, directly following the adoption of the IMF programme, another 889 enterprises with a combined workforce of 525,000 workers were subjected to bankruptcy procedures.[29] In other words, in less than two years "the trigger mechanism" (under the Financial Operations Act) had led to the lay-off of more than 600,000 workers (out of a total industrial workforce of the order of 2.7 million). The largest concentrations of bankrupt firms and lay-offs were in Serbia, Bosnia-Herzegovina, Macedonia and Kosovo.[30]

Many socially-owned enterprises attempted to avoid bankruptcy through the non-payment of wages. Half a million workers representing some 20 per cent of the industrial labour force were not paid during the early months of 1990, in order to meet the demands of creditors under the "settlement" procedures stipulated in the Law on Financial Organisations. Real earnings were in a free fall, social programmes had collapsed, with the bankruptcies of industrial enterprises. Unemployment had become rampant, creating within the population an atmosphere of social despair and hopelessness. "When Mr. Markovic finally started his programmed privatisation, the republican oligarchies, who all had visions of a national renaissance of their own, instead of choosing between a genuine Yugoslav market and hyperinflation, opted for war which would disguise the real causes of the economic catastrophe".[31]

The January 1990 IMF-sponsored package contributed unequivocally to increasing enterprise losses while precipitating many of the large electric, petroleum refinery, machinery, engineering and chemical enterprises into bankruptcy. Moreover, with the deregulation of the trade regime in January 1990, a flood of imported commodities contributed to further destabilising domestic production. These imports were financed with borrowed money granted under the IMF package (i.e. the various "quick disbursing loans" granted by the IMF, the World Bank and bilateral donors in support of the economic reforms). While the import bonanza was fuelling the build-up of Yugoslavia's external debt, the abrupt hikes in interest rates and input prices imposed on national enterprises had expedited the displacement and exclusion of domestic producers from their own national market.

Moreover, as in Eastern Europe, the strategy of the donors was either to destabilise large industrial enterprises or to break them up into smaller units in view of "increasing efficiency" and "fostering competition". This process referred to as "Reform by Dismemberment" consisted in breaking up an integrated system of public transportation or road haulage into a multitude of small individually-owned transport companies. The latter are referred to as "the successor enterprises".[32]

"Shedding Surplus Workers"

The situation prevailing in the months preceding the secession of Croatia and Slovenia (June 1991) (confirmed by the 1989-90 bankruptcy figures) points to the sheer magnitude and brutality of the process of industrial dismantling. The figures, however, provide but a partial picture, depicting the situation at the outset of the "bankruptcy programme". The latter has continued unabated throughout the period of the civil war and its aftermath. Similar industrial restructuring programmes were imposed by external creditors on Yugoslavia's successor states.

The World Bank had estimated that there were still in September 1990, 2,435 "loss-making" enterprises out of a remaining total of 7,531.[33] In other words, these 2,435 firms with a combined work-force of more than 1.3 million workers had been categorised as "insolvent" under the provisions of the Financial Operations Act, requiring the immediate implementation of bankruptcy procedures. Bearing in mind that 600,000 workers had already been laid off by bankrupt firms prior to September 1990, these figures suggest that some 1.9 million workers (out of a total of 2.7 million) had been classified as "redundant". The "insolvent" firms concentrated in the energy, heavy industry, metal processing, forestry and textiles sectors were among the largest industrial enterprises in the country representing (in September 1990) 49.7 per cent of the total (remaining and employed) industrial work-force.[34]

Whereas the Financial Organisations Law provided for automatic lay-off of workers of bankrupt enterprises without compensation, lay-offs in "profitable" enterprises, including those taken over under the privatisation programme, were governed by the provisions of the 1989 Labour Law. The latter, while allowing firms to "shed their surplus labour", had nonetheless maintained the clause pertaining to severance payments for redundant workers. The World Bank was of the view that the legal framework for "shedding surplus labour" under the Labour Law was unduly cumbersome and costly, namely that the severance costs incurred by the enterprise were considered as "prohibitive": "under the present law, the cost of retrenchment can be avoided only if an enterprise is declared to be bankrupt".[35]

To remedy the shortcomings of the Labour Law, the World Bank had suggested the setting up of a new system "to protect displaced workers", linking municipal, republican and federal agencies through the formation of a "social safety net" but also through the removal of "rigidities" in the labour market. To generate employment for displaced workers, the World Bank proposed the promotion of small and medium-sized private enterprises. This objective, however, was to be achieved under conditions of fiscal austerity and "tight credit" to industry.

Political Disintegration

Supporting broad strategic interests, the austerity measures had laid the basis for "the recolonisation" of the Balkans. In the multi-party elections in 1990, economic policy was at the centre of the political debate; the separatist coalitions ousted the Communists in Croatia, Bosnia-Herzegovina and Slovenia.

Following the decisive victory in Croatia of the rightist Democratic Union in May 1990 under the leadership of Franjo Tudjman, the separation of Croatia received the formal assent of the German foreign minister Mr. Hans Dietrich Genscher who was in almost daily contact with his Croatian counterpart in Zagreb.[36] Germany not only favoured secession, it was also "forcing the pace of international diplomacy" and pressuring its Western allies to grant recognition to Slovenia and Croatia.

The borders of Yugoslavia were in this regard, reminiscent of World War II when Croatia (including the territories of Bosnia-Herzegovina) was an Axis satellite under the fascist Ustasa regime: "German expansion has been accompanied by a rising tide of nationalism and xenophobia.... Germany has been seeking a free hand among its allies to pursue economic dominance in the whole of Mitteleuropa..."[37] Washington, on the other hand, favoured "a loose unity while encouraging democratic development... [US Secretary of State] Baker told [Croatia's president] Franjo Tudjman and [Slovenia's president] Milan Kucan that the United States would not encourage or support unilateral secession... but if they had to leave, he urged them to leave by a negotiated agreement"....[38]

Post-war Reconstruction

The prospects for rebuilding the newly independent republics appear bleak: debt rescheduling is an integral part of the peace process. The former Yugoslavia has been carved up under the close scrutiny of its external creditors, its foreign debt has been carefully divided and allocated to the republics, each of which is now strangled in separate debt-rescheduling and structural adjustment agreements. The republican leader has fully collaborated with the creditors: "All the current leaders of the former Yugoslav republics were Communist Party functionaries and each in turn vied to meet the demands of the World Bank and the International Monetary Fund, the better to qualify for investment loans and substantial perks for the leadership.... State industry and machinery were looted by functionaries. Equipment showed up in 'private companies' run by family members of the nomenclatura".[39] The privatisation programmes implemented under the supervision of the donors have contributed to a further stage of economic dislocation and impoverishment of the population. GDP had declined by as much as 50 per cent in four years (1990-93).[40]

Croatia, Slovenia and Macedonia had entered into separate loan negotiations with the Bretton Woods institutions. According to the IMF, the January 1990 "shock treatment" adopted prior to secession under Prime Minister Ante Markovic had not fully reached its objectives. Another round of "stabilisation cum restructuring" was required.

Under the agreement signed in 1993 with the IMF, the Zagreb government was not permitted to mobilise its own productive resources through fiscal and monetary policy. The latter were firmly under the control of its external creditors. The massive budget cuts demanded under the agreement had forestalled the possibility of post-war reconstruction. The latter could only be carried out through the granting of fresh foreign loans, a process which would fuel Croatia's external debt well into the 21st century. The cost of rebuilding Croatia's war-torn economy was estimated at some $23 billion.

Under the brunt of the 1993 IMF programme, Croatia's official unemployment rate increased from 15.5 per cent in 1991 to 19.1 per cent in 1994.[41] Eroded by inflation, wages had fallen to abysmally low levels. A new national currency, the kuna, was launched in October 1994. According to official figures, 95 per cent of the socially-owned enterprises had been transformed into joint stock companies.[42] A far more stringent Bankruptcy Law was instigated, together with procedures for the breaking up through "dismemberment" of large state-owned public utility companies. Also contained in its Letter of Intent to the Bretton Woods institutions, the Zagreb government is to restructure and fully privatise the banking sector with the assistance of the EBRD and the World Bank.

Negotiations with the Paris and London clubs, however, were stalled in 1994 over "how much of the former Yugoslav debt" would be assumed by Croatia. Recognition by Zagreb of its full share of the Yugoslav debt was a precondition both for debt rescheduling and the granting of fresh money. Also in 1995 a few months before the completion of the Dayton Peace Accord, the IMF acting on behalf of creditor banks and Western governments, proposed to redistribute the debt of former Yugoslavia roughly as follows: Serbia and Montenegro, 36 per cent; Croatia, 28 per cent; Slovenia, 16 per cent; Bosnia-Herzegovina, 16 per cent and Macedonia, 5 per cent.[43]

In Macedonia, the pattern was broadly similar: the auction of socially-owned enterprises has led to industrial collapse and rampant unemployment. A set of economic reforms were adopted in 1993 under an IMF-sponsored Systemic Transformation Facility (STF) with a view to compressing real wages and freezing credit. In an unusual twist, Mr. George Soros, the multi-billionaire business tycoon, acting as a private individual, had integrated the so-called International Support Group alongside the government of the Netherlands and the Bank of International Settlements. The money provided by the support group was not intended for the reconstruction of Macedonia. So-called "bridge financing" was provided to enable the Skopje government to reimburse its debt arrears with the World Bank.[44]

A second phase of structural adjustment was initiated in 1994 between the government of Prime Minister Branko Crvenkovski and the IMF. The head of the IMF mission Mr. Paul Thomsen expressed his satisfaction stating that "the results of the stabilisation program [under the STF] were impressive" particularly in view of "the efficient wages' policy" adopted by the Skopje government (under the Law on Wages). According to IMF negotiators, efforts to cut the deficit (which had already been slashed by 50 per cent in 1994) should be continued.[45] These endeavours, however, would inevitably require further compressions in social programmes and payments of old-age pensions. Under the agreement with the fund, the Skopje government was to reach debt-rescheduling agreements with the Paris and London clubs.

The IMF agreement specifically required the Skopje government to close down "insolvent" enterprises and lay-off "redundant" workers. In 1994, "every second company in Macedonia [was] a loss-producing one, increasing the number of such companies by 4,000".[46] The Finance Ministry confirmed, in this regard, that with bank interest rates at such high levels (under the donor-sponsored Law for Rehabilitation of the Banks) "it was literally impossible to find a company in the country which would be able to (...) cover the costs on account of the interest [rates]".[47] The IMF economic therapy for Macedonia constituted a coherent *"bankruptcy programme"* leading to the dismantling of the entire industrial sector. The most profitable assets were on sale on the Macedonian stock market which opened its doors in 1995. The stock market functions as an entity within the Privatisation Agency. The minister of finance Mr. Ljube Trpevski stated proudly in a press conference that "the World Bank and the IMF place Macedonia among the most successful countries in regard to current transition reforms".[48]

The Social Impact of the Reforms

The social impact of the IMF-World Bank economic therapy was candidly acknowledged. The World Bank confirmed in this regard that: "[a] sharp drop in public resources [was conducive] to unusually severe outbreaks [in Macedonia] of mumps and measles among infants and children (...) A growing share of the population, largely the uninsured, is being turned away from basic health services due to inability to pay. Recourse to such measures is indicative of the severity of the fiscal crisis, and is not without serious social and political consequences for a society which has long considered health to be a basic right of citizens and has prided itself on universal access to care."[49]

The proposed "solution" presented by the World Bank consisted of developing a "market-oriented" health-care system.

Rebuilding Bosnia-Herzegovina

With the Bosnian peace settlement holding under NATO guns, the West unveiled in 1995 a "reconstruction" programme which fully stripped Bosnia-Herzegovina of its economic and political sovereignty. This programme consisted largely in developing Bosnia-Herzegovina as a divided territory under NATO military occupation and Western administration.

Resting on the November 1995 Dayton Accord, the US and the European Union had installed a full-fledged colonial administration in Bosnia. At its head was their appointed high representative (HR), a non-Bosnian citizen.[50] The HR has full executive powers in all civilian matters, with the right to overrule the governments of both the Bosnian Federation and the Bosnian-Serb Republika Srpska. The HR was to act in close liaison with the IFOR Military High Command as well with donor agencies.[51]

An international civilian police force was under the custody of an expatriate commissioner appointed by the United Nations Secretary-General. Some 1,700 policemen from fifteen countries, most of whom had never set foot in the Balkans, were dispatched to Bosnia after a five-days training programme in Zagreb.[52]

While the West had underscored its support for democracy, the Parliamentary Assembly set up under the "constitution" and finalised under the Dayton Accord, acted largely as a "rubber stamp".[53] Behind the democratic facade, actual political power rested in the hands of a "parallel government" headed by the high representative and staffed by expatriate advisors.

Moreover, the constitution agreed at Dayton handed over the reigns of economic policy to the Bretton Woods institutions and the London-based European Bank for Reconstruction and Development (EBRD). Article VII stipulated that the first governor of the Central Bank of Bosnia and Herzegovina is to be appointed by the IMF and "shall not be a citizen of Bosnia and Herzegovina or a neighbouring State...".

Just as the governor of the Central Bank was an IMF appointee, the Central Bank was not allowed under the constitution to function as a central bank: "For the first six years (...) it may not extend credit by creating money, operating in this respect as a currency board" (Article VII). Neither was the new "sovereign" successor state allowed to have its own currency (issuing paper money only when there is full foreign-exchange backing), nor permitted to mobilise its internal resources.[54] As in the other successor republics, its ability to self-finance its reconstruction (without massively increasing its external debt) was blunted from the outset.

The tasks of managing the Bosnian economy had been carefully divided among donor agencies: while the Central Bank was under IMF custody, the EBRD headed the Commission on Public Corporations which supervises operations of all public-sector enterprises including energy, water, postal services, roads, railways, etc. The president of the EBRD appoints the chairman of the commission which also oversees public-sector restructuring, meaning primarily the sell-off of state and socially-owned assets and the procurement of long-term investment funds.[55]

One cannot sidestep a fundamental question: is the Bosnian Constitution formally agreed between heads of state at Dayton really a constitution? A sombre and dangerous precedent had been set in the history of international relations: Western creditors had embedded their interests in a constitution hastily written on their behalf; executive positions within the Bosnian state system were held by non-citizens who were appointees of Western financial institutions. No constitutional assembly, no consultations with citizens' organisations in Bosnia and Herzegovina, no "constitutional amendments"...

The Bosnian government had estimated in 1995 that reconstruction costs would reach US$47 billion. Western donors had pledged $3 billion in reconstruction loans. Only a fraction of this amount was actually disbursed. Moreover, part of this money was tagged to finance some of the local civilian costs of the Implementation Force's (IFOR) military deployment under the Dayton agreement as well as repay debt arrears with international creditors. Under the Dayton agreement, no taxes were paid by NATO personnel and several of the local costs of the military operation were met by the Bosnian government: "the Government of the Republic of Bosnia and Herzegovina shall provide, free of cost, such facilities NATO needs for the preparation and execution of the [NATO] Operation" (Annex 1-A).

In a familiar twist, "fresh loans" were devised to pay back "old debt". The Central Bank of the Netherlands has generously provided "bridge financing" of US$37 million. The money, however, was earmarked to allow Bosnia to pay back its arrears with the IMF, a condition without which the IMF will not lend it fresh money. But it is a cruel and absurd paradox: the sought-after loan from the IMF's newly created "Emergency Window" for so-called "post-conflict countries" was not to be used for post-war reconstruction. Instead it was applied to reimburse the Central Bank of the Netherlands which had coughed up the money to settle IMF arrears in the first place.[56]

While debt was building up, no new financial resources are flowing into Bosnia to rebuild its war-torn economy.

Multinationals have an Eye on Bosnia's Oil Fields

Of strategic importance to Western economic interests was the territorial partition of Bosnia-Herzegovina under the Dayton agreement. The latter was to enforce the "Inter-Entity Boundary Line" between the Federation of Bosnia-Herzegovina and the Bosnian-Serb Republika Srpska. Documents in the hands of Croatia and the Bosnian Serbs indicated that deposits of coal and oil had been identified on the eastern slope of the Dinarides Thrust, a region which "was the primary battlefront of this Summer's [1995] massive Croatian Army offensives against rebel Serbs in Bosnia and Croatia's Krajina region (...) According to Bosnian officials, Chicago-based Amoco (American Oil Company) was among several foreign firms that subsequently initiated exploratory surveys in Bosnia".[57] The West was anxious to develop these regions: "The World Bank – and the multinationals that conducted operations – are [August 1995] reluctant to divulge their latest exploration reports to the combatant governments while the war continues".[58] Moreover, there are also "substantial petroleum fields in the Serb-held part of Croatia just across the Sava river from the Tuzla region".[59] The latter under the Dayton agreement was part of the US Military Division with headquarters in Tuzla.

The territorial division under the Dayton agreement sanctions "ethnic cleansing". The deployment of nine heavily armed brigades of 70,000 troops (nearly as many as in the Vietnam War) was not intended to "enforce the peace" but rather to administer the territorial partition of Bosnia-Herzegovina in accordance with Western economic interests. This objective was also achieved through territorial fragmentation, – i.e. by entrenching socio-ethnic divisions in the structure of territorial partition thereby thwarting the united resistance of Yugoslavs of all ethnic origins against the recolonisation of their homeland.

Concluding Remarks

Macro-economic restructuring applied in Yugoslavia under the neoliberal policy agenda had unequivocally contributed to the destruction of an entire country. Yet since the onset of war in 1991, the central role of macro-economic reform had been carefully overlooked and denied by the global media. The "free market" had been presented as the solution, the basis for rebuilding a war-shattered economy. A detailed diary of the war and of the "peace-making" process had been presented by the mainstream press. The social and political impact of economic restructuring in Yugoslavia had been carefully erased from our social consciousness and collective understanding of "what actually happened". Cultural, ethnic and religious divisions were highlighted, presented dogmatically as the sole cause of the crisis when in reality they were the consequence of a much deeper process of economic and political fracturing.

This "false consciousness" had invaded all spheres of critical debate and discussion. It not only masks the truth, it also prevents us from acknowledging precise historical occurrences. Ultimately it distorts the true sources of social conflict. The unity, solidarity and identity of the Southern Slavs have their foundation in history, yet this identity had been thwarted, manipulated and destroyed.

The ruin of an economic system, including the take-over of productive assets, the extension of markets and "the scramble for territory" in the Balkans constitute the real cause of conflict.

What is at stake in Yugoslavia are the lives of millions of people. Macro-economic reform destroys their livelihood and derogates their right to work, their food and shelter, their culture and national identity. Borders are redefined, the entire legal system is overhauled, the socially-owned enterprises are steered into bankruptcy, the financial and banking system is dismantled, social programmes and institutions are torn down. In retrospect, it is worth recalling Yugoslavia's economic and social achievements in the post-war period (prior to 1980): the growth of GDP was on average 6.1 per annum over a twenty-year period (1960-80), there was free medical care with one doctor per 550 population, the literacy rate was of the order of 91 per cent and life expectancy was 72 years.[60]

Yugoslavia is a "mirror" of similar economic restructuring programmes applied not only in the developing world but also in recent years in the US, Canada and Western Europe. "Strong economic medicine" is the answer; throughout the world, people are led to believe that there is no other solution: enterprises must be closed down, workers must be laid off and social programmes must be slashed. It is in the foregoing context that the economic crisis in Yugoslavia should be understood. Pushed to the extreme, the reforms are the cruel reflection of a destructive "economic model" imposed under the neoliberal agenda on national societies throughout the world.

Endnotes

1. See the account of Warren Zimmerman (former US Ambassador to Yugoslavia), "The Last Ambassador, A Memoir of the Collapse of Yugoslavia", *Foreign Affairs*, Vol. 74, No. 2, 1995.
2. Milos Vasic et al, "War Against Bosnia", *Vreme News Digest Agency*, No. 29, 13 April 1992.
3. Sean Gervasi, "Germany, US and the Yugoslav Crisis", *Covert Action Quarterly*, No. 43, Winter 1992-93.
4. Dimitrije Boarov, "A Brief Review of Anti-inflation Programs, the Curse of Dead Programs", *Vreme New Digest Agency*, No. 29, 13 April 1992.
5. Sean Gervasi, op. cit., p. 42.
6. Ibid., p. 42.
7. World Bank, *Industrial Restructuring Study, Overview, Issues and Strategy for Restructuring"*, Washington DC, June 1991, pp. 10 and 14.
8. Dimitrije Boarov, "A Review of Anti-Inflation Programs, The Curse of Dead Programs", *Vreme News Digest Agency*, No. 29, 13 April, 1992.
9. Ibid.
10. Ibid.
11. Sean Gervasi, op. cit.
12. Ralph Schoenman, "Divide and Rule Schemes in The Balkans", *The Organiser*, 11 September 1995.
13. Sean Gervasi, op. cit., p. 44.
14. World Bank, *Yugoslavia, Industrial Restructuring*, p. viii.
15. Ibid., p. 28
16. See "Zagreb's About-turn", *The Banker* (London), January 1995, p. 38. Inflation figures for 1991-94 are for Croatia.
17. World Bank, op. cit., p. 10. The term GDP is used for simplicity, yet the concept used in Yugoslavia and Eastern Europe to measure national product is not equivalent to the GDP concept under the (Western) system of national accounts.

18. See Judit Kiss, "Debt Management in Eastern Europe", *Eastern European Economics*, May-June 1994, p. 59.
19. See Barbara Lee and John Nellis, *Enterprise Reform and Privatisation in Socialist Economies*, The World Bank, Washington DC, 1990, pp. 20-21.
20. Ralph Schoenman, "Divide and Rule Schemes in The Balkans", *The Organiser*, 11 September 1995.
21. For further details see World Bank, *Yugoslavia, Industrial Restructuring*, p. 33.
22. World Bank, *Yugoslavia, Industrial Restructuring*, p. 29.
23. Ibid., p. 23.
24. Ibid., p. 38.
25. Ibid., p. 39.
26. Ibid., p. 33.
27. Ibid., p. 33.
28. Ibid., p. 34. Data of the Federal Secretariat for Industry and Energy. Of the total number of firms, 222 went bankrupt and 26 were liquidated.
29. Ibid., p. 33. These figures include bankruptcy and liquidation.
30. Ibid., p. 34.
31. Dimitrije Boarov, op. cit.
32. See Esra Benathon and Louis S. Thompson, *Privatisation Problems at Industry Level, Road Haulage in Central Europe,* World Bank Discussion Paper No. 182, The World Bank, Washington DC, Chapter 3.
33. Ibid., p. 13. Annex 1, p. 1.
34. "Surplus labour" in industry had been assessed by the World Bank mission to be of the order of 20 per cent of the total labour force of 8.9 million, – i.e. approximately 1.8 million. This figure is significantly below the actual number of redundant workers based on the categorisation of "insolvent" enterprises. Solely in the industrial sector, there were 1.9 million workers (September 1990) out of 2.7 million employed in enterprises classified as insolvent by the World Bank. See World Bank, *Yugoslavia, Industrial Restructuring*, Annex 1.
35. World Bank, *Yugoslavia, Industrial Restructuring..*, p. 32.
36. Sean Gervasi, op. cit., p. 65.
37. Ibid., p. 45.
38. Zimmermann, op. cit.
39. Ralph Schoenman, "Divide and Rule Schemes in The Balkans", *The Organiser*, 11 September 1995.
40. Figure for Macedonia, *Enterprise, Banking and Social Safety Net,* World Bank Public Information Center, 28 November 1994.

41. "Zagreb's About Turn", *The Banker*, January 1995, p. 38.
42. Fifty per cent of the equity is private, 29 per cent is in the hands of the Croatian Privatisation Fund, the remainder is in State hands. See "Zagreb's Turn Around", *The Banker* (London), January 1995, pp. 38- 9.
43. In Croatia, the World Bank is supporting the development of a Capital Market including a Regulatory Framework favouring easy access by Western institutional investors and brokerage firms. See World Bank, *Croatia, Enterprise and Financial Sector Adjustment Loan,* Public Information Center, The World Bank, 16 February 1995.
44. See World Bank, *Macedonia Financial and Enterprise Sector*, Public Information Department, 28 November 1995.
45. According to the Macedonian Information Centre (MIC).
46. Macedonian Information and Liaison Service, *MILS News*, 11 April 1995.
47. Statement of Macedonia's Deputy Minister of Finance Mr. Hari Kostov, reported in *MAK News,* 18 April 1995.
48. *MILS News*, Skopje, 11 April 1995.
49. World Bank, *Macedonia, Health Sector Transition Project*, Public Information Department, 15 November 1995, Washington DC.
50. See Article 1 of the "Agreement on High Representative" of the Dayton Peace Accord.
51. Article II defines the mandate and powers. The High Representative convenes and chairs the "Joint Civilian Commission" to which he appoints as deemed necessary the representatives of civilian organisations and agencies, in addition to senior political representatives of the parties and the Commander of IFOR or his representative. Article V stipulates that "[t]he High Representative is "the final authority in theater regarding interpretation of this Agreement [on High Representative]".
52. According to a United Nations statement, United Nations, New York, 5 January 1996. See also Article II of the *Agreement on International Police Task Force* under the Dayton Peace Accord.
53. See Article IV of the Constitution of Bosnia and Herzegovina. Two billion dollars are allocated to finance the US contingent of 20,000 troops.
54. See International Monetary Fund, *Bosnia and Herzegovina becomes a Member of the IMF*, Press Release No. 97/70, Washington, 20 December 1995.
55. See the Agreement on Public Corporations under the Dayton Peace Accord, Art. 1, Commission on Public Corporations, Dayton Peace Accord, 15 November 1995.
56. See International Monetary Fund, *Bosnia and Herzegovina becomes a Member of the IMF*, Press Release No. 97/70, Washington, 20 December 1995.

57. Frank Viviano and Kenneth Howe, "Bosnia Leaders Say Nation Sit Atop Oil Fields", *The San Francisco Chronicle*, 28 August 1995. See also Scott Cooper, "Western Aims in Ex-Yugoslavia Unmasked", *The Organizer*, 24 September 1995.
58. Viviano and Howe, op. cit.
59. Ibid.
60. World Bank, *World Development Report 1991*, Statistical Annex, tables 1 and 2, Washington DC, 1991.

SELECTED BIBLIOGRAPHY

African Rights, 1993, *Somalia, Operation Restore Hope: A Preliminary Assessment,* London.

Addison Tony and Demery Lionel, 1987, "Alleviating Poverty under Structural Adjustment", *Finance and Development,* Vol. 24, No. 4.

Albanez, T., et al, 1989, *Economic Decline and Child Survival*, UNICEF, Florence.

Altmann, Jorn, 1990, "IMF Conditionality: the Wrong Party Pays the Bill", *Intereconomics*, May-June.

Alvarez, Elena, 1991, *The Illegal Coca Production in Peru: A Preliminary Assessment of its Economic Impact*, Institute of the Americas and University of California at San Diego, February 1991.

Anyiam, Charles and Robert Stock, 1991, *Structural Adjustment Programs and "Reality" of Living Conditions*, CASID annual meetings, Kingston.

Atta Mills, Cadman, 1989, *Structural Adjustment in Sub-Saharan Africa,* Economic Development Institute, World Bank, Washington DC.

Balassa, B., 1981, *Structural Adjustment Policies in Developing Countries,* World Bank, Washington DC.

Bamako Initiative Management Unit, 1990, *The Bamako Initiative Strategy in Mauritania,* New York.

Banco Intertamericano de Desarrollo, 1989, *Peru: informe economico,* Washington.

Barratt Brown, M., 1992, *Short-changed, Africa in World Trade,* Pluto Press, London.

Beardsley, Tim, 1993, "Selling to Survive", *Scientific American*, February.

Behrman, Jere and Anil B. Deolalikar, 1991, "The Poor and the Social Sectors during a Period of Macroeconomic Adjustment: Empirical Evidence from Jamaica", *World Bank Economic Review,* Vol. 5, No. 2.

Bell Michael and R. Sheehy, 1987, "Helping Structural Adjustment in Low Income Countries", *Finance and Development,* 24:4, December.

Beneria, Lourdes and Shelley Feldman, 1992, *Unequal Burden and Persistent Poverty,* Westview Press, Boulder.

Bennett, K., 1991, *Economic Decline and the Growth of the Informal Sector,* CASID Annual Conference, Kingston, Ont.

Bennett, Sara and Manengu Musambo, 1990, *Report on Community Financing and District Management Strengthening in Zambia,* Bamako Initiative Technical Report, UNICEF, New York.

Betz, J., 1990, "The Social Effects of Adjustment Policy in LDCs", *Intereconomics*, May-June.

Bianchi A. (editor), 1985, *La Deuda externa latino americana*, Grupo Editor Latino Americano, Santiago.

Boateng, E. Oti, *et al.*, undated, *A Poverty Profile for Ghana, 1987-1988,* World Bank, Washington DC.

Bourgoignie Georges and Marcelle Genné (editors), 1990, *Structural Adjustment and Social Realities in Africa,* University of Ottawa, Ottawa,

Brandt, H. *et al.*, 1985, *Structural Distortions and Adjustment Programmes in the Poor Countries of Africa,* Deutsches Institut fur Entwicklungs Politik, Berlin.

Brandt Commission, 1983, *Common Crisis, North-South Cooperation for World Recovery,* New York, Pan Books.

Bruno, Michael (editor), 1991, *Lessons of Economic Stabilisation and its Aftermath,* MIT Press, Cambridge Mass.

Canadian International Development Agency, 1987, *Sharing our Future*, Hull.

Canadian International Development Agency, 1990, *Working Paper on Poverty Alleviation for the 4As*, Hull.

Camen, Ulrich, 1991, *Country Paper Nepal: Macroeconomic Evolution and the Health Sector*, WHO, Geneva.

Cammen, Ulrich and Carrin, Guy, 1991, *Macroeconomic Analysis: Guinea, Macroeconomic Evolution and the Health Sector,* WHO, Geneva.

Campbell, Bonnie K., 1989, *Political Dimensions of the International Debt Crisis,* London, Macmillan.

Campbell, Bonnie K. and John Loxley (editors) 1990, *Structural Adjustment in Africa,* London, Macmillan.

Campodonico, Humberto, 1989, "La politica del avestruz", in Diego Garcia Sayan (editor), Lima, 1989.

Carrin, Guy and Kodjo, 1991, *The Basic Macro-economics of Government Health Sector Expenditures in Low Income Developing Countries,* WHO, Office of International Cooperation, Geneva.

Chauvier, Jean Marie, 1993, "Tourbillon de crises en Russie", *Le Monde diplomatique*, October.

Chossudovsky Michel, 1975, "Hacia el nuevo modelo economico chileno, inflacion y redistribucion del ingreso, 1973-74", *Trimestre Economico,* No. 122.

Chossudovsky, Michel, 1991, "The Globalisation of Poverty and the New World Economic Order", *Economic and Political Weekly,* Vol. 26, No. 44.

Comisión Economica para America Latina y el Caribe, 1990, *Magnitud de la Pobreza en America Latina en los Años Ochenta*, Santiago de Chile.

Commonwealth Secretariat, 1989, *Engendering Adjustment for the 1990s*, Report of a Commonwealth Expert Group on Women and Structural Adjustment, London.

Cornia, Giovanni A., 1989, "Investing in Human Resources: Health, Nutrition and Development for the 1990s", *Journal of Development Planning,* No. 19.

Cornia, Giovanni and Frances Stewart, *The Fiscal System, Adjustment and the Poor,* UNICEF, Innocenti Occasional Papers No. 11, Florence, 1990

Cornia, Giovanni A., Richard Jolly and Frances Stewart, 1987, *Adjustment with a Human Face,* Vol. 1, UNICEF, Oxford University Press, New York.

Cornia, Giovanni A. and Richard Strickland, *Rural Differentiation, Poverty and Agricultural Crisis in Sub-Saharan Africa, Towards an Appropriate Policy Response,* UNICEF, Florence.

Corrêa Linhares, Célia Maria and Maristela de Paula Andrade, 1992, "A Açao Oficial e os Conflitos Agrários no Maranhao", *Desenvolvimento e Cidadania*, No. 4, Sao Luis de Maranhao.

Cottarelli, Carlos, 1993, *Limiting Central Bank Credit to the Government*, IMF, Washington DC.

Cruz Rivero, C., *et al.*, 1991, *The Impact of Economic Crisis and Adjustment on Health Care in Mexico*, WHO, Florence.

Culpeper, Roy, 1987, *Forced Adjustment: The Export Collapse in Sub-Saharan Africa*, North-South Institute, Ottawa.

Culpeper, Roy, 1991, *Growth and Adjustment in Smaller Highly Indebted Countries*, the North-South Institute, Ottawa.

Dancourt, Oscar, 1987, "Cuando se abandona las politicas fondomonetaristas", in Herrera, C., Dancourt, O. and G. Alarco, *Reactivación y politica economica heterodoxa*, Fundación Friedrich Ebert, Lima.

Dancourt, Oscar *et al.*, 1990, " Una Propuesta de Reforma Monetaria para Acabar con la Inflacion", *Documentos de trabajo* No. 90, CISEPA, Pontificia Universidad Catolica del Peru, Lima, July 1990.

Dancourt, Oscar, and Ivory Yong, 1989, "Sobre hyperinflación peruana", *Economía*, XII:23, June 1989.

Devlin, Robert, 1990, "The Menu Approach", *IDS Bulletin*, Vol. 23, No. 2.

Didszun, Klaus, 1990, "On the Problem of Negative Net Transfers to Developing Countries", *Intereconomics*, May-June.

Drewnowski, Jan, 1965, *The Level of Living Index,* UNRISD, Geneva.

Ebel, Beth, 1991, *Patterns of Government Expenditure in Developing Countries during the 1980s*, UNICEF, Florence.

Edwards, S. 1988, *La Crisis de la deuda externa y las politicas de ajuste estructural en America Latina*, Estudios CIEPLAN, Santiago.

Elson, Diane, 1989, "How is Adjustment Affecting Women", *Development*, No. 1.

Faber, Mike and Griffith Jones, S., 1990, "Editorial on Approaches to Third World Debt Reduction", *IDS Bulletin*, Vol. 23, No. 2.

Fabricant, Stephen and Clifford Kamara, 1990, *The Financing of Community Health Service in Sierra Leone,* UNICEF, New York.

Ferroni, Marco and Ravi Kanbur, 1991, *Poverty Conscious Restructuring of Public Expenditure*, SDA Working Paper No. 9, World Bank, Washington DC.

Figueroa, Adolfo, 1989, "Integración de las politicas de corto y largo plazo", *Economía* XII:23, June.

Foxley, A., 1987, " Latin American Development after the Debt Crisis", *Journal of Development Economics*, Vol. 27, Nos. 1-2.

Garcia Sayan, Diego (editor), 1989, *Coca, cocaína y narcotrafico,* Comisión Andina de Juristas, Lima.

Gervais, Myriam, 1993, "Etude de la pratique des ajustements au Niger et au Rwanda", *Labour, Capital and Society*, Vol. 26, No. 1.

Gervasi, Sean, 1993, "Germany, US and the Yugoslav Crisis", *Covert Action,* No. 43, Winter 1992-93.

Ghai, Dharam, 1992, *Structural Adjustment, Global Integration and Social Democracy,* UNRISD, Geneva.

Glover, David, 1991, "A Layman's Guide to Structural Adjustment", *Canadian Journal of Development Studies*, Vol. 12, No. 1.

Goncalves, R. 1986, *Structural Adjustment and Structural Change: in Search of a Solution*, UNCTAD, Geneva.

Griffith-Jones, S. and O. Sunkel, 1986, *Debt and Development Crises*, Oxford, Clarendon Press,

Griffith-Jones, S., 1989, "Debt Reduction with a Human Face", *Development,* No. 1.

Griffith- Jones, S. (editor), 1989, *Debt Management and the Developing Countries,* UNDP, New York.

Grootaert, C. and Marchant T., *The Social Dimensions of Adjustment Survey,* World Bank, Washington DC.

Guichaoua, André, 1987, "*Les paysans et l'investissement-travail au Burundi et au Rwanda*", Bureau international du Travail, Geneva,

Guichaoua, André, 1989, *Destins paysans et politiques agraires en Afrique centrale*, L'Harmattan, Paris.

Haggard, Stephen *et al.*, 1992, *The Politics of Economic Adjustment,* Princeton University Press, Princeton.

Helleiner, G. K., 1987, "Stabilization, Adjustment and the Poor", *World Development,* 15:2 December.

Heller, Peter *et al.*, 1988, *The Implications of Fund-Supported Adjustment for Poverty,* IMF, Washington DC.

Hicks, R. and O. Per Brekk, 1991, *Assessing the Impact of Structural Adjustment on the Poor, the Case of Malawi*, IMF, Washington DC.

Hossein Farzin, 1991, "Food Aid: Positive and Negative Effects in Somalia?", *The Journal of Developing Areas,* January.

Hussein, Mosharaf, A. T. M. Aminul Islam and Sanat Kumar Saha, 1987, *Floods in Bangladesh, Recurrent Disaster and People's Survival,* Universities' Research Centre, Dhaka.

Instituto de Pesquisa Economica Aplicada (IPEA), O Mapa da Fome II: *Informaçoes sobre a Indigencia por Municipios da Federaçâo*, Brasilia, 1993.

Inter-American Development Bank, 1991, *Economic and Social Progress in Latin America, 1991 Report,* Washington.

International Labour Office, 1992, *Adjustment and Human Resource Development,* Geneva.

International Labour Organization, 1989, *Generating Employment and Incomes in Somalia,* Jobs and Skills Programme for Africa, Addis Ababa.

International Monetary Fund, 1988, *The Implications of Fund Supported Adjustment Programs for Poverty*, IMF, Washington DC.

International Monetary Fund, 1991, *Bangladesh: Economic Reform Measures and the Poor,* Washington, DC.

International Monetary Fund, World Bank, Organisation for Economic Cooperation and Development and European Bank for Reconstruction and Development, 1991, *A Study of the Soviet Economy*, Paris.

Jamal, V., 1988, "African Crisis, Food Security and Structural Adjustment", *International Labour Review*, 127:6.

Jesperson, Eva, 1991, *External Shocks, Adjustment Policies and Economic and Social Performance*, UNICEF, New York.

Johnson, John H., 1993, *Borrower Ownership of Adjustment Programs and the Political Economy of Reform,* World Bank, Washington DC.

Jolly, Richard, 1988, "Poverty and Adjustment in the 1990s", in Kallab and Feinberg (eds.), 1988, *Strengthening the Poor: What Have We Learnt*, Overseas Development Council, Transactions Books, New Brunswick, N J.

Kanbur, Ravi, 1989, *Poverty and the Social Dimensions of Adjustment in Côte d'Ivoire,* World Bank, Washington DC.

Kapeliouk, Amnon, 1993, "La détresse de la société russe", *Le Monde diplomatique*, September.

Kaufman, Bruce E., 1989, *The Economics of Labor and Labor Markets,* second edition, Orlando.

Khan, Mohsin, 1990, "The Macroeconomic Effects of Fund Supported-Adjustment Programs", *IMF Staff Papers,* Vol. 37, No. 2, Washington DC.

Killick, T. (editor), *Adjustment and Financing in the Developing World: the Role of the IMF,* IMF, Washington DC.

Killick, T., 1993, *The Adaptive Economy, Adjustment Policies in Low Income Countries*, World Bank, Washington DC.

Kisic, Drago and Veronica Ruiz de Castilla, 1989, "La Economia peruana en el contexto internacional", *CEPEI*, Vol. 2, No. 1, January.

Krasner, Stephen D., 1985, *Structural Conflict: The Third World Against Global Liberalism,* Berkeley, University of California Press.

Kreuger, Ann, 1987, "Debt, Capital Flows and LDC Growth", *American Economic Review*, 77:2.

Kreuger, Ann, *et al.,* 1990, "Developing Countries' Debt Problems and Efforts at Policy Reform", *Contemporary Policy Issues,* January.

Langoni, Carlos, 1987, *The Development Crisis*, International Center for Economic Growth, San Francisco.

Lifschutz, Lawrence, 1979, *Bangladesh, the Unfinished Revolution*, Zed Press, London.

Lopez Acuña, Daniel, *et al.*, 1991, *Reforma del Estado y Desarrollo Social en America Latina*, PAHO/OPS, Washington DC.

Lora, G., 1988, *Politica y burguesia narcotraficante*, Mi Kiosco, La Paz.

Loxley, John, 1986, *Debt and Disorder, External Financing for Development*, Westview Press.

Loxley, John, 1991, *Ghana's Recovery: An Assessment of Progress, 1987-1990,* The North-South Institute, Ottawa.

Madrid Declaration of Alternative Forum, 1994, *The Other Voices of the Planet*, Madrid.

Malpica, Carlos, 1989, *El poder economico en el Peru*, Vol. I, Mosca Azul Editores, Lima.

Manley, M. and W. Brandt, 1985, *Global Challenge, From Crisis to Cooperation,* Pan Books, London.

Martirena Mantel, A. M. (editor), 1987, *External Debt, Savings and Growth in Latin America,* International Monetary Fund-Instituto Torcuato di Tella, Buenos Aires.

Maya, R. S., 1988, *Structural Adjustment in Zimbabwe: Its Impact on Women*, Zimbabwe Institute of Development Studies, Harare.

McAfee, Kathy, 1991, *Storm Signals, Structural Adjustment and Development Alternatives in the Caribbean*, South End Press, Boston, Mass.

Mendosa, Teresa, Rebosio Guillermo, and Alvarado, Carmen, 1990, *Canasta optima alimentaria,* Centro de Estudios Nuevaa Economia y Sociedad, Lima.

Miller, M. 1989 *Resolving the Global Debt Crisis,* United Nations Development Programme, New York.

Morales, Juan Antonio, 1987, "Estabilisación y Nueva Politica Economica en Bolivia", *El Trimestre Economico*, Vol. 54.

Morales, Juan Antonio, 1989, *The Costs of the Bolivian Stabilisation Programme,* documento de trabajo, No. 01/89, Universidad Catolica Boliviana, La Paz.

Morales, Juan Antonio, 1990, *The Transition from Stabilisation to Sustained Growth in Bolivia,* paper presented at "Lessons of Economic Stabilisation and Its

Aftermath", Bank of Israel and Interamerican Development Bank, Jerusalem, January-February 1990.
Moser, Caroline O. N., 1989, "The Impact of Recession and Structural Adjustment on Women: Ecuador", *Development*, No. 1.
Mosley, 1990, *Increased Aid Flows and Human Resource Development in Africa*, UNICEF, Florence.
Murray, C., 1987, "A Critical Review of International Mortality Data", *Soc. Scie. Med.*, Vol. 25, No. 7.
Nagaraj, K., *et al.*, 1991, "Starvation Deaths in Andhra Pradesh", *Frontline*, 6 December.
Nahimana, Ferdinand, 1993, *Le Rwanda, Emergence d'un État*, L'Harmattan, Paris.
Nelson, Joan M. (editor), 1990, *Economic Crisis and Policy Choice: The Politics of Adjustment in the Third World*, Princeton University Press.
Newbery, David, 1989, "The Debt Crisis", *Development*, No. 1.
North-South Institute, 1988, *Structural Adjustment in Africa: External Financing in Development*, Ottawa, The North-South Institute.
Nuqui, Wilfredo, 1991, *The Health Sector and Social Policy in the Philippines since 1985,* UNICEF, Florence.
Oyejide T. A., 1985, *Nigeria and the IMF*, Heinemann, Ibadan.
Panamerican Health Organization, 1990, *Development and Strengthening of Local Health Systems,* Washington DC.
Panamerican Health Organization, 1991, *Health Conditions in the Americas,* Vol. 1, Washington.
Pandhe, M. K., 1991, *Surrender of India's Sovereignty and Self-Reliance*, Progressive Printers, New Delhi.
Pastor, Manuel, 1987, "The effects of IMF programs in the Third World", *World Development,* 15:2.
Peet, Richard (editor), 1987, *International Capitalism and Industrial Restructuring.*
Pirages, Dennis C., 1990, *Transformations in the Global Economy,* London, Macmillan.
Polanyi-Levitt, Kari, 1989, *Some Reflections on the LDC Debt Crisis*, Department of Economics, McGill University, Working paper 2/89, Montreal.
Portes, Richard, 1990, "Development Versus Debt: Past and Future", *IDS Bulletin*, Vol. 23, No. 2.
Pronk, Jan, 1989, "Adjustment and Development: Bridging the Gap", *Development*, No. 1.
République Rwandaise, Ministère des Finances et de l'Économie, 1987, *L'Économie rwandaise, 25 ans d'efforts (1962-1987)*, Kigali.
Rhodes, W., 1990, "The Debt Problem at the Crossroads", *IDS Bulletin*, Vol. 23, No. 2.
Ribe, Helen *et al.*, 1989, *How Adjustment Programs can Help the Poor,* World Bank, Washington DC.
Ritter A. and Pollock, D., 1985, *The Latin American Debt Crisis: Causes, Consequences and Prospects*, North-South Institute.
Rumiya, Jean, 1992 *Le Rwanda sous le régime du mandat belge (1916-1931)*, L'Harmattan, Paris.
Russell, Robert, 1990, "The New Roles and Facilities of the IMF", *IDS Bulletin,* Vol. 23, No. 2.

Sachs, Jeffrey (editor), 1989, *Developing Country Debt and the World Economy,* University of Chicago Press.

Sandifor, Peter, *et al,* 1991, "Why do Child Mortality Rates Fall, An Analysis of the Nicaraguan Experience", *American Journal of Public Health,* Vol. 81, No. 1.

Schadler, Susan, *et al.,* 1993, *Economic Adjustment in Low Income Countries,* IMF, Washington.

Seshamani, V., 1990, *Towards Structural Transformation with a Human Focus, The Economic Programmes and Policies of Zambia in the 1980s,* UNICEF, Florence.

Sobhan, Rehman, 1991, *The Development of the Private Sector in Bangladesh: a Review of the Evolution and Outcome of State Policy,* Research report No. 124, Bangladesh Institute of Development Studies.

Socialist Republic of Vietnam, 1993. *Vietnam: A Development Perspective* (main document prepared for the Paris Donor Conference), Hanoi.

Squire, Lyn, 1991, "Introduction: Poverty and Adjustment in the 1980s", *The World Bank Economic Review,* Vol. 5, No. 2.

Standing Committee on External Affairs, 1990, *Securing Our Global Future: Canada's Unfinished Business of Third World Debt,* Ottawa: House of Commons.

Streeten, P. 1987, "Structural Adjustment: A Survey of the Issues and Options", *World Development,* 15:22, December.

Suarez, Ruben, 1991, *Crisis, Ajuste y Programas de Compensación Social: Experiencias de los Fondos Sociales en Países de America Latina y el Caribe,* Organización Panamericana de la Salud, Washington DC.

Tarp, Finn, 1993, *Stabilisation and Structural Adjustment*, Routledge, London.

Tomann, H.,1988, "The Debt Crisis and Structural Adjustment in Developing Countries", *Intereconomic* 23:5.

UNICEF, 1989, "Revitalising Primary Health Care/Maternal and Child Health, the Bamako Initiative", report by the Executive Director, New York,

United Nations Conference on the Least Developed Countries, 1990, *Country Presentation by the Government of Rwanda*, Geneva.

United Nations Development Programme, 1992, *Human Development Report, 1992,* New York.

United Nations Economic Commission for Africa, 1989, *African Alternative Framework to Structural Adjustment Programmes for Socio-Economic Recovery and Transformation,* ECA, Addis Ababa.

UNICEF, 1991a, *The State of the World's Children, 1991,* New York.

UNICEF, 1991b, *The Bamako Initiative, Progress Report and Recommendation Submitted to Executive Board, 1991 Session*, New York.

Vietnam Ministry of Education, UNDP, UNESCO (National Project Education Sector Review and Human Resources Sector Analysis), 1992, *Vietnam Education and Human Resources Analysis*, Vol. 1, Hanoi.

Wagao, Jumanne H., 1990, *Adjustment Policies in Tanzania, 1981-1989, the Impact on Growth, Structure and Human Welfare*, UNICEF, Florence.

Weisner, W., "Domestic and External Causes of the Latin American Debt Crisis", *Finance and Development*, 22:1, March 1985.

Williams, Maurice, 1989, "Note on the Structural Adjustment Debate in Africa", and "Options for Relieving Debt of Low Income Countries", *Development*, No. 1.

Williamson, John (editor), 1984, *IMF Conditionality,* Institute for International Economics.

Williamson, John, 1990, "The Debt Crisis at the Turn of the Century", *IDS Bulletin,* Vol. 23, No. 2.

World Bank, 1983, *Yugoslavia: Adjustment Policies and Development Perspectives,* Washington DC.

World Bank, 1989a, *Peru, Policies to Stop Hyperinflation and Initiate Economic Recovery,* Washington DC.

World Bank, 1989b, *Adjustment Lending, An Evaluation of Ten Years of Experience,* Washington DC.

World Bank, 1989c, *Sub-Saharan Africa, From Crisis to Sustainable Growth,* Washington DC.

World Bank and UNDP, 1989, *Africa's Adjustment and Growth in the 1980s,* Washington DC.

World Bank, 1990a, *Social Dimensions of Adjustment Priority Survey,* SDA Working Paper No: 12, Washington DC.

World Bank, 1990b, *Assistance Strategies to Reduce Poverty,* Washington DC.

World Bank, 1990c, *Making Adjustment Work for the Poor,* Washington DC.

World Bank, 1990d, *World Development Report, 1989*, Washington DC, Oxford University Press.

World Bank, 1990e, *Analysis Plans for Understanding the Social Dimensions of Adjustment*, Washington DC.

World Bank, 1991a, *World Development Report, 1991,* Washington DC, Oxford University Press.

World Bank, 1991b, *The Poverty Handbook,* discussion draft, Washington DC.

World Bank, 1991c, *Human Development, A Bank Strategy for the 1990s,* Washington DC.

World Bank 1993a, *World Development Report, 1993*: *Investing in Health*, Washington DC.

World Bank, 1993b, *Viet Nam, Transition to Market Economy*, Washington DC.

World Bank, 1993c, *Vietnam, Population, Health and Nutrition Review*, Washington DC.

World Bank 1994, *Adjustment in Africa*, Washington DC, Oxford University Press.

Yoder, R. A., Are People Willing and Able to Pay for Health Services, *Social Science and Medicine,* Vol. 29.

Zuckerman, Elaine, 1989, *Adjustment Programs and Social Welfare*, World Bank discussion paper No. 44, Washington DC.

Index